Women on the Front Lines

JESSIE ALLEN AND ALAN PIFER
Editors

Preface by Gail Sheehy

Kimberly Allshouse
Robert J. Blendon
Jack A. Brizius
Marianne C. Fahs
Susan E. Foster
Ruth Harriet Jacobs
Jo-Ann Lamphere-Thorpe
Julianne Malveaux
Paula Rayman
Cynthia M. Taeuber

Women on the Front Lines

Meeting the Challenge of an Aging America

THE URBAN INSTITUTE PRESS
Washington, D.C.

THE URBAN INSTITUTE PRESS
2100 M Street, N.W.
Washington, D.C. 20037

Library of Congress Cataloging in Publication Data

Women on the Front Lines: Meeting the Challenge of an Aging America/Jessie Allen and Alan Pifer, editors.
    1. Aged women—United States—Social conditions. 2. Aged women—United States—Economic conditions. 3. Aged women—Government policy—United States. 4. Caregivers—United States. I. Allen, Jessie, 1957– .
II. Pifer, Alan J.

HQ1064.U5W617	1993	92-34290
305.42—dc20		CIP

ISBN 0-87766-575-3 (alk. paper)
ISBN 0-87766-574-5 (alk. paper; casebound)

Urban Institute books are printed on acid-free paper whenever possible.

Printed in the United States of America.

Distributed by:
    National Book Network

4720 Boston Way   3 Henrietta Street
Lanham, MD 20706   London   WC2E 8LU   ENGLAND

THE URBAN INSTITUTE PRESS is a refereed press. Its Editorial Advisory Board makes publication decisions on the basis of referee reports solicited from recognized experts in the field. Established and supported by The Urban Institute, the Press disseminates policy research on important social and economic problems, not only by Institute staff but also by outside authors.

Women on the Front Lines: Meeting the Challenge of an Aging America, edited by Jessie Allen and Alan Pifer, is a product of the Project on Women and Population Aging, sponsored by the Southport Institute for Policy Analysis.

Conclusions are those of the authors and do not necessarily reflect the views of staff members, officers, trustees, advisory groups, or funders of The Urban Institute or the Southport Institute.

CONTENTS

List of Tables

List of Figures

ACKNOWLEDGMENTS

The material in this book was developed through the Project on Women and Population Aging of the Southport Institute for Policy Analysis, in Washington, D.C. The project was launched in 1989 to inform the policy community on the many ways in which the aging of the U.S. population affects the problems, choices, resources, and needs of women and their families.

The Southport Institute is a nonprofit, nonpartisan public policy research organization whose program focuses primarily on issues affecting human resource development. The Project on Women and Population Aging is supported in part by The Commonwealth Fund.

The editors wish to express their appreciation to Felicity Skidmore, director of The Urban Institute Press, for her strong support of this project and her acute editorial eye. Thanks are also due our project advisers, Sara Rix, Linda Tarr-Whelan, and Fernando Torres-Gil, who gave generously of their time and wisdom. Finally, the indispensable support and hard work of Kit Ober, Forrest Chisman, and Carmelita Cooksey of the Southport Institute are gratefully acknowledged.

I recently indulged in a fantasy. It is twenty years from now, the year 2012. The United States already has been surpassed by the economic ascendency of Japan and Germany. Now the Cantonese and Hong Kong Chinese, liberated by the breakup of China, threaten to render the United States a fourth-rate power. Our work force, devastated by functional illiteracy, AIDS, and unaffordable health care, is down to the lowest productivity rate in American history. A new government finally hits upon the key to regaining the nation's position in the world. It will invest in the productivity of its greatest asset: long-living women in an aging society.

In the year of my fantasy, 2012, the baby boom is between the ages of 47 and 66. The women routinely look forward to living into their 90s and possibly to 100. As a result of greatly increased political representation in Congress and at the state and local levels, accelerated research into older women's health has made breast cancer, heart disease, and osteoporosis easily preventable. Women—who arrive at the age of 50 with their own pensions and savings plans, anticipating good health and high energy for another 40 or 50 years, and being at the peak of mental health and self-confidence—are demanding high quality paid work to tap their sense of mission.

The country's new leader informs Congress she intends to spearhead a VL Bill to tap these Veterans of Life to transform public education and public health. Low-cost loans will allow them to further their own liberal education or professional training. Then our society will engage them as teachers, health professionals, community organizers, and paid nurturers of its no-parent children and the aging aged.

Big business, too, has recognized that older women are particularly well-suited to handling money and holding the line on budgets: Women by 2012 will represent over half the nation's chief financial officers. And as the Western medical establishment has been pushed by boomers to incorporate the popular practices of Eastern medicine, older women have been rediscovered as natural healers. Salty, worldly-wise public women are sought after to host radio talk shows. Organized religion, shaken up by losing market share to such talk shows, has been forced to ordain women as priests, as well as to deploy them in new roles as spiritual and psychological counselors.

Farfetched? Perhaps. But at least half my fantasy is supported by the fact that unprecedented numbers of women are already surviving into very old age. American women are beginning to view the approach of menopause, not as a marker to the end, but as a bridge to their Second Adulthood. Even by today's longevity standards, the average woman has as many years to use in her liberated, post-reproductive life as she has already enjoyed as a fertile woman, when she was so busy just getting from A to B to C. If 45 is the old age of youth, 50 is the youth of a woman's Second Adulthood.

How are they using their expanded life cycle? *Women on the Front Lines*, edited by Jessie Allen and Alan Pifer, addresses that question and the disturbing issues that flow from it. First, more and more women are expending a greater portion of their lives in the paid work force. That key trend will continue, as shown in the Census Bureau data amassed by Cynthia Taeuber and Jessie Allen in their chapter on "The Demographic Outlook." By the year 2005, of all the women in the country between the ages of 25 and 54, fully 82% are expected to be in the work force. The norm will be paid outside employment throughout a woman's First Adulthood, combined with child and family responsibilities. But even in their mid-50s most women aren't retiring. Many women of the Silent Generation (now in their 50s) started their income-producing work much later than men. They can't afford to stop working before their mid-60s. Indeed, while more and more men are taking early retirement, women in their mid- to late 50s are more likely to be out working full time than ever before! By the year 2000, employees aged 55 to 64 will be the fastest growing segment of the work force. Women of the baby boom are expected to spend nearly *three-quarters of their adult lives* in the labor force.

That's the good news for American productivity. The bad news is that the social adjustments being made to the aging of America— arguably the most profound social and economic change of our times—have not been to women's benefit. Rather, they have created new burdens for women.

This prophetic book provides startling data to document this phenomenon. Most middle-aged and young-old Americans today still have living parents, a change in family dynamics with no precedent in history. Traditionally, women in the middle years have always been depended upon to do the work of unpaid caregiving to the disabled elderly at home. But women now fill nearly half the paid positions *outside* the home. And yet, as the book points out, astonishingly, no reforms in public policy or work scheduling or paid family leave have been instituted to help middle-aged women deal with this double burden. The authors show how, due to traditional policies of hiring, retirement and pension benefits, health care, and marriage norms— all designed around the typical male life cycle—many of these same caregiving women are set up for drastic reductions in living standards in their old age. They can expect to outlive their support systems.

If one probes just beneath the calm, composed surface of middle-aged women—even those of some means—one finds many who have bag-lady fears. They begin to notice the older women at the margins of our society who are invisible to most others. I mean those women who have to quit their jobs and give up health insurance and pension coverage to nurse a parent or in-law through the long twilight of chronic illness. (Or to nurse themselves through a bout with breast cancer.) When they try to reclaim their professional positions or re-enter the job market, they run into the wall of ageism. Many end up picking from the dregs of low-pay, no-benefits, high-turnover jobs.

Why should the rest of society care about them? Because if their enormous contribution to the care of the new "aging aged" is not acknowledged by changes in public policy, these vital, productive middle-aged Americans will be stripped of their own defenses against dependency in their older years. The choice for women in their 40s and 50s today is often between spending their financial resources on their mother's old age, or on their own middle age. If they decide to do the work of angels, without help, they will ultimately become a dead weight on the resources of the society that ignored their contribution.

Women on the Front Lines is a wake-up call. It is not too late to make the inexorable aging of our population a source of new dynamism. Just because they will be longer and longer, women's lives need not be harder. Indeed, what could be more propitious for all Americans than to invest in the protection and enhancement of one of the nation's greatest natural resources—the mothers, aunts, and grandmothers who will outlive us all?

Gail Sheehy

Chapter One

THE FRONT LINES

Jessie Allen

On any given day, every major newspaper in the United States probably contains at least one article relating to the aging of the nation's population. A network of social changes is becoming more and more apparent: growing numbers of older Americans, the extension of the normal life-course to older and older ages, an aging work force, the increasing likelihood that a family will have to provide extended care for a disabled elderly member. These issues all spring from the well-recognized aging trend, but they are also linked by another common factor: in each case, the people whose lives are most immediately and profoundly affected are women.

Women are on the front lines of our aging society for three main reasons: first, they are a majority among the elderly; second, they provide most of the care for disabled elderly Americans; and third, they face economic disadvantages at older ages. The most dramatic demographic effects of the aging trend will not occur until the baby boom generation reaches retirement age in the second and third decades of the next century. However, focusing on the situation of women reveals the problems and opportunities that this trend is already creating and the urgency of developing policy responses in the near term.

Well before the baby boom retires, there will be significant changes, especially in the numbers of the very old. By just 2010, there will be twice as many Americans aged 85 and older as there were in 1990. This is the age group most likely to need care for chronic disabilities, care that is provided mainly by women. Meanwhile, the average age of women continues to rise. In 1990, women aged 50 and over made up 39 percent of adult women (aged 21 and older). By 2010 nearly half (48 percent) of all adult women will be at least 50 years old.

After 2010, the entry of the baby boom into the elderly age groups will rapidly swell the numbers of Americans aged 65 and over. There were about 32 million elderly Americans in 1990, representing 13 percent of the total population. By 2020, their numbers will rise to over 52 million, and by 2030 more than one in five Americans will be elderly. More than 8 million of these people will be aged 85 and over, most of them women (U.S. Bureau of the Census 1989).

This book covers a wide range of issues of importance to women, including high rates of poverty among the elderly who live alone, middle-aged women's struggles to combine family care with paid work outside the home, increasing competition for Medicaid funds, women's prospects in the growing healthcare occupations, the controversial cost-effectiveness of preventive medicine, and older women's status in the labor force. Population aging affects all these matters, and policies intended to address them will need to factor in the aging trend in order to succeed. If we want to build effective social policy for the future of the work force, healthcare, and family care in the United States, we must not overlook the impact of population aging on American women.

THREE POINTS OF FOCUS

The most obvious reason why the aging trend has particular meaning for women is that most older people *are* women. Because of their longer life expectancy, women make up a majority of the elderly, and they outnumber men by nearly three to one past age 85. In fact, the rapid growth of the oldest age group is primarily due to the unprecedented numbers of women who are surviving into very old age. But it is not only elderly women whose lives are affected by population aging.

The second important point is that women continue to do most of the unpaid caring work in our society, even though they now constitute nearly half the paid labor force. The growing numbers of frail and disabled elderly Americans thus represent a major life issue for women of all ages that also has implications for women's future economic status and work-force productivity. Women's longer lives and lifelong roles as caregivers—in a society where labor, healthcare, and retirement norms and policies often overlook these circumstances—contribute to older women's economic disadvantages.

The third core issue is that many elderly women lack the economic resources for a comfortable life. Nearly a third of women aged 65 and over have incomes below 150 percent of the poverty level, and women constitute about three-quarters of the elderly poor.

The chapters following articulate a number of specific consequences of the aging trend for women, and ultimately for the whole society. They point to the need for policy initiatives, from both the public and private sectors, that address work and family issues, health-care, and the socioeconomic status of older women.

Despite many areas of consensus among the contributing authors in this volume, they do not all interpret the aging trend and its policy implications in the same way. For example, Cynthia M. Taeuber and Jessie Allen, in chapter 2, stress the probable future increase in women's pension coverage rates, whereas Julianne Malveaux, in chapter 7, emphasizes the likely continued gap between the amounts of retirement income received by women and men. Neither of these projections is certain, but both are likely. Both need to be taken into account in any responsible analysis of future Social Security and pension policies. It was an editorial decision to preserve such differences in interpretation and emphasis, allowing readers the benefit of multiple perspectives on the issues.

CROSS-CUTTING THEMES

Despite differences of perspective, and although the chapters cover a wide range of subjects, a few centrally important ideas emerge repeatedly in different contexts. In particular, four cross-cutting themes appear: the differences among the elderly population and the policy implications of these differences; the widespread changes in society that will be necessary to accommodate the demand for eldercare; the conflict between the nurturing approach to life to which women are socialized and a society that does not value that approach; and the importance of women as a link between generations.

Theme I: Differences among the Elderly

A major theme throughout this book is the need for policy to recognize differences among the growing elderly population. The differences between older men and older women are especially significant for policy decisions, and some policies that were thought to be gender neutral have been found to effectively discriminate against older women. In chapter 6, Rayman, Allshouse, and Allen describe the ways in which Social Security policies tend to privilege the work and marital experience of older men, contributing to poverty among elderly women. At the same time, it is necessary to recognize differences among older women related to factors such as race and ethnicity, age, and family status.

The tendency to view the elderly as a homogeneous group has been particularly detrimental to older women, who often fall outside what attitudes and policies regard as normal patterns of aging. It is true, for instance, that the majority of older Americans are married and that most have incomes well above the poverty level. But it is equally true that not all the elderly fall into these categories, and that those who do not tend to be women. As the demographic overview in chapter 2 demonstrates, older women (aged 65 and over) are far less likely than men to be married: 42 percent versus 77 percent, respectively, in 1990. At the upper ages, the gap widens: in 1990 only 26 percent of women aged 75 and over were married, compared with 70 percent of men that age.

Several chapters examine the sources of the economic problems faced by elderly women and the prospects for future change. Significant economic differences are reported among elderly women along the lines of race and ethnicity. As chapter 7, by Malveaux, shows, elderly black women are three times as likely as elderly white women to be poor, and elderly Hispanic women have poverty rates about double those of white women. Poverty in old age is also strongly correlated with marital status. Chapter 7 contains the grim statistic that 60 percent of elderly black women who live alone are poor. When this figure is contrasted with the 4 percent poverty rate for white married couples, as reported in chapter 2, a sharp picture of the economic disparities among the elderly by sex, age, race, and living status emerges.

The older a woman is, the less likely she is to be living with a husband. Women's longer life expectancy, typical marriage-age patterns, and high divorce rates all lead to elderly women's lone status. What is more, retirement and pension policies create more favorable conditions for married people—thus, for elderly men. Yet when an older woman ends up alone and poor, society continues to treat her as a tragic accident. In fact, the impoverishment of elderly women is often a logical outcome of a whole set of work, retirement, healthcare, and family care norms and policies that, while gender-neutral in language, are designed around typical male life patterns and, as a result, disadvantage women.

Unless significant policy reforms are forthcoming, economic differences by sex and living status among the elderly are expected to persist and may even widen in the future. One study has concluded that, "without further initiatives, the gap between elderly women living alone and all other elderly persons will increase over the next 30 years. By the year 2020, poverty among elderly Americans will be confined primarily to women living alone" (Commonwealth Fund Commission 1987: OR-2).

Differences in health status among the elderly are also significant. In chapter 4, Jo-Ann Lamphere-Thorpe and Robert J. Blendon speculate that health differences among older Americans may actually become more pronounced, noting that "there may be an increasing proportion of individuals in good health up to the point of death, as well as an increasing proportion with prolonged severe functional limitations." Marianne C. Fahs emphasizes in chapter 5 that this diversity is critical for structuring effective health policy in our aging society. As she points out, for preventive healthcare programs to be cost-effective in terms of the years of healthy life that are saved, they must include high proportions of users who are at high risk for the conditions such programs are designed to prevent. Risk differences often coincide with factors of social and economic status, gender, race and ethnicity, and age.

The practical policy issue here is that money spent to identify and ensure the participation of high-risk individuals will be recouped in the increased cost-effectiveness of a prevention program. Yet, differences among older women are often ignored in health policy. Fahs points to the fact that black women aged 65 to 74 are nearly twice as likely to die of heart disease as white women in this age group. However, black women have not been identified as a group at particular risk for heart disease. Moreover, there have been no studies of the effectiveness of preventive strategies for reducing risk factors for heart disease in women over age 65. With few exceptions, research on the prevention of heart disease has focused exclusively on younger men.

Theme II: Effects of the Rising Demand for Eldercare

The second theme that surfaces repeatedly in this volume is the pervasive social change that will occur because of the rising numbers of the very elderly, many of whom are disabled and need care. Unless adjustments are made in workplace structures and public policies, the enormous increase in the demand for eldercare could interfere with women's work-force participation, slow women's economic progress, and make the lives of many women and their families much harder. Through its impact on women, this trend also has implications for healthcare access and financing, labor-force productivity, and the welfare of children. The increased demand for eldercare could add to the economic woes of future generations of older women. Middle-aged women may have to sacrifice income, health insurance, and pension coverage when they assume the job of caring for disabled elderly relatives. Chapter 3, by Susan E. Foster and Jack A. Brizius, and chapter 9, by Jessie Allen, analyze these issues in depth. However, the effects of the increasing demand for eldercare are so widespread that every chapter in the book considers some aspect of this major social trend.

Theme III: Caring and Social Values

A related theme that emerges is the conflict between the caring, nurturing approach to life to which women are socialized and a society that does not value that approach, even though it depends upon it to maintain its standard of living. Chapter 3 points out that, despite protestations to the contrary, caregiving continues to be viewed with disdain and is not valued economically. This is a conflict that goes beyond the distribution of caring work—paid and unpaid—and affects the choices women make and the obstacles they continue to face in education and throughout the labor force.

Many of the chapters suggest that one of the keys to maintaining a high quality of life in an aging society will be a revaluation of, and increased support for, the "ethic of caring" that the authors of chapter 6 observed among the older women they interviewed—an ethic based on the perception of connections among individuals and their mutual dependence. Yet, to a large extent, the social and political gains women have made over the last century have been founded on a perception of their increased autonomy. A sense of our society's ambivalent attitude toward nurturing comes through in chapter 8 by Ruth Harriet Jacobs, when she asserts that while we seek to expand the social roles available to older women we must also recognize the vital contributions they have made through traditional nurturing roles. Do we view caregiving as productive work? Is the goal to free women from the constraints of traditional roles by making new roles accessible or by revaluing the old ones, or both? What are the society's priorities in this regard?

An aging society needs to find ways to promote both gender equity and an ethic of care. The question is how. A number of approaches are proposed or implied in the chapters that follow. They include socializing boys and men to more nurturing attitudes and perceptions of interdependence, shifting business structures to accommodate family care, monetarizing more caring work, redistributing caregiving equally between the sexes, and raising economic compensation for caring work.

These are big issues without easy solutions. The chapters in this book point out how they will be influenced by the social effects of the aging trend's impact on women.

Theme IV: Linking Generations

The fourth recurrent theme in this book is women's position as a link between generations—both individually as family caregivers and societally as a group whose economic problems span the life-course. An examination of the situation of women in our aging society tends to undermine the notion that most significant conflict over resources will be intergenerational. After all, it is women who are the primary caregivers to both the frail elderly and to children. It is also true that both elderly single women and young single mothers are disproportionately represented among poor Americans. In the work, education, and health policies that would support family care and improve women's economic position, the interests of children and the elderly overlap. Further, the belief that the economic disadvantages of children are a result of unfair transfers of income and services to the elderly depends to some extent on a universalizing view of the elderly as an affluent, or at least relatively secure, population. When one recognizes the economic obstacles older women will continue to face, especially older women who live alone and older women of color, it is difficult to support that view.

POLICY PRIORITIES FOR WOMEN IN AN AGING SOCIETY

Population aging is drawing attention to the problems faced by older people and their caregivers and is increasing the likelihood of some policy action on their behalf. The danger is that this action may follow an ineffectual cycle like the one Ruth Harriet Jacobs describes in chapter 8, in which reforms are fragmented, superficial, and quickly relinquished, leaving underlying problems unsolved.

However, the kind of bold, basic policy changes many of the chapters suggest are hard to accomplish. Substantial political opposition exists toward some of these reforms, and in other cases there is bitter debate about who will bear the costs. The primary purpose of this book is to present a comprehensive analysis of the complex effects of the aging trend for women, and to define those effects in a way that will help stimulate an integrated and broad-based approach to policy reform. The aim is to provoke new thought about some reforms that have been suggested in the past, and to suggest new angles on old problems that may lead to creative solutions.

The challenge will be to create new policy initiatives that genuinely empower and integrate older women in our aging society, provide true workplace equity for women, increase the adequacy and fairness of the retirement system, effectively and equitably provide long-term care, and take advantage of the productive capacities of an aging population. To accomplish this, it will be necessary to keep in mind the way in which the aging trend intersects women's changing roles. This convergence has meaning for policy decisions on many levels, whether one is framing family and medical leave legislation, designing an employee retraining program, considering which type of national health insurance plan to support, or making a decision about one's own pension and retirement plans.

Many general accounts of the aging trend emphasize its long-range trajectory and projected peak in the middle of the next century. This perspective naturally tends to dampen any sense of urgency in policy response. However, this volume's analysis of the trend's impact on women underscores the extent to which the effects of population aging are being felt right now—and the force they will increasingly exert just in the next 10 to 20 years on some longstanding social norms.

In particular, the pressure of the growing demand for eldercare at a time when most women are in the paid labor force tends to expose the contradictions underlying the treatment of all dependent care in our society. It is clearly unfair for women to be expected to provide care while being penalized in an economic system that devalues the very care it relies on for its perpetuation. Yet, to date, little progress has been made in addressing this paradox and the extensive social problems it creates. If one central message emerges from this volume, it is that the way in which dependent care of all kinds is approached— both as paid and unpaid work—is self-contradictory, inequitable, and inefficient. The consequences for women, their families, and work- force productivity are already damaging. With the increased pressure of the aging trend, and in the absence of corrective policies, these consequences could soon be devastating.

SEQUENCE OF CHAPTERS

Women on the Front Lines opens with a demographic overview of women's situation in an aging United States and a chapter on the central issue of caregiving policy.

Chapter 2, by Taeuber and Allen, provides the statistical background needed to place the discussion in subsequent chapters in proper perspective. Its purpose is to review the changing characteristics of the growing elderly population, especially those of women. It discusses disability and dependency trends that will affect caregiving demand, and it highlights educational and employment trends among younger women that will partly determine how population aging influences their lives. The increasing diversity of our aging society is stressed throughout.

Chapter 3, by Foster and Brizius, projects a crisis in dependent care triggered by the growing numbers of disabled elderly Americans. This is a major theme of the book and reappears in different contexts again and again. The chapter argues for a comprehensive national approach to caregiving issues, replacing the categorical nature of today's policies. A number of basic policy goals are identified and examined.

Two chapters on healthcare and women's health follow. Chapter 4, by Lamphere-Thorpe and Blendon, examines some of the most urgent health policy issues our country is facing from a new point of view. The authors analyze women's two-fold roles as consumers and providers of healthcare to explore such issues as containing Medicare costs, dealing with healthcare labor shortages, providing healthcare coverage to uninsured Americans, and separating long-term care from Medicaid.

Chapter 5, by Fahs, addresses economic and health policy issues that affect the development of preventive services for older women. The chapter analyzes the future consequences for older women and society if we fail to invest in greater prevention efforts while the elderly population continues to expand.

The next three chapters address the socioeconomic status of older women—their work and retirement experiences, differences by race, and the need to expand their social roles. In chapter 6, Rayman, Allshouse, and Allen focus on the convergence of women's increasing labor-force participation and the aging of the U.S. population. Interviews from focus groups provide perspectives on the infrequently studied experiences of older minority women in the labor force. Pol-

icies to improve the work and retirement outlook for future generations of older women are suggested.

Malveaux, in chapter 7, examines in detail the economic status of
older minority women. The chapter analyzes economic differences
among older women of color by living status and age and investigates
the relationship between minority women's income sources and their
disproportionate poverty, speculating on possible areas of future
change.

Chapter 8, by Jacobs, analyzes a number of factors that contribute
to the social marginalization of older women. The chapter takes a
pragmatic approach to social change, offering numerous concrete suggestions for ways to expand the very limited roles now available to
most elderly women.

The final two chapters draw out certain philosophical and policy
implications of the discussions in the earlier chapters. Chapter 9, by
Allen, suggests aspects of the growing demand for eldercare that—if
recognized and incorporated in policy reforms—might be used to
shift the unequal burden of care women now carry, possibly leading
to increased gender equity.

Chapter 10, by Pifer, lays out a set of premises for a policy analysis
of the aging trend's effects on women and, through those effects, on
human resource issues. The chapter then suggests a series of broad-
based policy goals that develop from a review of the preceding chapters.

References

Commonwealth Fund Commission on Elderly People Living Alone. 1987. *Old,
    Alone, and Poor: A Plan for Reducing Poverty among Elderly People
    Living Alone.* Baltimore, Md.: Commonwealth Fund Commission on
    Elderly People Living Alone, Johns Hopkins University.
U.S. Bureau of the Census. 1989. "Projections of the Population of the United
    States, by Age, Sex and Race: 1988 to 2080," by Gregory Spencer.
    Current Population Reports, ser. P-25, no. 1018. Washington, D.C.:
    U.S. Government Printing Office.

Chapter Two

WOMEN IN OUR AGING SOCIETY: THE DEMOGRAPHIC OUTLOOK

Cynthia M. Taeuber and Jessie Allen

Everyone is affected by the changes that accompany an aging society. This chapter examines the demographics of population aging in the United States and its present and future intersection with various aspects of the experience of women.

Our main focus is on the growing elderly population, especially the varying level of needs, abilities, and resources of elderly women. We use the characteristics of today's younger adult women to help provide a view of elderly women in the future. We also explore the implications of the overall aging trend on physical and economic dependency. These issues have multiple implications for women, young and old, in part because of women's long life expectancy and their roles as caregivers. Changes in disability levels mean a growing demand for long-term care, paid and unpaid. Most of this care continues to be provided by women and received by the "oldest-old" women. Finally, we briefly consider some trends among women of all ages that will influence the outcome of population aging in women's lives. We focus on changes in women's education and labor-force participation, changes that affect the ability of women to provide unpaid long-term care, and the cost of such care to women and society at large.

THE GROWING ELDERLY POPULATION

Diversity and growth are two terms that define America's elderly population. The population aged 65 and over is commonly grouped together under the label, "the elderly,"[1] and yet, this is a heterogeneous population. Elderly women tend to have life circumstances quite different from those of elderly men. Some older people, especially single oldest-old women, tend to have significant financial and health problems. Others, especially young-old men and married couples, are generally more secure. In short, the elderly, like other age groups, are diverse in their needs, abilities, and resources.

Numerical Growth

In 1900, 1 in 25 Americans was elderly. In 1990, the proportion had risen to 1 in 8, and by 2030, it is likely to be more than 1 in 5. Eventually, we may well have more grandparents than youths in our society. Most of these grandparents will be grandmothers, since elderly women outnumber elderly men. Within the expanding older population, the rate of growth of the oldest old (85 years and over), most of whom are women, is stunning. The number of oldest old increased fivefold from 1950 to 1990 and will double again by 2010 under the assumptions of the U.S. Bureau of the Census middle series population projections model.[2]

CHANGES IN AGE COMPOSITION

Changes in age composition can have dramatic political, economic, and social effects on a nation. In the past, declines in the number of births have been the most important contributor to the long-term aging trend. Now, however, the improved chance of survival to the oldest ages, especially for women, is the most important factor in the growth of the very old population (Rosenwaike and Dolinsky 1987). The volume of net migration has traditionally had the smallest role in changing age distributions. In the next century, however, past immigration, especially of young Hispanics, will become an additional important element in the eventual rapid growth and greater diversity of the elderly population.[3] Because of relatively low birthrates from the 1920s through World War II, growth in the size of the elderly population will be steady but undramatic until after 2011, when members of the baby boom (born 1946 to 1964) begin to reach age 65.

In 1990, the baby-boom generation was aged 26 to 44 years and constituted nearly one-third of the American population (see figure 2.1). There were 31.1 million people aged 65 or older (see table 2.1). Of these, 18.6 million, or 60 percent, were elderly women. Among the elderly in 1990, the oldest old were a small but rapidly growing group. Their numbers are already sufficient to have a major impact on the nation's health and social service systems. The 1990 Census counted 2.2 million women 85 or older (table 2.1). They make up nearly 2 percent of the total female population and one of nine elderly women. By 2010, nearly one in five elderly women would be aged 85 or older.

Figure 2.1 U.S. POPULATION: 1990

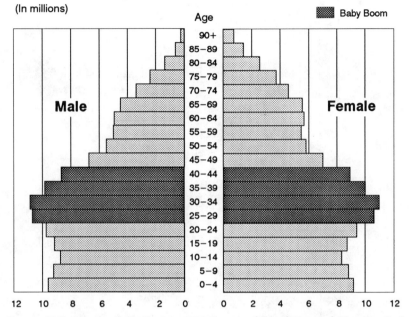

Source: U.S. Bureau of the Census, 1990 Census of Population and Housing, Series CPH-L-74, "Modified and Actual Age, Sex, Race, and Hispanic Origin Data."

In 2010, the members of the baby boom will be aged 45 to 64 (see figure 2.2). From 2011 to 2050, growth in the elderly population will be more dramatic as the baby boom becomes the grandparent boom. From 2011 to 2030, the baby-boom generation will be the young old and the aged (65 to 74 years old and 75 to 84 years old). During these two decades, the female population aged 65 to 84 would grow 68 percent whereas the female population aged 85 and over would grow 29 percent. Meanwhile, the female population under age 65 would decrease 3 percent. About one in seven women were elderly in 1990, but about one in four women would be elderly by the year 2030 (table 2.1).

After 2030 (see figure 2.3), we will witness the final phase of the gerontological explosion. The growth of the young old would decelerate as the smaller cohorts born after the baby boom, from 1965 to 1984, reach ages 65 through 84 in 2050. That age group is projected to decrease from 57 million in 2030 to 53 million in 2050, although the total elderly population would continue to grow slowly.

Table 2.1 U.S. POPULATION BY AGE, SEX, RACE, AND HISPANIC ORIGIN: 1990–2050 (Numbers in thousands)

Sex and Age Groups	All Races				Black				Hispanic Origin[a]			
	1990	2010[b]	2030[b]	2050[b]	1990	2010[b]	2030[b]	2050[b]	1990	2010[c]	2030[c]	2050[c]
Both Sexes:												
All ages	248,710	282,575	300,629	299,849	30,483	38,833	44,596	47,146	22,354	41,918	67,733	96,142
65 years and over	31,079	39,362	65,604	68,532	2,492	3,860	7,784	9,571	1,146	2,708	6,952	12,060
75 years and over	13,033	18,323	29,616	36,942	994	1,584	3,071	4,724	431	1,165	2,909	6,220
85 years and over	3,021	6,115	8,129	15,287	223	478	788	1,817	91	343	877	2,492
Percentage 65 and over	12.5	13.9	21.8	22.9	8.2	9.9	17.5	20.3	5.1	6.5	10.3	12.5
Percentage 75 and over	5.2	6.5	9.9	12.3	3.3	4.1	6.9	10.0	1.9	2.8	4.3	6.5
Percentage 85 and over	1.2	2.2	2.7	5.1	0.7	1.2	1.8	3.9	0.4	0.8	1.3	2.6
Females:												
All ages	127,471	144,241	154,086	154,529	16,063	20,231	23,269	24,690	10,966	20,539	33,228	47,512
65 years and over	18,586	22,991	37,010	39,225	1,535	2,262	4,418	5,440	671	1,580	3,809	6,615
75 years and over	8,447	11,643	18,030	22,621	651	994	1,866	2,854	268	733	1,772	3,676
85 years and over	2,180	4,324	5,568	10,201	156	330	532	1,193	59	239	607	1,635
Percentage 65 and over	14.6	15.9	24.0	25.4	9.6	11.2	19.0	22.0	6.1	7.7	11.5	13.9
Percentage 75 and over	6.6	8.1	11.7	14.6	4.1	4.9	8.0	11.6	2.4	3.6	5.3	7.7
Percentage 85 and over	1.7	3.0	3.6	6.6	1.0	1.6	2.3	4.8	0.5	1.2	1.8	3.4

Males:												
All ages	121,239	138,333	146,543	145,320	14,420	18,602	21,328	22,456	11,388	21,379	34,506	48,630
65 years and over	12,493	16,372	28,594	29,307	957	1,598	3,366	4,131	475	1,128	3,142	5,445
75 years and over	4,586	6,681	11,585	14,321	343	590	1,204	1,870	163	431	1,137	2,545
85 years and over	841	1,791	2,560	5,086	66	148	256	624	32	104	270	857
Percentage 65 and over	10.3	11.8	19.5	20.2	6.6	8.6	15.8	18.4	4.2	5.3	9.1	11.2
Percentage 75 and over	3.8	4.8	7.9	9.9	2.4	3.2	5.6	8.3	1.4	2.0	3.3	5.2
Percentage 85 and over	0.7	1.3	1.7	3.5	0.5	0.8	1.2	2.8	0.3	0.5	0.8	1.8
Ratio (males per 100 females):												
All ages	95.1	95.9	95.1	94.0	89.8	91.9	91.7	91.0	103.8	104.1	103.8	102.4
65 years and over	67.2	71.2	77.3	74.7	62.3	70.6	76.2	75.9	70.8	71.4	82.5	82.3
75 years and over	54.3	57.4	64.3	63.3	52.7	59.4	64.5	65.5	60.8	58.8	64.2	69.2
85 years and over	38.6	41.4	46.0	49.9	42.3	44.8	48.1	52.3	54.2	43.5	44.5	52.4

Sources: Data for 1990: U.S. Bureau of the Census, 1991, "Modified and Actual Age, Sex, Race, and Hispanic Origin Data," 1990 Census of Population and Housing, ser. CPH-L-74 (Washington, D.C.: U.S. Government Printing Office). Data for 2010–2050: U.S. Bureau of the Census, 1989, "Projections of the Population of the United States, by Age, Sex, and Race: 1988 to 2080," by Gregory Spencer; *Current Population Reports*, ser. P-25, no. 1018 (Washington, D.C.: U.S. Government Printing Office [middle series]). Hispanic origin data for 2010–2050: U. S. Bureau of the Census 1986, "Projections of the Hispanic Population 1983 to 2080," by Gregory Spencer; *Current Population Reports*, ser. P-25, no. 995 (Washington, D.C.: U.S. Government Printing Office [highest series]).

a. People of Hispanic origin may be of any race.

b. Assumes an ultimate total fertility of 1,800; life expectancy at birth in 2050 of 76.4 years for males and 83.3 years for females; and an ultimate net migration of 500,000 per year.

c. Assumes an ultimate total fertility rate of 2,300; life expectancy at birth in 2050 of 76.4 years for males and 83.3 years for females; and an ultimate net migration of 361,500 per year.

Figure 2.2 U.S. POPULATION: 2010

(In millions)

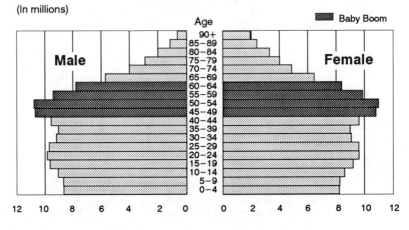

Source: U.S. Bureau of the Census (1989).

Figure 2.3 U.S. POPULATION: 2030

(In millions)

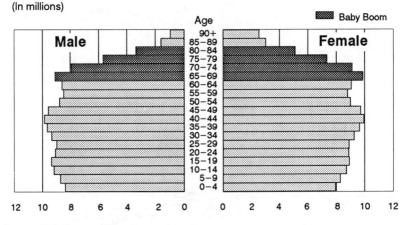

Source: U.S. Bureau of the Census (1989).

The size of the oldest-old population will be remarkable after 2030 as the aging of the aged, the great grandparent boom begins. The population aged 85 and over is expected to grow from 3 million in 1990 to 8 million in 2030 and to nearly double in size again by 2050 (figure 2.4), to over 15 million, as the survivors of the baby-boom reach the oldest ages. The oldest old would then be 5 percent of the total population. The number of oldest-old women will increase from

Figure 2.4 U.S. POPULATION: 2050

(In millions)

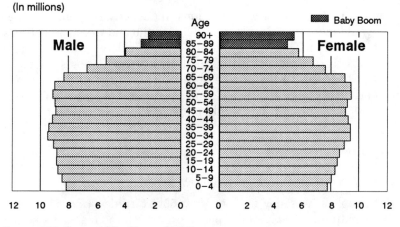

Source: U.S. Bureau of the Census (1989).

2.2 million in 1990 to 5.6 million in 2030 and to over 10 million in 2050.

The Census Bureau's middle series projections assume that it will be increasingly difficult to reduce mortality rates further, and anticipate a slow, incremental rise in life expectancy at older ages. If mortality rates decrease at a faster rate, particularly among the oldest old, the numbers given earlier could be much higher. With such demographic facts staring us in the face, some policymakers and business leaders are becoming more attentive to how an aging society affects us all. An additional factor to consider is the changing racial and ethnic composition of older age groups.

RACE AND HISPANIC ORIGIN OF THE ELDERLY

Although the elderly population is predominantly white, we can expect to see more racial diversity and more persons of Hispanic origin (who may be of any race) within America's elderly population in the coming years. Persons of races other than white constituted about 1 in 10 elderly persons in 1990. By 2050, the proportion may increase to about 2 in 10. From 1990 to 2050, the number of elderly blacks would nearly quadruple and their proportion of the total elderly population would increase from 8 to 14 percent. The black population aged 85 and over would increase from only 223,000 in 1990 to 1.8 million by 2050. The proportion of Asians, Pacific Islanders, American Indians, Eskimos, and Aleuts combined would increase from less than 2 percent of the total elderly population to 7 percent from 1990 to 2050.

Under the highest series projections, the elderly Hispanic population would more than double from 1990 to 2010 and would be 10 times greater by 2050. The proportion of Hispanic elderly would increase from less than 4 percent of the total elderly population in 1990 to nearly 18 percent by the middle of the next century. About one-fifth of elderly blacks and elderly Hispanics were aged 80 or older in 1990. By 2050, these proportions would increase to almost one-third.

Longevity

Trends in Life Expectancy and Survival

Most people alive today will see their 65th birthday. Under the mortality conditions of 1989, life expectancy at birth had reached a record high of 75.3 years (National Center for Health Statistics 1991: table 15).[4] Eighty percent of newborns will survive to age 65. The most dramatic recent reductions in mortality have occurred among women and the oldest old. This is primarily because of reductions in mortality rates from major cardiovascular diseases (Fingerhut 1984).

Mortality differs significantly by race. Under the mortality conditions of 1979–81, 80 percent of whites and Hispanics would survive to age 65, compared with only 66 percent of blacks and 71 percent of American Indians[5] (National Center for Health Statistics 1985; Spencer 1989; Handler 1984). White women aged 65 in 1989 had an expected additional 19 years of life. For elderly black women, it was just over 17 years. One in three white women died at age 85 or older in 1989, compared with about one in five black women. At age 85, both black and white women have an average of 6 to 7 years of life remaining (National Center for Health Statistics 1990 [table 6-1]; 1992 [table 4]).

The female advantage in life expectancy may abate in the next century if recent mortality trends continue. Men aged 85 and over are expected to increase their numbers relative to women, but because women would still be more likely than men to survive to the oldest ages, the health, social, and economic problems of the oldest old are likely to remain primarily the problems of women.

Implications of Longevity

As life expectancy continues to increase, we increasingly confront quality-of-life issues for older people. The number of years of good health in relation to the number of years of chronic illness is important. The financial soundness of retirement plans could be critical to an ever-larger proportion of the population (Metropolitan Life Insurance 1988: 15). At age 65, women might need to consider how to finance an additional 20 or more years of life. We can expect to see more long-term chronic illness, disability, and dependency. More people may live long enough to suffer from the cognitive diseases of senile dementia and Alzheimer's. More young-old people will have oldest-old family members who need care and attention.

Economic Characteristics

WORK AND RETIREMENT

Relatively few elderly women or men work for pay. Only 16 percent of elderly men and 9 percent of elderly women were labor-force participants in 1990. More and more men retire early, that is, before the age when they receive full benefits. For example, in 1967, 90 percent of men aged 55 to 59 were in the labor force; by 1990, only 80 percent were. Women aged 55 to 59, however, are more likely to be in the labor force than ever before. In 1967, 48 percent were in the labor force compared with 55 percent in 1990, when women made up 43 percent of all workers aged 55 and older (U.S. Department of Labor 1991a: table 3).[6]

In the future, a greater proportion of elderly women can be expected to have pensions, which may reduce their desire or need to work. The U.S. Bureau of Labor Statistics (BLS) has projected that only 16 percent of men and less than 9 percent of women aged 65 and older will be in the labor force in the year 2005 (Fullerton, Jr. 1991).[7] Among those aged 55 to 64, the BLS has projected that 68 percent of men and 54 percent of women will be in the labor force, which would make women a larger part of a shrinking older work force.

Occupations of older women workers   Older women have traditionally been at the greatest disadvantage in the labor market. They have tended to have less work experience than men and less education than younger people (Rones and Herz 1989: 38). This situation may change for older women who want to work in the future, because more will have had more education and will have been in the labor force continuously.

Labor force participation rates of women aged 55 and over are nearly the same for whites, blacks, and Hispanics (who may be of any race). In 1987, the labor force participation of women in this age group was

21.5 percent for whites, 24.7 percent for blacks, and 22.2 percent for Hispanics. Black and Hispanic women, however, are more concentrated in relatively few low-paying occupations (Herz 1988: 10 and table 6). In 1987, for example, about half (49.3 percent) of employed black women 55 to 64 years old and nearly one-third (31.1 percent) of Hispanic women in that age range worked in service occupations, compared with one in six (15.9 percent) white women (Herz 1988: table 6).[8]

It is unlikely that the occupational differences between older black and white women will be as pronounced in the future. This is because a high proportion of today's elderly black women were employed in their younger years as service workers with low wages and few benefits. Black women under age 45 in 1991 were typically employed in technical, sales, and administrative support occupations (50 percent) and as professionals and managers (19 percent). Such jobs are more likely to be covered by pensions and health insurance (Taeuber and Valdisera 1988: 22, figure 23).

Pension coverage and effect on future labor force participation
Because women are increasingly joining the labor force and because men are increasingly likely to live at least into their 70s, we can expect in the future to see more married couples with two private pensions in addition to Social Security benefits. In December 1986, 12.4 million retirees (of any age) received private pension benefits; two-thirds were men.

Men have higher pension benefits than women. The combined mean Social Security and pension income received by male retirees was $1,160, 45 percent higher than the mean of $800 for women. Part of this difference is because female retirees are older on average than male retirees, and older retirees tend to receive less pension income. Age is not the sole answer, however. For each age interval, men have higher mean pension income than women (Short and Nelson 1991: 2, 3, 7).[9] Older black women, compared with older white women, are less likely to receive a pension, to have completed high school, to own their homes or other valuable assets, or to be married; hence, they have fewer resources for retirement (Woods 1989: 10–11). There are overall differences in resources between black women and white women even at the same educational level, differences that could reflect the effects of past discrimination.

Some researchers believe we are now seeing the "golden age of the golden years" (Weinstein 1988: 7), and that baby-boom retirees will be less well off than today's retirees. There are many indicators that the personal savings and retirement benefits of the elderly may be less in the future. One study (Woods 1989: 2–19) showed limited evidence of a shift in pension coverage from traditional defined contribution plans to plans that allow pretax employee contributions (such as 401(k) plans). Also, workers in smaller firms were less likely to be covered than those in larger firms. Industries with low rates of coverage included construction, retail trade, nonprofessional services, and agriculture.

As a result of the greater likelihood of women working now than in the past, young and middle-aged women are likely to have been in the labor force long enough to have savings, pensions, and Social Security in their own names, which could make a significant difference in their economic status as they age. In 1987, 64 percent of women wage and salary workers were covered by a pension plan and 40 percent were vested[10] (33 percent were entitled to future benefits and 7 percent were entitled to lump-sum payments). Sixty-nine percent of men were covered by a pension plan, and 49 percent were vested. Pension coverage rates of workers under 30 years of age were identical for men and women, whereas men aged 35 to 64 had higher coverage and vesting rates than did women in that age group. The disparity in earnings between men and women is one factor in the different coverage and vesting levels (Short and Nelson 1991: 3).

Despite these changes, it is difficult to predict whether, in the future, as large a proportion of people in their early 60s will be able to afford to retire early as do now. There have been definite signs that pension plans will be less generous in the future. Additionally, the recent growth of part-time and temporary employment that carries few benefits could also depress pension coverage among future retirees. Also, workers are supporting an increasing portion of the cost of their retirement plans. It seems likely that men will continue to have higher benefit levels than women for some time to come, although this could change by the time the youngest members of the baby boom reach old age.

INCOME AND DIFFERENCES AMONG SUBGROUPS

The overall economic position of elderly men and women has improved significantly since the 1970s. Not everyone within the elderly population has shared equally in the income gains, however.

Elderly women are generally less secure economically than elderly men. We may see some relative improvement in the future as more women become better educated and have a history of long-term employment. In 1990, median income was $14,183 for elderly men and

$8,044 for elderly women (DeNavas and Welniak 1991: table 26). White men had much higher median incomes than other groups. The 1990 median income for white men aged 65 and over was more than double that of elderly black and Hispanic women (figure 2.5). The differences in median income were not statistically significant between black and Hispanic women or between white women and Hispanic men.

Living arrangements and marital status are related to how well older people fare economically. Elderly married couples saw their annual real incomes rise by 21 percent, from a median of $17,330 to $20,996, from 1979 to 1987 (1987 dollars). The median annual income of elderly female unrelated individuals (most living alone) increased by only 13 percent over that period, from $6,966 to $7,863 (Ryscavage 1991: 9–11).

The Urban Institute's Dynamic Simulation of Income Model (DYNASIM) projects what income characteristics would be like for future elderly populations based on the behavior and characteristics of the population that existed in the 1980s. The results also assume a future continuation of current government policies and the state of the economy when the model was designed. Many uncertainties are associated with asset income, an income source held by many elderly people and one that is affected by the economy. DYNASIM assumes that, "on average, real growth in financial assets will track real growth in GNP, and that income from assets will match the expected rate-of-return on U.S. Treasury notes" (Zedlewski et al. 1990: 98).[11]

The DYNASIM model presents a continuing mixed-income picture for the elderly. Under the model's assumptions, the effects on income of the stronger attachment of women now under age 45 to the labor force and their increased likelihood of receiving pensions would not

Figure 2.5 MEDIAN INCOMES OF PERSONS AGED 65 AND OVER IN THE UNITED STATES, BY SEX AND RACE: 1990

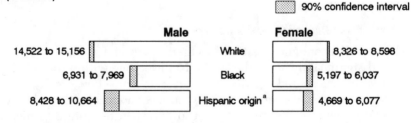

Source: DeNavas and Welniak (1991: table 26).
a. People of Hispanic origin may be of any race.

be especially evident until after 2010. Unmarried elderly women, most of whom are widowed and relatively old, would continue to be at financial risk compared with men and married couples (who tend to be among the young old). From 1990 to 2010, the rate of increase of real median income would be slower for unmarried elderly women (35 percent) than for married couples (57 percent) or unmarried men (51 percent). The 2010 real median annual income level for unmarried women would remain much lower ($8,100 [1988 dollars]) than for elderly married couples ($24,400). Half of elderly unmarried women would have pension benefits that averaged $1,200 annually, compared with $6,300 for married couples and $4,000 for unmarried men. Sixty-eight percent of unmarried women would have annual incomes of less than $10,000 in 2010, compared with 44 percent of unmarried men and 3 percent of married couples (Zedlewski et al. 1990: 73–74, tables 3.1, 3.7, 3.11.).[12]

After 2010, the income level of unmarried elderly women would improve somewhat but would continue to be lower than for married couples and unmarried elderly men. Pensions would be held by more elderly women, but levels would remain much lower than those for men or married couples. The authors of the DYNASIM model concluded that substantial numbers of elderly women would remain at financial risk in the future, especially as they reach the oldest ages, and when living alone with the possibility of limitations in their activities of daily living (ADLs) (Zedlewski et al. 1990: 73–74, tables 3.1, 3.7, 3.11).[13]

POVERTY STATUS

There has been a dramatic reduction in the last 30 years in the overall proportion of the elderly who are poor. In 1959, 35 percent of elderly people were poor. In 1990, 12 percent were poor. Nevertheless, there are important differences among subgroups. The economic situation for elderly black women who are poor has been particularly intractable; their poverty rates did not improve over the decade of the 1980s (Ryscavage 1991: 9–11).

Poverty rates for subgroups   The elderly poor are disproportionately female, black, and Hispanic. Women constituted 58 percent of the elderly population but 74 percent of the elderly poor in 1990. Black women made up 5 percent of the elderly population and 16 percent of the elderly poor (Littman 1991: tables 1, 3, 5). The poverty rate for all elderly women was 15 percent, double the rate for elderly men. Among those 75 years of age and older, nearly 20 percent of women were poor, again twice the rate for men in the same age group. Among the elderly aged 75 and older, the 1990 poverty rate for black women (44 percent) was more than double that for white women (17 percent) and more than five times that for white men (8 percent). Poverty is especially high for black women aged 75 and older who live alone or with unrelated individuals. In 1990, there were 280,000 such women, and over half were poor.

In 1990, among elderly whites, poverty rates increased with age. Poverty was lowest for elderly white men aged 65 to 74. Black and Hispanic women aged 65 to 74 had higher poverty rates than white women in that age group. For blacks and Hispanics, poverty rates were not effectively different for women aged 65 to 74 compared with those aged 75 and over (figure 2.6); likewise, there was no statistical difference when the two age groups were compared for men. Poverty rates for Hispanic men aged 75 and over were not statistically different from any group other than black women aged 75 and over (Littman 1991: table 5).

Poverty rates from the 1980 Census for people aged 85 and over varied from 8 percent for women living in families to 73 percent for the nearly 31,000 black women who lived alone.[14] Data from the 1980 Census also showed that poverty rates among elderly American Indian women were similar to those for black women. By contrast, the overall

Figure 2.6 PERCENTAGE OF POOR ELDERLY IN THE UNITED STATES IN 1990, BY AGE, SEX, RACE, AND HISPANIC ORIGIN

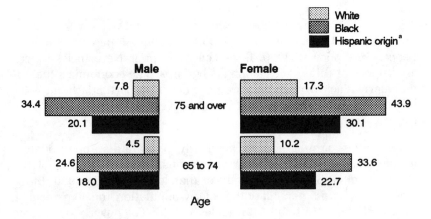

Source: Littman (1991: table 5).
a. People of Hispanic origin may be of any race.

rates for Asian and Pacific Islander[15] women were closer to the relatively low rates of white elderly women.

The elderly who did not live with relatives ("unrelated individuals" in census terminology, most of whom live alone) were more likely to be poor in 1990 (24.7 percent) than elderly married-couple family householders (5.0 percent). For unrelated individuals, poverty rates were lower among white elderly women (24.0 percent) than for elderly women who were black (60.1 percent) or Hispanic (49.7 percent) (figure 2.7). In married-couple households with an elderly householder, poverty rates were lower where the householder was white (3.8 percent) than black (21.5 percent) or Hispanic (15.7 percent).

Education is closely associated with lifetime economic status. Poverty rates drop dramatically as the educational level of the elderly increases. Of the 3.7 million poor elderly in 1990, 1.8 million were elderly women who never finished high school. This is especially important for the future, because a greater proportion of women of the baby boom have completed high school and college than have today's elderly women (Littman 1991: table 11).

Figure 2.7 PERCENTAGE OF POOR ELDERLY IN THE UNITED STATES IN 1990, BY HOUSEHOLD RELATIONSHIP, RACE, AND HISPANIC ORIGIN

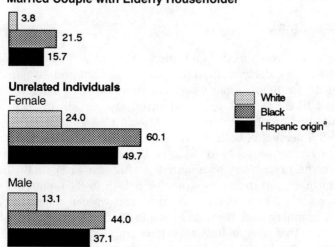

Married Couple with Elderly Householder

3.8
21.5
15.7

Unrelated Individuals
Female

24.0
60.1
49.7

☐ White
▨ Black
■ Hispanic origin[a]

Male

13.1
44.0
37.1

Source: Littman (1991: table 5).
a. People of Hispanic origin may be of any race.

Elderly with incomes below 150 percent of the poverty threshold   A higher proportion of the elderly than of adults aged 25 to 64 had incomes concentrated between 100 percent and 150 percent of their respective poverty thresholds. This was especially the case for women. Of the 7.9 million elderly people with such incomes in 1990, almost 7 in 10 were women (5.5 million) (Littman 1991: table 6). In all, 32 percent of elderly women had incomes below 150 percent of their respective poverty thresholds. This figure was 40 percent for women 75 years and older and 50 percent for elderly women living alone. A total of 4.4 million elderly who lived alone had incomes below 150 percent of their respective poverty thresholds. Of these, about 3.7 million were elderly women, most were white, and most were residents of metropolitan areas (Littman 1991: tables 6, 7).

Social Characteristics

Marital status, living arrangements, and educational attainment vary considerably within the older population and will change in future generations. Elderly men are much more likely than women to be married and living in a family setting. The older population is becoming increasingly better educated, which has important implications for future health and economic status as well as the need for and delivery of services. We discuss these characteristics in more detail next.[16]

MARITAL STATUS

Differences between men and women   Most elderly men are married, whereas most elderly women are not (74 percent and 40 percent, respectively, in 1990). Elderly women in 1990 were more than three times as likely as men to be widowed (14 percent of men and 49 percent of women) (Saluter 1991: 12, table 1).

About 5 percent of both elderly men and women were divorced and had not remarried in 1990 (Saluter 1991: 12, table 1). For divorced women, the probability of remarriage after age 45 is small. In 1985, only 29 of 10,000 divorced women aged 45 to 64 remarried during the year. Only 5 of 10,000 elderly divorced women remarried during 1985 (Uhlenberg and Boyd 1990: table 2). The implication of these numbers is that most elderly men have a spouse for assistance, especially when health fails, and the majority of elderly women do not.

The marriage patterns of older and younger women differ considerably. There is evidence that the divorce rate has peaked and may subside somewhat, but it is still expected to remain much higher than was experienced by today's elderly. First-marriage and remarriage rates have declined steadily since the 1970s. It now seems likely that 10 percent of women will never marry, compared with the historical rate of 5 percent (Norton and Miller 1991: 5–6). Even more striking is the growing difference between white and black women. Only 75 percent of black women in their late 30s had ever been married by June 1990, compared with 91 percent of white women of that age. For Hispanic women, the figure was 89 percent. This does not mean that all these women will be childless and without family support in their elder years. A disproportionate share in the growth of one-parent families in recent years has been accounted for by never-married women. The trend indicates long-term economic strains that could affect the eventual economic status of women as they age. This trend also leads us to expect continued high rates of participation by women in the labor force.

Age differences   Living arrangements and marital status shift considerably with advancing age, and the patterns differ between men and women and by race. From age 65 to 74, most men and most white women are married and living with their spouse (figure 2.8). In 1990, among the noninstitutionalized population aged 65 to 74, white males were the most likely to be married and living with their spouse (80.3 percent), whereas black females were the least likely (29.6 percent). At 85 and older, within the noninstitutionalized population, half (48.7 percent) of white men were still married in 1990. By contrast, only 10.3 percent of oldest-old white women were married.

Future marital status   The remarkable changes in marriage patterns over the last quarter of a century will continue to profoundly affect women's lives. As table 2.2 projects, however, we would see little change in the proportion of married elderly men and women well into the next century. There would be a decline in the proportion widowed, especially among women as men improve their chances of survival beyond age 65. The projected decreases in widowhood would occur for women aged 65 to 74 (from over one-third in 1990 to one-fifth by 2020), as well as for women aged 75 and over (from two-thirds in 1990 to just over half in 2020). There would be significant increases in the proportion divorced, however, from 5 percent of elderly men and women in 1990 to 8 percent of elderly men and 14 percent of elderly women in 2020.

One model (Schoen et al. 1985) has projected that baby-boom women will experience widowhood at around age 65 on average, later

Figure 2.8 PERCENTAGE OF PERSONS AGED 65 AND OVER IN THE UNITED
STATES WHO ARE MARRIED, SPOUSE PRESENT, BY AGE, SEX, RACE,
AND HISPANIC ORIGIN: 1990

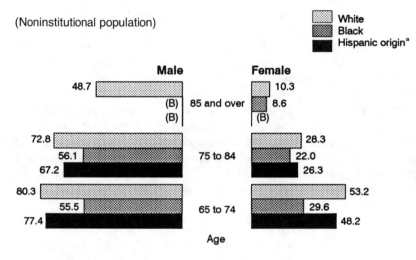

Source: Saluter (1991: table 1).
Note: B, base is less than 75,000.
a. People of Hispanic origin may be of any race.

than elderly women of today. Members of the baby boom would be
about twice as likely as the current generation of oldest old to experience divorce over their lifetime. On average, baby-boom women
would live about 15 years as widows, and less than 1 in 10 would
remarry.

LIVING ARRANGEMENTS

Living alone   Elderly women are more likely than elderly men to live
alone, and as they age, the likelihood increases. In 1990, 9.2 million
persons aged 65 or older lived alone; 8 in 10 of these (78.8 percent)
were women (Saluter 1991: tables 2, 7).

Among noninstitutionalized persons aged 65 to 74, one-third of
both black and white women lived alone. These groups were more
likely to live alone than Hispanic women. Black men were more likely
to live alone than white men.[17] For noninstitutionalized persons aged
85 and over in 1990, white women were twice as likely to live alone
as white men (58 percent and 30 percent, respectively).

Data from the 1980 Census show that the overall proportion of
elderly American Indians, Eskimos, and Aleuts living alone (males,

Table 2.2 MARITAL STATUS OF PERSONS IN THE UNITED STATES AGED 65 AND OVER, BY AGE AND SEX: 1990–2040 (Percentage distribution)

Age, Year	Female				Male			
	Never Married	Married[a]	Widowed	Divorced	Never Married	Married[a]	Widowed	Divorced
65 Years and Over:								
1960	8.5	37.1	52.9	1.5	7.1	72.5	18.8	1.6
1970	7.7	35.4	54.4	2.3	7.5	73.1	17.1	2.3
1980	5.9	39.5	51.2	3.4	4.9	78.0	13.5	3.6
1990	4.9	41.5	48.6	5.1	4.2	76.5	14.2	5.0
2000	4.2	41.2	46.6	8.0	4.5	75.0	14.5	6.0
2020	5.0	43.9	36.7	14.3	6.1	74.2	11.9	7.8
2040	7.3	42.2	37.2	13.2	10.4	69.2	12.9	7.4
65 to 74 Years:								
1960	8.4	45.6	44.4	1.7	6.7	78.9	12.7	1.7
1970	7.8	45.2	44.0	3.0	8.0	78.0	11.3	2.7
1980	5.6	50.0	40.4	4.0	5.2	82.1	8.4	4.3
1990	4.6	53.2	36.1	6.2	4.7	80.2	9.2	6.0
2000	3.9	55.6	30.1	10.4	5.2	79.5	8.5	6.8
2020	6.0	55.9	21.8	16.3	7.8	76.5	6.9	8.8
2040	7.7	57.9	21.5	12.9	12.6	72.9	6.4	8.1
75 Years and Over:								
1960	8.6	21.8	68.3	1.2	7.8	59.1	31.6	1.5
1970	7.5	20.6	70.3	1.3	6.6	64.3	27.7	1.4
1980	6.4	23.4	67.9	2.4	4.2	69.8	23.7	2.2
1990	5.4	25.4	65.6	3.6	3.4	69.9	23.7	3.1
2000	4.4	27.7	62.1	5.8	3.5	68.7	22.9	4.9
2020	3.9	28.9	55.5	11.7	3.1	69.9	21.0	5.9
2040	7.0	30.8	48.7	13.5	8.2	65.4	19.6	6.7

Sources: Data for 1960: U.S. Bureau of the Census, 1960, "Marital Status and Family Status: March 1960, Current Population Reports, ser. P-20, no. 105 (table 1) (Washington, D.C.: U.S. Government Printing Office. November). Data for 1970 and 1980: unpublished revised data replacing data published in appropriate P-20 report. Data for 1990: Saluter (1991: table 1). Projections for 1990–2040: Alice Wade, 1989, Social Security Area Population Projections: 1989 (33–35), Actuarial Study 105, SSA Pub. No. 11-11552, Alternative II (intermediate projections) (Washington, D.C.: U.S. Department of Health and Human Services, Social Security Administration, June).
Note: Data are for civilian noninstitutional population for March 1960–1990; Social Security Area population January 1, 2000–2040.
a. Includes separated.

24 percent; females, 42 percent) was about the same as for blacks (males, 24 percent; females, 40 percent). The proportion of elderly Asians and Pacific Islanders living alone (males, 16 percent; females, 37 percent) was more similar to that for Hispanics (males, 17 percent; females, 31 percent) (Taeuber and Smith 1987).

Living arrangements in the future   It would make demographic sense if women married men at least seven years younger than they are— but they rarely do (Rawlings 1990: table 14).[18] Most younger women are sticking to tradition and marrying men several years older than they are, therefore tending to survive their husbands by 10 or more years. Remarriage is not common among elderly women. In addition, more women (especially black women) are entering their elder years as divorced or never married. Thus, it is likely that elderly women living alone will be part of the future. The absolute numbers are likely to increase along with the increasing size of the aged female population, although a countertrend is improving life expectancy for men, especially white men aged 65 to 74. The Census Bureau projects that by the year 2000, women will maintain over half the households with householders aged 75 and over.[19]

The elderly in institutions   Most elderly people live in the community, but institutionalization increases with age. In 1990, nearly 1.8 million people (all ages) lived in nursing homes. The majority of nursing home residents are oldest-old women.

The increasing number of aged and the increased labor-force participation of women (the primary care providers for the disabled aged) lead many analysts to believe that the number and proportion of elderly Americans living in institutions will increase. Certainly the number may grow simply because the size of the elderly population is growing. The percentage increase in the size of the U.S. nursing home population over the last decade was less than the increase in the size of the oldest-old population. This may be a hopeful sign, but certainly the data available now are not sufficiently detailed to allow us to do more than surmise.

One study (Murtaugh, Kemper, and Spillman 1990) estimated that, if past utilization rates continue, the lifetime risk of institutionalization for those reaching age 65 in 1990 would be 43 percent. Most admissions are for less than one year. Over half of women and one-third of men would use a nursing home before death. If survival rates improve at the oldest ages, it is likely that the risk of institutionalization would also increase.

Research has shown that the better educated also tend to be better off economically and to stay healthier longer.[20] Thus, it is important that the proportion of the elderly population with at least a high school diploma is increasing. The differences in educational attainment between elderly men and women are not substantial. The data shown in the following subsection, therefore, are for the total elderly population rather than women alone.

Future educational attainment of the elderly   The proportion of all elderly Americans with at least a high school education will increase in the coming decades. In 1989, only 55 percent of the noninstitutionalized elderly had at least a high school education, compared with 82 percent of the population aged 25 to 64. Nearly 30 percent of the elderly had only an eighth-grade education or less, compared with about 8 percent of adults aged 25 to 64. This relatively low level of educational attainment was particularly acute among elderly blacks (57.3 percent) and Hispanics (63.9 percent) (U.S. Bureau of the Census 1990: table 1). As for higher education, 11 percent of the elderly in 1989 had completed four or more years of college, compared with 18 percent of people aged 55 to 59 and 24 percent of those aged 45 to 49.

Future improvements in the levels of educational attainment among the elderly will come more slowly for blacks and Hispanics than for whites. For example, more than four in five (82.8 percent) of whites aged 45 to 49 have a high school education and about one-fourth (23.8 percent) have had four or more years of college. By comparison, two-thirds (65.5 percent) of blacks and half (46.8 percent) of Hispanics aged 45 to 49 have a high school diploma. Only one in seven (14.8 percent) blacks that age have completed four or more years of college, as have 9.9 percent of Hispanics (U.S. Bureau of the Census 1990: table 1).

POPULATION AGING AND PATTERNS OF DEPENDENCY

It is increasingly likely that more and more people in their 50s and 60s will have surviving parents, aunts, and uncles. The four-generation family will become common. Children will know their grandparents and even their great-grandparents. And more people, especially the young old, will face the concern and expense of caring for very old, frail relatives. Old people without children may face institutionalization at earlier ages than those with surviving adult children.

There is no historical precedent for the experience of most middle-aged and young-old people having living parents. It has been estimated that one in three 50-year-old women had living mothers in 1940, and that by 1980, that proportion had doubled to two in three (Menken 1985).

The experience and problems of the young old caring for the oldest old will become more and more familiar throughout society. The physical condition of the young old, especially of women, since they provide most of the care, may become a serious issue as they try to help frail elderly people move from beds to baths and toilets. Need for a greater diversity of mechanical aids for private homes and increased demands for access to public buildings for the disabled are likely.

Parent Support Ratio

Future patterns of dependency can be inferred from a parent support ratio,[21] defined here as the number of persons aged 85 years and over per 100 persons aged 50 to 64 years. The parent support ratio tripled from 1950 to 1990 (from 3 to 9), and would triple again over the next six decades (to 28 in 2050). It is highest for whites.

As medical technology provides more ways to save and extend lives, we can expect to see the duration of chronic illness, and consequently the need for help, to increase even more. The strain of caring for frail elderly relatives could affect worker productivity. Women in particular may have to leave the work force or work part-time to care for frail relatives at just the time when they want to work for retirement benefits for their own old age. Other women will be responsible for frail relatives while adjusting to their own retirement, widowhood, and reduced incomes.

Social Support Ratios

The total social support ratio (S.S.R.) is defined as the number of youth (under age 20) and elderly in relation to the working-age (aged 20 to 64) population. The S.S.R. was about 70 young and elderly people per 100 working-age people in 1990 (figure 2.9). From 1990 to 2050, there will be a profound shift in the composition of the total S.S.R. as the elderly population increases and the young population decreases for all groups. For example, for the white population, there would be some decrease in the youth S.S.R., but the elderly S.S.R.

Figure 2.9 RATIOS OF YOUTH AND ELDERLY TO OTHER ADULTS, BY RACE,
AND HISPANIC ORIGIN: 1990 AND 2050
(Number of persons of given age per 100 persons aged 20 to 64)

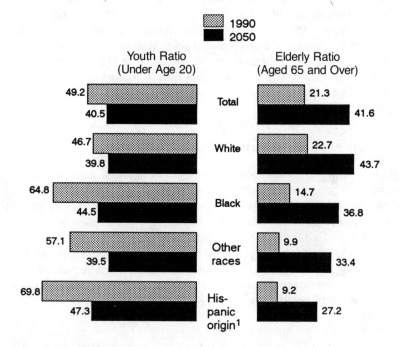

[1]People of Hispanic origin may be of any race.
Note: Youth Ratio is the number of persons under age 20 divided by the number of
persons aged 20–64 times 100. Elderly Ratio is the number of persons age 65 years and
over divided by the number of persons aged 20–64 times 100.
Source: U.S. Bureau of the Census, Data for 1990 from 1990 Census of Population and
Housing, Series CPH-L-74, *Modified and Actual Age, Sex, Race, and Hispanic Origin
Data*; data for 2050 from *Projections of the Population of the United States, by Age,
Sex, and Race: 1988 to 2080*, Current Population Reports, Series P-25, No. 1018. U.S.
Government Printing Office, Washington, DC, 1989 (middle series projections). His-
panic origin data from *Projections of the Hispanic Population: 1983 to 2080*, Current
Population Reports, Series P-25, No. 995. U.S. Government Printing Office, Washington,
DC, 1988 (middle series projections).

would nearly double. Of course, not all youths and elderly people
require support, nor do all working-age people actually work or provide direct support to young or elderly family members (workers do
provide indirect support through taxes and social welfare programs).
The ratios are most useful as indicators of future periods when we

can expect the age distribution to affect the need for distinct types of social services, housing, and consumer products.

The most telling point about the elderly S.S.R. is that it includes a growing proportion of those aged 75 and over who are more likely than those aged 65 to 74 years to have health problems and reduced economic resources. For each racial and ethnic group, those aged 65 to 74 years constituted the largest proportion of the elderly S.S.R. in 1990. By the year 2050, however, the population 75 years of age and over could be about half the elderly S.S.R. (and more than half for whites).

Disability and Dependency

Chronic illnesses increase with age and are more common among women. Among people aged 85 and over, almost one in four live in an institution because of serious health problems. Of the noninstitutionalized oldest old, about one in five is unable to carry on a major activity, and two in five have a condition that limits their activities (Havlik, Liu, and Kovar 1987: 20). In a 1990 study (Harpine, McNeil, and Lamas 1990: table A),[22] 4.4 million elderly people needed assistance with one or more everyday activities. Within each age category, women were more likely to need assistance than men.

ESTIMATES OF THE SIZE OF THE DEPENDENT ELDERLY POPULATION

Functional limitations are higher for women than men and increase with age. As a result of this and the shorter life expectancy of men, women have more years of expected dependency than men.

A study by Hing and Bloom (1990: 6–7, table 5) found that one-third (34 percent) of elderly women were functionally dependent, compared with one-fifth (22 percent) of elderly men.[23] This study found that by age 85, 36 percent of functionally dependent men lived with their spouse, compared with only 4 percent of their female counterparts. Functionally dependent women aged 65 to 84 were most likely to live alone (38 percent). Among functionally dependent oldest-old women, however, 30 percent lived with someone other than a spouse, and 38 percent lived in a nursing home.

Regardless of race or sex, functional dependency increases with age, but at different rates for different groups. The rate of functional limitation is highest among elderly black women. Among the elderly, 74–84 percent of black women had one or more limitations, compared with 62–76 percent of black men, 58–62 percent of white women, and 50–54 percent of white men (data shown in 90-percent confidence intervals). About half of elderly black women had severe limitations, compared with about 30 percent of black men and white women and 20 percent of white men (McNeil and Lamas 1986: table B).[24]

Functional limitations are highest among those with relatively low incomes. There are also differences in the distribution of income between elderly whites and blacks who have one or more functional limitations. Of that group, less than one in three white men aged 65 to 74 had monthly incomes below $900, compared with more than two in three black women that age. White women and black men were in between the two extremes (Taeuber 1992: table 3-10).

Analysts disagree strongly about projections of the future health status of the elderly. One view (Manton 1986) falls midway between the most optimistic and the most pessimistic views. It holds that the prevalence of disability will increase as mortality rates decrease, but that the rate of increase will slow as we learn more about the management of disease and disabilities as well as prevention and rehabilitation (Riley and Riley 1989). If medical advances slow mortality rates among the elderly but not disability rates, the number of elderly disabled would increase in the future just from the increased number of surviving oldest old (Zedlewski et al. 1990: 44–70, 84).[25]

RETIREMENT AND WORK DISABILITIES

Retirement age is being raised to keep pension plans and the Social Security system solvent. But, as reported in the 1984 Survey of Income and Program Participation (SIPP) (reported in 90-percent confidence intervals), a significant minority of all persons aged 65 to 72 had disabilities that prevented them from working. From 25 to 30 percent of white men and women aged 65 to 72 were prevented from working because of a disability, compared with well over one-third of black men and black women (the difference between men and women within a race group is not statistically significant) (Taeuber 1992: table 3-11).

IMPLICATIONS OF HEALTH STATUS FOR LONG-TERM CARE

The increasing size of the oldest-old population alone suggests that in the future more Americans will seek long-term care as they move from independent living, to assisted living at home, to institutional care. The greatest effects would not come until after 2030, when members of the baby boom reach the oldest ages.

The number of elderly people requiring services for functional disabilities can be expected to increase substantially unless there are dramatic medical advances on several fronts. For example, in the

Urban Institute's DYNASIM model, if the disability rates of the 1980s continued into the future, the number of persons with two or more limitations in activities of daily living (ADLs) would increase from 4 million in 1990 to nearly 6 million in 2010 and then to 9 million in 2030. These numbers focus on physical limitations and tell us little about cognitive disabilities that could also affect the need for long-term care (Zedlewski et al. 1990: 54, table 2.10).

It is not clear whether the percentage of the oldest-old population that requires care will increase. The need for nursing home care turns to a large degree on whether medical technology can prevent severe disability as life expectancy is increased among the oldest old. There may be more demand for community care to support the less severely disabled.

THE FUTURE FOR WOMEN IN AN AGING AMERICA

The aging of America, and developments among its elderly population, will not occur in a vacuum but will affect and interact with other simultaneous demographic, social, and economic trends. This section briefly considers projected trends for women's work and education that will affect the experience of women in an aging society and the overall impact of the aging trend itself.

Labor Force Participation

Today, most women work for pay. In 1991, 57 percent of women 16 years and over (56.7 million) participated in the labor force. This is an increase of 20 percentage points over the last three decades. Labor-force participation was highest among women in the prime-working ages (25 to 54): 74 percent compared with 70 percent for women aged 20 to 24 and 23 percent for women aged 55 and older (U.S. Department of Labor 1991b: table 1).

The women of the baby boom, many of whom delayed marriage and childbirth while establishing themselves in the labor force, are more likely to be in the labor force than women of their mother's generation. Fifty-nine percent of married women were labor force participants in 1991, as were 62 percent of women who maintained families. Three in four employed women worked full time in 1991.

The attachment of women under age 45 to the labor force is unprecedented. Women retiring in 1980 averaged 45 percent of their adult life in the labor force. The Social Security Administration projects that women retiring in the year 2000 will have spent 54 percent of their adult life in the labor force, and that this will increase to 71 percent for women retiring in 2020 (Reno 1985: 24). The increased commitment to the labor force has implications for women's lifetime earnings, pension coverage, and ability to provide significant levels of care for frail elderly relatives.

The worklife expectancy of women is less than that of men. There is little difference between white and black women in this regard. The most recent study available (Smith 1986: tables 3, 4, pp. 7, 33) has shown that in 1980, women had a worklife expectancy of 29 years compared with 39 years for men.[26] Worklife expectancy has edged upward for women. In 1900, women had a worklife expectancy of 6 years, about 13 percent of their total life expectancy of 48 years. In 1950, worklife expectancy was 15 years, about one-fifth of the expected lifetime of women. Based on the mortality and work histories of 1980, women would spend 38 percent of their lives in the labor force. The increase reflects women being more continuously involved in the labor force as young women and at ages over 55.

An important factor affecting the worklife of women is higher education, which encourages longer, more continuous careers. In 1980, women who had 15 years or more of schooling had a worklife expectancy of 35 years, compared with 22 years for women who had not completed high school. As women add years of education, the opportunity costs of alternative activities are driven up. Higher education is also associated with later retirement for both men and women.

Occupations

The overall labor force remains sharply segregated by sex. Women have made some progress entering management and the professions. The majority of women, however, are still in traditional, low-paying occupations where more than half the workers are women. The number of women in high-paying jobs remains small relative to men. Women continue to be overrepresented in clerical and service occupations. They are underrepresented in production, craft, and laborer occupations. The largest improvement in occupational mix has been among younger women.

Education, Employment, and Earnings

As already described here, women have made headway in their educational qualifications. The improvements have occurred regardless of race, but Asian and white women are still those most likely to graduate from high school and college.

In 1989–90, women earned the majority of associate, bachelor's, and master's degrees; more than one-third of doctorate degrees; and nearly two-fifths of first-professional degrees. Two-thirds of those aged 25 years and over enrolled in college were women, an indication that older women are moving to catch up to the proportion of men with higher education (National Center for Educational Statistics 1991: tables 27–31).

The largest increases in labor-force participation have been among the best educated. As a result of improved educational status, more women are more qualified for better jobs than ever before. Higher education is associated with higher incomes. In 1990, women with four or more years of college who worked year-round and full-time (YRFT) had a median income of $29,000, compared with $17,400 for women who had graduated from high school only (DeNavas and Welniak 1991: table 29).

At similar educational levels, a gap remains in the income of men and women. For example, for YRFT workers who had completed four or more years of college, women had 70 percent the income of men. The income gap is smaller between black men and women and for younger cohorts. For example, among YRFT workers 35 to 44 years old with four or more years of college, white women had incomes that were 70 percent of those of white men, whereas black women's income was 81 percent that of black men's. For college-educated YRFT workers aged 25 to 34 years old, the gaps were smaller: white women's income was 83 percent of white men's; and black women's income was 96 percent of black men's.

The income gap is partly explained by the concentration of college-educated women in lower-paying occupations such as teaching, social work, and nursing. There is more variety in the occupational distribution of younger women, which is reflected in their improved income relative to men.

Working women have improved their salaries relative to men over the decade of the 1980s. Median weekly earnings of women employed in full-time wage and salary jobs were $373 in the fourth quarter of 1991. This was 74 percent of men's earnings, compared with 63 percent in 1979. This ratio is an overall average that does not take into consideration differences between men and women in work history, educational attainment, skills, and family responsibilities, all of which play a part in the wage gap. The median is greatly affected by the higher concentration of women in relatively low-paying occupations as compared with men. Some women choose to take lower-paying jobs for personal reasons (such as family responsibilities). Others do not have the choice. The fact that women and men tend to take different courses of study in school is also a factor in different occupational patterns. Observed wage differences could partly reflect the effects of past and present discrimination. The wage gap ratio can be used to show change in the relative differences between the wages of men and women. By itself, it is not an indicator that women are paid less for doing the same work as men.

Labor Force Projections

Women constituted 40 percent of the labor force in 1975, 45 percent in 1990, and would be 47 percent by the year 2005 under the moderate growth projections of the Bureau of Labor Statistics. These projections include an increase of 26 percent in the number of women partici-pating in the labor force from 1990 to 2005. In 1975, 55 percent of women aged 25 to 54 were in the labor force. In 1990, 74 percent were. The BLS projects that labor-force participation of women in these prime working ages will jump to 82 percent by 2005 (Fullerton, Jr. 1991: tables 1, 2). The 1990-to-2005 increase in làbor-force participa-tion by women is modest compared with the 1975-to-1990 period, because women of the baby boom will be nearing the ages of peak participation.

Women in an Aging United States

In an increasingly interdependent and aging world, the United States is remarkable for the diversity of its female population. It is never easy to arrive at a shared vision when there are such strong differences, but that is the challenge. The pace and direction of demographic changes will create compelling social, economic, and ethical choices for individuals, families, and governments into the next century. The directions we choose, the decisions we make, will directly affect the quality and vitality of our lives for many decades.

We face critical policy questions. Will more people be at risk of extended years of disability, or will the onset of chronic illness be postponed to older ages? Such issues have many implications for the lives of women—young and old—at all social and economic levels. What will happen if large numbers of people have Alzheimer's dis-ease, for example? Is it inevitable? Preventable? Who will care for the physically and economically dependent aged? Will care programs take into account cultural differences? Can public education assume a larger role in informing individuals about the long-term physical and economic effects of their life-styles in the younger years?

This book describes the changing situation for women in an aging United States. The lives they lead as young women will affect their prospects in old age. As such, it is wrong to assume that tomorrow's older women will have the same characteristics as today's elderly women. A look at the characteristics younger of women can help predict some of the likely changes. For example, educational attainment is much higher for the women of the baby-boom generation. Young minorities in the labor force are employed in occupations covered by Social Security and retirement plans more often than is true of their mothers (Taeuber and Valdisera 1986: 22). There may be implications for economic status in retirement for those young women who have experienced long-term unemployment. Changes in marriage patterns, the increase in single motherhood, and changes in pension eligibility are additional aspects of younger women's lives that will influence their experiences as older women.

For women in an aging society, their own health is not the only issue. The health of others, and the provisions made for care of the frail elderly, will affect the quality of the daily lives, choices, and movements of women of all ages.

Whether we plan for it or not, within the next two decades, the United States will have a much larger, and more varied, older population. This is a certainty. Individual women, and all of us as a society, face the challenge of anticipating and preparing for the changing needs and desires of a diverse, aging America.

Notes

1. This chapter defines the elderly as persons aged 65 and over. Where possible, we show component age groups: the "young old" (65 to 74 years); the "aged" (75 to 84 years); and the "oldest old" (85 years and over). The term "frail elderly" refers to elderly people with significant physical and/or cognitive health problems.

2. Throughout, population projections for the period 2000 to 2050 are middle series projections from U.S. Bureau of the Census (1989). The middle series projections indicate what would happen to the age distribution if fertility, mortality, and net migration trends remained roughly the same as those of the mid-1980s continuing into the next century. For the base year, 1986: lifetime births per 1,000 women, 1,825; life expectancy at birth, 75.0; yearly net immigration, 662,000. Assumptions for the year 2050 are, respectively: 1,800; 81.2; and 500,000.

3. The term "Hispanic" refers to persons who identify themselves as being of Spanish-speaking background and trace their origin or descent from Mexico, Puerto Rico, Cuba, Central and South America, and other Spanish-speaking countries.

4. Life expectancy is defined as the average number of years of life remaining to a person if he or she were to experience the age-sex-race-specific mortality rates of the specified year throughout the remainder of his or her life.

5. Unpublished life table values for Hispanics are from Gregory Spencer, Population Division, U.S. Bureau of the Census. Life table values for American Indians and Alaskan Natives are from Handler 1984 for 28 reservation states (which include 67 percent of American Indians) for 1979–81.

6. Data for 1967 from the Bureau of Labor Statistics, unpublished annual averages from the 1967 Current Population Survey. See also: U.S. Department of Labor (1981: table A-3); Herz (1988: table 1); and Tuma and Sandefur (1987).

7. These are moderate growth projections.

8. Unpublished data for Hispanics from 1987 Current Population Survey available from Diane Herz, Bureau of Labor Statistics.

9. The Survey of Income and Program Participation (SIPP) universe for retirement consisted of all persons 25 years old and over who had retired from a job and received income as a retiree, a survivor, or a dependent during December 1986.

10. A covered worker is one whose employer had a retirement plan for any of its employees; these figures include workers who choose not to participate in the pension plan offered. A vested employee is one with pension rights that cannot be forfeited.

11. Assumptions of the model are described in Zedlewski et al. (1990). The results are conditional on the assumptions of the model and are not a definite statement of the future. The model results are for the entire elderly population, rather than separately for those living in the community versus those in institutional group quarters; this has substantial impact on the income results. Assumptions about assets are detailed on pp. 97–98.

12. For the figures in this paragraph, income is in 1988 dollars, is pretax, and includes earnings, Social Security benefits, private and government pensions, asset income, and Supplemental Security Income. Average pension income includes units with zero income from pensions.

13. Activities of daily living in the DYNASIM model include bathing, dressing, transferring, using the toilet, and eating.

14. U.S. Bureau of the Census, special tabulations from the 1980 Census of Population (tabulations funded by the National Institute on Aging), available from Age and Sex Statistics Branch, Population Division, Bureau of the Census (telephone: 301-763-7883). Poverty rates from the decennial census and the Current Population Survey are not strictly comparable.

15. Only data for the total Asian and Pacific Islander population were available when this chapter was written. An overall average for this group masks the great diversity among the specific nationality groups (for example, Japanese, Chinese, Vietnamese, Cambodian, and so forth). One cannot conclude that women in all Asian/Pacific Islander groups have an economic status similar to whites.

16. Data in this section are for noninstitutionalized elderly persons, except where specifically noted otherwise. In the March 1990 Current Population Survey, there were 29.6 million persons in the noninstitutional population 65 years and over.

17. For those aged 65 to 74, the following are not statistically significant differences: white and Hispanic men; black men and Hispanic women; white women and black women; black men and Hispanic men; and Hispanic men and Hispanic women.

18. For the curious, 0.1 percent of men aged 65 to 69 in 1990 had wives under age 35, 0.7 percent had wives aged 35 to 44, 5.9 percent had wives aged 45 to 54, and 10.8 percent had wives aged 55 to 59.

19. U.S. Bureau of the Census, unpublished work tables prepared by Robert Grymes in conjunction with Grymes (1986).

20. For example, see Kitagawa and Hauser 1973: esp. 11, 14, 157).

21. The ratio is used as an estimate of elderly generations, even though persons who are part of the age group in the numerator are not necessarily in the same families as the age group for the denominator. Thus, the ratio is only a rough indication of need for family support over time.

22. The questions on need for personal assistance were whether a noninstitutionalized person required the help of another person, because of a health condition that had lasted three months or longer, to (1) take care of personal needs such as dressing, eating, or personal hygiene, (2) get around outside the household, (3) do light housework, (4) prepare meals, and (5) keep track of bills and money. These are referred to as "everyday activities" and are somewhat different from the lists of activities included in two other measures used frequently, activities of daily living (ADLs) and instrumental activities of daily living (IADLs).

23. Estimates are based on data collected in the Supplement on Aging to the 1984 National Health Interview Survey and the 1985 National Nursing Home Survey. See Hing and Bloom (1990) for definitions of functional dependency.

24. Limitations are severe if the person is unable to perform one or more of the activities of daily living.

25. Zedlewski et al. (1990) use an activities of daily living (ADL) index as a measure of disability. This is an index of five ADLs that includes people who said they had difficulty performing the activity. The index excludes continence as an ADL.

26. Worklife expectancy measures summarize the number of years during which an average cohort member would be attached to the labor force if prevailing rates of mortality and labor-force entry and exit remained in effect throughout his or her lifetime. The measures include periods of unemployment. The estimates do not control for differences in hours worked among the demographic groups.

References

DeNavas, Carmen, and Edward Welniak. 1991. "Money Income of Households, Families, and Persons in the United States: 1990." *Current Population Reports*, ser. P-60, no. 174. U.S. Bureau of the Census. Washington, D.C.: U.S. Government Printing Office, August.

Fingerhut, L.A. 1984. "Changes in Mortality among the Elderly, United States, 1940–1978, Supplement to 1980." In *Vital and Health Statistics* (National Center for Health Statistics, U.S. Public Health Service), ser. 3, no. 22a, DHHS Pub. No. (PHS)82-1406a. Washington, D.C.: U.S. Government Printing Office, April.

Fullerton, Howard N., Jr. 1991. "Labor Force Projections: The Baby Boom Moves On." *Monthly Labor Review* 114 (11, November): 31–44.

Grymes, Robert. 1986. "Projections of the Number of Households and Families: 1986 to 2000." *Current Population Reports*, ser. P-25, no. 986. Washington, D.C.: U.S. Government Printing Office.

Handler, Aaron. 1984. "American Indian and Alaskan Native Life Expectancy, 1979–81." Washington, D.C.: Indian Health Service.

Harpine, Cynthia, John McNeil, and Enrique Lamas. 1990. "The Need for Personal Assistance with Everyday Activities: Recipients and Caregivers." *Current Population Reports*, ser. P-70, no. 19. U.S. Bureau of the Census. Washington, D.C.: U.S. Government Printing Office, June.

Havlik, R.J., B.M. Liu, M.G. Kovar. 1987. "Health Statistics on Older Persons, United States, 1986." In *Vital and Health Statistics* (National Center for Health Statistics, U.S. Public Health Service), ser. 3, no. 25. DHHS Pub. No. (PHS)87-1409. Washington, D.C.: U.S. Government Printing Office, June.

Herz, Diane E. 1988. "Employment Characteristics of Older Women, 1987." *Monthly Labor Review* (September) (U.S. Department of Labor, Bureau of Labor Statistics).

Hing, E., and B. Bloom, 1990. "Long-Term Care for the Functionally Dependent Elderly." In *Vital and Health Statistics* (National Center for Health Statistics, ser. 13, no. 104. Hyattsville, Md.: U.S. Public Health Service.

Kitagawa, Evelyn M., and Philip M. Hauser. 1973. *Differential Mortality in the United States: A Study in Socioeconomic Epidemiology.* Cambridge, Mass.: Harvard University Press.

Littman, Mark S. 1991. "Poverty in the United States: 1990." *Current Population Reports*, ser. P-60, no. 175. U.S. Bureau of the Census. Washington, D.C.: U.S. Government Printing Office.

Manton, Kenneth. 1986. "Past and Future Life Expectancy Increases at Later Ages: Their Implications for the Linkage of Chronic Morbidity, Disability, and Mortality." *Journal of Gerontology* 41(5): 672–81.

McNeil, J.M., and E. Lamas. 1986. "Disability, Functional Limitations, and Health Insurance Coverage: 1984/85." *Current Population Reports*, ser. P-70, no. 8. U.S. Bureau of the Census. Washington, D.C.: U.S. Government Printing Office.

Menken, Jane. 1985. "Age and Fertility: How Late Can You Wait?" Presidential address delivered at annual meeting of the Population Association of America, March 28, Boston.

Metropolitan Life Insurance. 1988. "New Longevity Record in the United States." *Statistical Bulletin* 69 (3, July-Sept.).

Murtaugh, C., P. Kemper, and B. Spillman. 1990. "The Risk of Nursing Home Use in Later Life." *Medical Care* 28 (10, Oct.): 952–62.

National Center for Educational Statistics, Office of Educational Research and Improvement. 1991. *Projections of Education Statistics to 2002.* NCES 91-490. Washington, D.C.: U.S. Government Printing Office, December.

National Center for Health Statistics. 1985. U.S. *Decennial Life Tables for 1979–91,* vol. 1, no. 1. U.S. Public Health Service. DHHS Pub. No. (PHS) 85-1150-1. Washington, D.C.: U.S. Government Printing Office, August.

————. 1990. *Vital Statistics of the United States, 1988,* vol. 2. Washington, D.C.: U.S. Government Printing Office.

————. 1991. *Health, United States, 1990.* DHHS Pub. No. (PHS) 91-1232. Hyattsville, Md.: U.S. Public Service.

————. 1992. *Monthly Vital Statistics Report* 40 (8, suppl. 2, Jan. 7) (U.S. Public Health Service).

Norton, Arthur J., and Louisa F. Miller. 1991. "Marriage, Divorce, and Remarriage in the 1990s." U.S. Bureau of the Census. Paper presented at annual meeting of the American Public Health Association, November, Atlanta.

Rawlings, Steve W. 1990. "Household and Family Characteristics: March 1990 and 1989." *Current Population Reports,* ser. P-20, no. 447. Washington, D.C.: U.S. Government Printing Office, December.

Reno, Virginia. 1985. "Women and Social Security." *Social Security Bulletin* 48 (2, Feb.). Social Security Administration: 17–26.

Riley, Matilda White, and John W. Riley, Jr. 1989. "The Quality of Aging: Strategies for Interventions." *The Annals* 503 (May).

Rones, Philip L., and Diane E. Herz. 1989. *Labor Market Problems of Older Workers.* Report of the Secretary of Labor. Bureau of Labor Statistics. Washington, D.C.: U.S. Government Printing Office, January.

Rosenwaike, Ira, and Arthur Dolinsky. 1987. "The Changing Demographic Determinants of the Growth of the Extreme Aged." *Gerontologist* 27 (3, June): 275–80.

Ryscavage, Paul. 1991. "Trends in Income and Wealth of the Elderly in the 1980s." Paper presented at annual meeting of the American Society on Aging, March 18, New Orleans.

Saluter, Arlene F. 1991. "Marital Status and Living Arrangements: March 1990." *Current Population Reports,* ser. P-20, no. 450. U.S. Bureau of the Census. Washington, D.C.: U.S. Government Printing Office, May.

Schoen, Robert, William Urton, Karen Woodrow, and John Baj. 1985. "Marriage and Divorce in 20th Century American Cohorts." *Demography* 22 (2, Feb.): 101–114.

Short, Kathleen, and Charles Nelson. 1991. "Pensions: Worker Coverage and Retirement Benefits, 1987." *Current Population Reports,* ser. P-70, no. 25. U.S. Bureau of the Census. Washington, D.C.: U.S. Government Printing Office, June.

Smith, Shirley J. 1986. "Worklife Estimates: Effects of Race and Education." *Bulletin* 2254. Bureau of Labor Statistics, U.S. Department of Labor. Washington, D.C.: U.S. Government Printing Office.

Spencer, Gregory. 1989. Unpublished projection tabulations, U.S. Bureau of the Census.

Taeuber, Cynthia M. 1992. "Sixty-Five Plus in America" *Current Population Reports*, ser. P-23, no. 178. U.S. Bureau of the Census. Washington, D.C.: U.S. Government Printing Office.

Taeuber, Cynthia M., and Denise Smith. 1987. "Minority Elderly: An Overview of Characteristics and 1990 Census Plans." U.S. Bureau of the Census, Washington, D.C. Photocopy.

Taeuber, Cynthia M. and Victor Valdisera. 1986. "Women in the American Economy." *Current Population Reports*, ser. P-23, no. 146. U.S. Bureau of the Census. Washington, D.C.: U.S. Government Printing Office.

Tuma, N.B., and G.D. Sandefur. 1987. "Trends in the Labor Force Activity of the Aged of the United States, 1940–1980." Photocopy, May.

Uhlenberg, Teresa Cooney, and Robert Boyd. 1990. "Divorce for Women after Midlife." *Journal of Gerontology* 45 (1, Jan.): 53–511.

U.S. Bureau of the Census. 1989. "Projections of the Population of the United States, by Age, Sex, and Race: 1988 to 2080," by Gregory Spencer. *Current Population Reports*, ser. P-25, no. 1018. Washington, D.C.: U.S. Government Printing Office.

————. 1990. "Educational Attainment in the United States: March 1989 and 1988." *Current Population Reports*, ser. P-20, no. 451. Washington, D.C.: U.S. Government Printing Office.

U.S. Department of Labor, Bureau of Labor Statistics. 1981. *Employment and Training Report of the President*. Report to Congress. Washington, D.C.: U.S. Government Printing Office.

————. 1991a. *Employment and Earnings*. Washington, D.C.: U.S. Government Printing Office, January.

————. 1991b. *Employment in Perspective: Women in the Labor Force*. Report 822, Fourth Quarter 1991. Washington, D.C.: U.S. Government Printing Office.

Weinstein, Mark H. 1988. "The Changing Picture in Retiree Economics." *Statistical Bulletin* 69 (3, July-Sept.).

Woods, John R. 1989. "Pension Coverage among Private Wage and Salary Workers: Preliminary Findings from the 1988 Survey of Employee Benefits." *Social Security Bulletin* 52 (10): 2–19.

Zedlewski, S.R., R.O. Barnes, M.R. Burt, T.D. McBride, and J.A. Meyer. 1990. *The Needs of the Elderly in the 21st Century*. Urban Institute Report 90-5. Washington, D.C.: Urban Institute Press.

Chapter Three

CARING TOO MUCH? AMERICAN WOMEN AND THE NATION'S CAREGIVING CRISIS

Susan E. Foster and Jack A. Brizius

Men just don't have the knack for caring for the sick and dying.
—Male caregiver
(In Sommers and Shields 1987)

As America's caregivers, women hold the family together and maintain the social structure of the country. But recent changes in economic and demographic realities have begun to turn women's nurturing into nightmare.

In the past, caregiving was limited by several factors that have now changed. First, women did not have to spend as much time caring for a parent. Life expectancies were shorter, and parents of adult women often died before children were out of the home. Today, more people are living longer. Most adult women must care for aging parents, either while they are caring for their own children or after their children have left home. Elderly spouses and other relatives need care, often for extended periods. In the past, caregiving usually did not have to compete with breadwinning, because most women worked in the home. Now, the majority of women are in the labor force, and it is expected that by the year 2000 at least 60 percent of American women will be working outside the home (Johnston et al. 1987). For some women, these factors can combine to produce caregiving situations that provoke emotional, physical, and financial stress.

The combination of increased survival rates, lower mortality at very old ages, and women's increased labor force participation means that caregiving is no longer a potentially satisfying, if burdensome, way of life but, instead, a crisis for an expanding proportion of women in America. This chapter briefly explores the dimensions of that crisis and examines ways in which public policy might be formulated to alleviate at least part of the burden of caregiving, which is sure to increase in the near future as our population ages.

THE CAREGIVING CRISIS: THREE TRENDS CONVERGE

Changing economic and demographic realities have converted caregiving into a national crisis. Three trends have contributed:

The American family is changing. By the year 2000, less than 10 percent of American families will resemble the family depicted on "Ozzie and Harriet"—a family where the father is the breadwinner and the mother keeps the home and raises two children (Hodgkinson 1989). Growing numbers of families are headed by single parents, usually women, and multigeneration households are becoming more common (Hodgkinson 1989). Middle-aged parents are increasingly responsible for the care of frail elderly family members.

The American labor force is changing. The work force is growing more slowly, and the average age of the work force is rising as the pool of younger workers is shrinking. In the coming decades more women will be in the labor force than ever before. As more women work, and as more workers are middle-aged, caregiving and work responsibilities will clash more often. The need for a more family-responsive workplace will grow. Efforts toward increased productivity may founder because of workers' conflicts between caring for family members and job responsibilities.

The American population is aging. The number of elderly people is growing rapidly, but—more importantly—the number of very elderly people is growing faster. The supply of long-term care facilities has not grown, implying that more and more families are responsible for caring for the frail elderly. The numbers behind these trends are examined next.

Children and Families

The number of children under age five is expected to continue to increase until the late 1990s, when the "baby boom echo" recedes. As of 1987, about half of the 18.5 million children under the age of five had mothers who were employed. Of these young children, about 30 percent were cared for in the home by fathers (15.3 percent), 5.1 percent by grandparents, 3.3 percent by other relatives, and 6.2 percent by nonrelatives. Over 35 percent of young children with mothers in the labor force were cared for in another home by grandparents (8.7 percent), other relatives (4.5 percent), or nonrelatives (22.4 percent). Thus, over 65 percent of young children who received care while their mothers worked elsewhere were cared for in a private home. Nearly 37 percent of these children were cared for by a relative or another family member (O'Connell and Bachu 1990).

Increasing numbers of families are headed by single women, who often have few economic resources with which to procure care for their young children. There are more children who need care at the same time that other forces are working to make it more difficult for families to provide that care.

Women in the Labor Force

Women's labor-force participation has been increasing throughout the past 20 years, and is expected to continue to increase during the 1990s. By the year 2005, 63 percent of women aged 16 and over are expected to be in the labor force, constituting 47 percent of the work force (Fullerton, Jr. 1992). More extensive discussions of women's work-force situation are found elsewhere in this volume. An important issue that stands out here is that since the caregiving role is still firmly established for women, their increasing participation in all occupations means that they must more often perform dual roles.

Population Aging

Population aging is the major driving force in the caregiving crisis in America. Although the number of children needing care is also growing, it is the rapidly expanding elderly population that presents the most important challenge. From 1950 to 1990, the population aged 75 and over grew from about 3.5 million to over 13 million, and the number aged 85 and older grew from less than 600,000 to over 3 million.

The fact that more of us are living longer means that more Americans have elderly family members who need care. The startling estimate that 2 out of 3 fifty-year-old women have living mothers is presented by Taeuber and Allen in chapter 2. Further, it has been estimated that more than 1 in 10 people aged 65 and older today have a child at least 65 years of age (Select Committee on Aging 1988). Although most older Americans are healthy enough to live independently, the very elderly are much more likely to need care. Most do not need institutional care, however, and the task of caring for these older people in their homes usually falls to women, daughters, wives, daughters-in-law, or other relatives or friends.

PEOPLE NEEDING CARE

Large numbers of people, both young and old, will require care in the future. More children will need care because more mothers will be working outside their homes. And many more elderly people will require care because they are living longer.

The number of children under the age of five with mothers in the labor force is expected to increase from 9.5 million in 1990 to 10.1 million by the year 2010—about a 6 percent increase (U.S. Bureau of the Census 1989). Children under the age of 15 with mothers in the labor force are expected to increase from 28.5 million in 1990 to 32.0 million by 2010—over a 12 percent increase (O'Connell and Bachu 1990).

The largest increase in persons needing care will occur in the elderly (age 65 and over) population. According to an Urban Institute report, the number of elderly requiring institutional care is expected to more than triple by 2030 if current disability rates persist (Zedlewski et al. 1990). The number with limitations in activities of daily living (ADLs) is expected to more than double. If rates of disability decline modestly, the number of elderly requiring institutional care would still more than double. The same report points out that tremendous diversity will probably exist among the elderly in their ability to pay for care or the insurance that covers it.

In the future, more and more people in their 50s and 60s will have elderly relatives who will require care. Further, the type of care required is likely to be more intensive, since (as shown by Taeuber and Allen in chapter 2) by 2050 over half of the elderly population is expected to be 75 years of age or older.

CAREGIVING IN AMERICA

For many American women, caring for children, disabled family members, and/or aging parents is their most consuming job. This work takes multiple forms. Caregiving is arranging for a grandmother to stay with an infant while a mother goes to work. Caregiving is cleaning up after a victim of Alzheimer's disease, making sure that a bedridden husband receives his insulin, or managing the family finances for an elderly parent. Caregiving is visiting a parent in a nursing home, and then running home to put the children to bed. Caregiving is also a full-time job for many older women, who provide nearly round-the-clock care for their chronically ill husbands or other family members.

If we are to develop a comprehensive caregiving policy, we must focus on the growing demand for care caused by population aging. According to the report of the Select Committee on Aging (1988), family or "informal" caregiving provides 80 percent to 90 percent of medical and personal care, household maintenance, transportation, and shopping needed by the elderly. This chapter's examination of caregiving for the elderly is intended to provide a perspective on caregiving in general, and on its integration with labor force partici- pation. The problems faced by women in caring for the elderly are similar in some degree to the problems of arranging child care or caring for younger disabled adults.

Who Are the Caregivers for the Elderly?

The providers of eldercare are overwhelmingly women: mostly wives, daughters, and daughters-in-law. However, husbands and sons account for about 21 percent of caregivers (Select Committee on Aging 1988).

According to one study, both black and white elderly people are most often cared for by daughters and spouses, though these groups are slightly more likely to provide care in white families. Black sib- lings, other relatives, and nonrelatives are all more likely to provide care for black elderly people than are the corresponding groups for elderly white people (White-Means 1990).

An analysis of data from the 1982 National Long-term Care Survey (Select Committee on Aging 1988) found that the average age of care- givers of elderly disabled people is 57. Thirty-six percent are aged 65 or older. According to another study of those survey data (Stone, Cafferata, and Sangl 1987), the majority of caregivers provide unpaid care for one to four years, but fully 20 percent provide care for five years or more. Caregiving provides no holidays: 80 percent of all caregivers provide care seven days a week. The study estimated that caring for elderly parents forces large numbers of working daughters to rearrange their work schedules (35 percent), cut work hours (23 percent), and take time off without pay (25 percent). For some women, the conflicts inherent in trying to care for elderly family members and keeping a paying job are too much; Stone et al. (1987) found that 12 percent of women who are responsible for caring for elderly parents quit their jobs to provide care. Caregivers of the elderly are less likely to be employed than their age peers in the general population. Another smaller study of caregiving daughters found that 13 percent had quit paid work in order to care for their disabled mothers (Brody et al. 1987). On the whole, caregivers are in middle-income brackets, but female caregivers are much more likely to be economically disadvantaged than their peers in the general population (Select Committee on Aging 1988).

A recent study of female workers who care for elderly dependents underscored the difficulties of women who carry responsibilities as both breadwinners and caregivers. The researchers studied 40 women (daughters and daughters-in-law) who were primary caregivers for dependent elderly family members over the age of 70. These family members also received some home-care services from agencies in Massachusetts (Gibeau 1989). The researchers reported the following findings:

☐ As primary caregivers, the women spent an average of 12 hours per week caring for elderly family members and 26 hours per week caring for their homes, in addition to holding full-time jobs. If the elderly disabled person lived with the caregivers, the combined work of caring for the home and the elderly family member averaged 35 hours weekly.

☐ Most of these women had been in the labor force before assuming the caregiving responsibilities. Most had worked over 20 years, and most had cared for the elderly relative for at least five years.

☐ The major conflicts with work reported by these women were having to leave or miss work to help arrange medical care, and the general level of emotional strain and fatigue. Over half of the women in the sample had missed work an average of seven times within the last year.

For some of the caregivers, the cumulative hours amounted to three full-time jobs (Gibeau 1989). Most women in the study reported that if they were unable to receive any help outside the family for dependent care, they would have to quit their jobs. They ranked the availability of cafeteria-style benefits for eldercare as their highest priority for additional help, if it could be provided.

Paid Caregivers

Although most eldercare is provided by "informal" caregivers, a growing amount of care is the work of paid caregivers, most of whom are middle-aged women. According to a report published by the Older Women's League and the American Federation of State, County and Municipal Employees (AFSCME), about 1.5 million paid caregivers work in more than 25,000 nursing homes and 12,000 home health agencies (Quinlan 1988).

In just a decade, the number of nursing aides grew by over 300,000 workers (see table 3.1). Women make up 90 percent of these workers; over 30 percent of these workers are black and nearly 7 percent are Hispanic. In 1987, the labor force as a whole was about 45 percent female, 10 percent black, and 7 percent Hispanic. There were about 300,000 home health aides working in the United States (Silvestri and Lukasiewicz 1992). Over 90 percent of them are female, and they are also disproportionately from minority groups (Quinlan 1988).

As stated, most paid caregivers are middle-aged. The average age of home health workers has ranged from about 47 to the mid-fifties in several studies. Nursing aides in long-term care facilities are in their mid-thirties on average. Most have only a high school education or less, and have worked in the caregiving field about five years (Quinlan 1988).

In general, nursing aides and other paid caregivers, such as home health aides, work for low wages. In a 1987 study, average hourly wages of nursing aides were reported in the $4–$5 per hour range in most of the metropolitan areas studied. Wages in rural areas are probably lower. About three-quarters of home health aides earned less than $10,000 per year (Quinlan 1988). Many paid caregivers work part-time, and do not receive health coverage or pension benefits. Because wages are low and caregiving is a difficult job, turnover among paid caregivers is high. According to Quinlan (1988: 17), "among nursing home workers, . . . it is not uncommon for half the aides to leave their

Table 3.1 SELECTED CHARACTERISTICS OF NURSING AIDES, ORDERLIES, AND ATTENDANTS IN THE UNITED STATES: 1977–87

Year	Number Employed	Women (%)	Black (%)	Hispanic (%)
1987	1,324,000	90.4	30.8	6.6
1986	1,299,000	90.5	29.5	5.0
1985	1,242,000	89.9	29.2	4.9
1984	1,235,000	90.4	29.0	4.9
1983	1,269,000	88.7	27.3	4.7
1982	1,136,000	87.1	31.3[a]	
1981	1,116,000	86.6	28.3	
1980	1,093,000	87.5	28.8	
1979	1,024,000	87.5	30.6	
1978	1,037,000	87.0	27.6	
1977	1,008,000	86.3	26.5	

Source: U.S. Department of Labor, 1978–88, "Employed Persons by Detailed Occupation, Sex, and Race" (annual averages). In *Employment and Earnings*, vols. 25–35 (Washington, D.C.: U.S. Government Printing Office).

a. Designated "black and other" through 1982.

jobs within the first six months. On average the turnover rate is 60% for 'paraprofessionals' who work in home care; 80% to 90% leave within two years."

The low level of pay for these caregivers raises an important question, posed by Quinlan (1988: 22): "Is the real issue the disdain in which caregiving and nurturing is held? Since 'anyone can do it' is the general perception and those who do are nearly all women, the work is not truly valued. In contemporary American society, that means it is not valued economically."

What Do Caregivers Do?

Caregivers assist with shopping and transportation, perform household chores, help with finances, and administer medication or change bandages. Two-thirds of caregivers attend to personal needs, such as bathing, eating, dressing, and going to the toilet. Slightly less than half of caregivers help individuals get in or out of bed or move around the home. As Sommers and Shields (1987: 16) pointed out, the term *caregiving* "covers a wide spectrum of services, depending on the degree of disability, living arrangements, and economic circumstances. . . . frequently, as the disability increases, there is a progression from sporadic chores to round-the-clock care."

Women appear to provide more high-intensity care than do men who are caregivers. Women are much more likely than men to take care of the personal hygiene needs of the care recipient, including bathing, dressing and toileting, and to clean and cook (Select Committee on Aging 1988). Among blacks, more nonrelatives and relatives other than spouses and children perform more intimate tasks for elderly people than do unrelated white caregivers for white elderly people (White-Means 1990).

Along with the physical services, caregivers provide emotional support. Sommers and Shields (1987) cited case after case of both the rewards of nurturing and the conflicts felt by caregivers. Typical was Carol, who spent many years taking care of her father: "I did the best I could for Dad," she reports, "and I'm proud I did it. If I had it to do over again, which I may have to do with my husband's family, I would. When you are a caregiver you are probably doing the most noble thing you could possibly do for somebody who really needs the help" (41). At the same time, caregiving can be emotionally and physically draining. Dorothy reported that caring for her dying father and her sick mother "was a time full of anxiety and guilt, mostly due to our inexperience. I was not prepared for the dying process, for our society does not teach us to die, only to be born and to be young and beautiful. It was appalling to watch the wasting of my father's body . . . . In retrospect, I wonder how I survived. I am not a nurse, merely a human being with no choice in what was happening to me" (31).

Caregiving can provide substantial personal satisfaction. Most family caregivers report that this work makes them feel useful. Spousal caregivers are especially likely to view caregiving as important to their sense of self-worth. At the same time, caregiving can be a tremendous burden. Caregivers have less time for themselves. They have less privacy than before they began to give care. Their social life declines. They feel conflicts over other roles, such as caring for their own children or providing support for their families. Stone and Kemper (1989) estimated that about 1.7 million women must care for both elders and children. Over half of spouses and children of disabled elders work full-time, representing 9.2 percent of the full-time work force of the country (Stone and Kemper 1989).

The conflict between work and caregiving not only causes increased stress for caregivers, but it may be a substantial drag on national productivity in a period when shortages of skilled labor are growing. Data from the 1982 National Long-Term Care Survey showed that nearly 11 percent of caregivers had left the labor force expressly to provide unpaid care. About 40 percent of these people had been unemployed for two to four years, and a little more than a third had been out of the labor force for five years or more (Select Committee on Aging 1988). Greater percentages of blacks than whites appear to quit their jobs to give care (White-Means 1990). The aging of the work force is likely to increase this drain in the future.

Quitting a job is not the only response to the need to find time for caregiving. Absenteeism is higher among caregivers, since they often have to stay home for unexpected emergencies. Many caregivers seek part-time employment, which usually does not provide the same level of health and pension benefits as full-time employment (Select Committee on Aging 1988).

ADDRESSING THE CRISIS IN CAREGIVING

If we are to address the crisis in caregiving in America, we need a comprehensive caregiving policy, not only to assist women caregivers whose lives are being adversely affected but also for the good of the economy and of society. We need to look at caregiving comprehensively because many of the broad issues are the same for caregivers, whether they are caring for young children, disabled young adults, or the frail elderly. These issues include improving the choices available to caregivers, ensuring the quality of care, and financing care. In addition, the issues of pay equity for women and the role of men in providing care are common to all forms of caregiving.

What issues must be resolved before developing an effective caregiving policy?

First, we must begin to look at caregiving as part of the life cycles of families and develop policies that address the issues from that perspective. Second, we must view caregiving as a matter of choice. Caregivers now have few choices in dealing with these issues; they need more choices. Third, we must decide if, and how much, we want to pay people to take on jobs that women now do on an unpaid basis. Fourth, we must make some tough decisions about how we spend our money. Fifth, we must develop policies that consider the caregiving needs and responsibilities of men as well as of women. In the discussion that follows, each of these assertions is examined from the perspective of a comprehensive caregiving policy.

Caregiving as a Life-Cycle Issue

For many women, life is a lifetime of caregiving. Any effective caregiving policy must thus deal with the caregiving demands made of women during their entire adult lives. Since their lives are spent in the context of families, this implies that we must look at the caregiving needs of families as they evolve over time. Caregiving policy must recognize the diversity among family structures, the burgeoning number of single-parent families, the fact that many caregivers are divorced, and that there are many more older women than men. Caregiving policy must also recognize the needs of older women who have spent their lives as caregivers and now need care themselves. For over half the women in America, issues of participation in the labor force must be overlaid on this picture.

Expanding Choices for Caregivers

The purpose of caregiving policies should be to increase the choices available to caregivers. Caregivers today often have to "choose" between providing care themselves at home (and losing job, income, opportunities) or arranging for institutional care (at a cost that usually pauperizes an elderly family member). Other options are limited.

Most caregivers for the elderly report that they would not want to be relieved of the responsibility, even if full-time substitute care were available. Patients and families see nursing home care as a last, desperate option. A similar story is told by mothers who cannot find adequate, affordable child care and whose children come home from school to an empty house. Americans' frustration over this lack of choice is perhaps the most important political impetus to the solution of the caregiving problem.

Shifting to Paid Caregiving

Giving caregivers more choices will require us to decide in a broad sense how much of informal caregiving we want to convert to paid work. For some services, such as child care, we are paying people to do work so that other people can do other, and presumably more "productive," work. For others, we would be paying people to do work to free up time for caregivers who would not be doing paid work. In this sense, substituting paid work for unpaid work would be buying "leisure" time for caregivers, or at least time that would allow them to reduce their stress and perhaps remain healthy longer.

Some may argue that converting the unpaid work of women to paid work that is likely to be performed by other women is unnecessary, that we should simply get the men to pull their own weight. Although it appears that some men are taking on more of the household and child-raising responsibilities, change in this area is exceedingly slow. There is an international movement to add housework, including caregiving, to the gross national product (GNP). So far, no country has taken this step, but France and Norway have created "satellite" GNP estimates that include it. The inequality of job compensation between men and women exacerbates the problem. When a couple has to decide which of them will quit a job or reduce hours to allow time for caregiving, the woman's job is often the first to go because it is usually the lowest paid.

Deciding How to Spend Money for Care

Solving the caregiving problem will require substantial resources. If we convert much of the unpaid work now accomplished by informal caregivers to paid work, the price will be high. This implies that we must shift priorities in both public and private spending to address the caregiving issue. Four principles should guide this effort:

1. **We must view spending on caregiving as an investment.** Some spending will pay off in increased productivity by women in the workplace. Corporations are investing in eldercare benefits, flexible

work hours, job sharing, and other innovations because they believe that productivity will increase and their labor shortage problems will be solved through these actions. Investments in developmental child care, after-school programs, and other programs for children will pay off in improved education, a better-trained labor force in the future, and reduced special education costs. Investments in respite care services, home healthcare, and other eldercare services will pay off in reduced nursing care costs, especially if they delay the onset of very expensive institutional care. These investments may also reduce healthcare costs for caregivers themselves.

We must begin to estimate the cost of these investments and the savings that would result in order to make judgments about the relative investment value of different components of a caregiving spending policy.

2. **We must invest in preventive measures as part of the solution to the caregiving problem.** One way to relieve the burden of future caregivers would be to prevent the conditions that require care. (For a more extensive discussion of prevention strategies, see chapter 5, by Fahs, in this volume.) Prevention cannot be a total solution, however, because preventing some diseases can lead, in the long run, to situations in which people live longer only to fall victim to diseases that are even more disabling and require more care for longer time periods.

3. **We must find a way to shift priorities in medical care spending.** Institutional care is expensive, and will become even more so as standards of care are raised. At the same time, spending on services that can help delay the onset of institutional care has not grown at the same rate as spending for institutional care. Public policymakers are reluctant to open access to funding for home-based care services to families who already provide these services "informally." The other side of the argument is that these are the areas where we should invest to help solve the caregiving crisis, before the rising tide of frail elderly people ends up in nursing homes at an even greater cost to them, their families, and the society at large.

Another mismatch of priorities in the current care system involves the large amounts of resources spent on terminal care. Issues such as the right to die, the growing use of living wills, and other measures to set individual priorities at the end of life are symptoms of the irrationality of our current system. We now spend vast resources on heroic measures in the final month of life, while relatively little is invested in the quality of life during the final 5 to 10 years.

4. **We must find ways to finance paid caregiving over the life cycle of the family.** Viewed as a periodic need during the growth of a family, the financing of caregiving choices seems amenable to a social insur-

ance approach, whereby investments in caregiving would be financed by savings during the productive years. Unlike Social Security, however, some caregiving expenditures, such as child care, will occur in the early years, while others, such as home healthcare for the elderly, will occur later. This implies that we should spread out the saving and spending patterns of families through a social insurance scheme that works at both ends of the age spectrum.

We need to be able to finance caregiving through a strategy that recognizes that the family's needs peak at certain periods and recede during others. A single mother, for example, may need child care when she is in her 20s, but may not require other caregiving assistance until she is in her late 40s and her parent becomes ill. Our ability to finance paid caregiving at those two periods could be enhanced if we could find a way for this woman to contribute toward those needs during her peak earning years between the ages of, say, 30 and 45.

Caregiving Needs and Responsibilities of Men

Men as well as women are victims of the caregiving crisis. Men's quality of life is impaired by disability and by the lack of options for quality care. When long-term care costs threaten the family's economic security, men's savings as well as women's are threatened. Still, much of the caregiving burden will involve women taking care of other women.

Strategies that enable and encourage men to take on more of the caregiving responsibilities will be necessary. Many men shirk caregiving responsibilities by claiming, as does the man quoted at the beginning of this chapter, that caregiving is "naturally" women's work. It is also true that the current wage structure and values of our society are so skewed that it is economically irrational and socially unacceptable for most men to take time out from jobs to give care. Adopting policies of equal pay for comparable work will help remove the economic disincentive for men to consider caregiving roles and address the economic imbalance that caregiving compounds for women. Developing a more family-responsive workplace will help free men as well as women to provide care. Finally, the provision of paid care will help men take more financial responsibility for caring for aging parents.

TOWARD A NATIONAL CAREGIVING POLICY

Based on our analysis of the caregiving crisis, it is possible to suggest some broad approaches to developing a national caregiving policy.

Our discussion is organized around three necessary aspects of such a policy: prevention, choices, and fairness.

Prevention

The goal of prevention in caregiving is not to eliminate the need for care but to reduce the severity of conditions that require care, and to limit expense. Many of the underlying issues that should be addressed to prevent the need for high levels of care are not usually seen as related to caregiving, or to the welfare of women. Yet these issues are crucial to providing women with options in the face of the economic and emotional demands of caregiving. To this end, the following series of steps, all major policy initiatives in their own right, could help reduce the societal need for caregiving.

   1. Provide adequate prenatal care and other maternal and child health services.   We know how to prevent the majority of conditions that cause us to have to care for young children in special ways. Good prenatal care reduces the incidence of prematurity and of low birth-weight babies, as well as the incidence of a variety of developmental problems in young children. We can reduce the costs of early childhood caregiving substantially simply by making sure that young mothers have access to prenatal care. This step will also pay off in reduced special education costs and many other benefits. Providing better prenatal care is particularly important to black and other minority Americans, whose lack of access to prenatal care has caused significantly higher rates of disability among children of color than among white families.

   2. Reduce the incidence of teenage pregnancy and parenthood.   Children who have children are more likely to have low birth-weight babies, are less able to care for them, are more likely to seek public assistance, and are more likely to require outside help in caring for them. Large savings in the costs of caregiving for children could accrue if state governments and the federal government mounted a significant effort to reduce the incidence of teenage pregnancy and parenthood.

   3. Reduce the incidence of injury and disability.   During the 1980s, the rates of occupational illness and disability began to rise after a decade-long slide (U.S. Department of Labor 1989c). We need to redouble our efforts to improve workplace safety, consumer safety, and safety in the home. Many of the most disabling conditions, requiring the highest levels of care, for nonelderly adults result from injuries in the home, in the car, or in the workplace. Steps such as requiring air bags in cars, reducing drunk driving and smoking, ensuring that Occupational Safety and Health Administration (OSHA) standards are met, and reducing the exposure of workers to toxic environments will have significant effects on the demand for long-term caregiving.

When we invest in prevention strategies for occupational illness and all types of injuries, we seldom consider the costs of caregiving, informal or paid, in reckoning the benefits of reducing the incidence of these conditions. Although we have largely eliminated black lung disease through protective steps for workers in coal mines, we are still paying for years of care provided by women in coal fields. Each disability condition that is allowed to continue costs society not only in terms of the pain and suffering of the victim of the condition but also in terms of the burdens of long-term caregiving.

Equally important would be efforts to reduce the incidence of accidental injury among the elderly. Making residences safer for the elderly, for example, could reduce the chances that they would fall or otherwise injure themselves and require more care. Many elderly people who are otherwise healthy and require little or no care can suddenly require significant amounts of care if they fall or otherwise injure themselves.

4. Invest in research to postpone, prevent, and cure Alzheimer's and other diseases of aging. By current estimates, as many as 47 percent of people over the age of 85 will contract Alzheimer's disease or another form of dementia. The number of the elderly with severe dementia is expected to increase by 60 percent over the next 40 years. If prevention or cures cannot be found, by the year 2030, over 7.4 million Americans will be afflicted with this condition (Schwab 1989). The implications of these data are staggering. Unless progress is made to prevent or cure these diseases of the frail elderly, caregiving burdens could grow substantially in the next decades, even if we can provide more and better alternatives to informal caregiving.

Improving the Choices of Caregivers

Caregivers need choices. Families coping with caregiving responsibilities have varied characteristics; they do not need the same set of services or the same level of services to function effectively. Individual situations vary widely, and cultural and economic differences also argue for a caregiving strategy involving choice. Unfortunately, our traditional way of identifying specific needs and providing categorical assistance for families fails to recognize the importance of choice in caregiving.

Most of the debate in recent years has been about the role of the public sector in providing services that will take some of the burden off of caregivers. Issues surrounding the availability of home health-care, respite care, adult day care, child care, and other paid care-giving services have dominated the discussion of caregiving policy. But there are other important issues in providing choices for caregivers. What follows is a list of suggested steps to improve those choices.

1. Develop a more family-responsive workplace. Employers are beginning to recognize that the demands of caregiving are reducing the productivity of workers just when their companies and the economy as a whole must become more productive to meet global competition. Labor shortages have also contributed to a movement toward a more family-responsive workplace. Public policies are being considered that would require employers to provide a work environment that allows families to meet caregiving needs more easily and effectively. Here are brief descriptions of some programs and policies that can assist people in the labor force who are also caregivers.

Dependent care. Increasingly, child care and care for dependent adults may be provided at the workplace or through employer-supported dependent-care arrangements. We will need to forge a partnership of business, labor, and government to expand the supply of high-quality care. How can the public and private sectors help workers provide high-quality care for young children, disabled family members, and the frail elderly? A survey in the mid-1980s found that only about 3,500 out of a total of about 200,000 large firms provide child care at the workplace or child-care benefits. Yet, provision of child care in the workplace is growing. Companies offering child care assistance to families do so in a variety of ways. John Fernandez (1986) lists the following types of assistance for child care: subsidies for existing off-site day care; company-provided day care; support for family day care; care for school-age children; care for sick children; and paid time off for doctor and dentist appointments. In addition, some companies allow employees paid time off to visit schools for parent-teacher conferences and otherwise attend to education-related problems of their children.

The relatively high cost of child care has apparently prevented many smaller firms from offering company-provided child care, but increasingly child-care subsidies are being offered as part of cafeteria-style benefit programs. Under these programs, employees can choose which of several employee benefits they will use, within a fixed amount of benefit dollars available to each employee. These plans make child care a bit more affordable, but do little to expand the supply or convenience of good child care.

Anecdotal evidence and a few recent studies point to a growing demand for a new workplace benefit—eldercare. A 1985 survey of employees of the Travelers Insurance Company showed that at least 20 percent of those employees were helping an elderly relative, mostly parents or parents-in-law (Friedman 1986).

Victor Barocas and Deborah Lewis (1990) noted that recent surveys of senior executives show that employees of large corporations report a need for help in caring for elderly relatives and that senior executives themselves have similar responsibilities. The combination, they believe, will cause increasing numbers of companies to consider adding eldercare to their benefit packages.

Eldercare programs, to date, have focused mostly on information and referral help, but a few companies are subsidizing home health-care for disabled elderly adults, respite care, and adult day-care services. Table 3.2 depicts a range of eldercare programs and policy options provided by some large corporations.

Child care and eldercare will assume increasingly equal places in benefits available to workers as the population ages, and workers should be able to choose among a variety of dependent-care benefits as part of their compensation packages.

Leave and work scheduling. At present, people who combine family caregiving responsibilities with paid work face limited, unpleasant choices. If the stress of the dual role becomes too great, they must either quit their jobs or stretch existing leave and work schedule policies, trying to find time to fulfill both responsibilities.

A more family-responsive workplace would provide a third alternative: a work environment that combines new types of work schedules and leave policies to allow people to continue working even when their caregiving responsibilities are severe. Policies to permit more flexible work schedules and different types of referral and informational programs have been adopted by some large corporations, as shown in table 3.2.

Leave policies set conditions under which an employee may vacate a job for a period of time and then return to the same job or a similar one with the same employer. Leave can be either paid or unpaid, although most of the public policy discussion has focused on the issue of unpaid leave. Several types of leave policies have been discussed:

☐ Parental leave: provides time off for either parent to care for a newborn or newly adopted child.

Table 3.2 SAMPLING OF ELDERCARE ASSISTANCE PROGRAMS OFFERED BY U.S. COMPANIES

Type of Program	Type of Assistance	Companies that Have Implemented Program
Information and training	Training, newsletters, seminars, videocassettes, information kiosks/fairs	Pepsico, Travelers, Champion, Wang, McNeil Consumer Products
Referral and linkage	Assisting the caregiver to obtain necessary help in the elderly person's home community	American Express, IBM
Direct care	Day-care centers, consortia, respite care	Hallmark, Stride Rite, Aerospace
Support of community services	Support (financial or personnel) to local agencies that provide services to the elderly	Allied Corporation, Gateway Bank (Conn.)
Health promotion and employee assistance programs	Support groups, information seminars, individual or family counseling	Levi Strauss, Aerospace, Good Samaritan Hospital (Oregon)
Human resource and personnel policies	Flextime, part-time/sharing, family leave	Honeywell, Pitney Bowes, Atlantic Richfield, State of New York
Financial assistance or employee subsidies	Flexible benefits, S125 spending accounts, respite care, reimbursement accounts	Remington, Hewitt Associates, American Express

Source: Barocas and Lewis (1990). Reprinted by permission of *The Human Resources Professional*, published by Faulkner and Gray, New York, NY.

☐ Family leave: allows time off for the care of a seriously ill family member, usually limited to a child, spouse, or parent.
☐ Medical leave: offers time off for an employee's own serious illness or injury, even when the illness or injury is not job-related.

Although President George Bush recently vetoed a federal bill that would have mandated unpaid parental, family, and medical leave for workers in the private sector, a number of states have taken action to provide such policies. Table 3.3 shows the status of leave policies among the states as of June 1992.

Part-time work. Women make up about two-thirds of the voluntary part-time work force. Part-time employment has been advantageous to

Table 3.3 LEAVE POLICIES AMONG STATES, JUNE 1992

State	Family and Medical Leave	Parental and Family Leave	Parental Leave	Maternity Leave
Alaska[a]	x			
California		x		x
Connecticut	x			
Florida[a]		x		
Georgia[a]	x			
Hawaii[a]		x		
Illinois[a]		x		
Iowa				x
Louisiana				x
Maine	x			
Maryland[a]		x		
Massachusetts				x
Minnesota			x	
Montana				x
New Jersey		x		
North Dakota[a]		x		
Oklahoma[a]		x		
Oregon		x		x
Rhode Island	x			
Tennessee				x
Vermont	x			x
Virginia[a]			x	
Washington		x		
West Virginia[a]		x		
Wisconsin	x			

Source: Center for Policy Alternatives (1992).
a. Policy covers state and/or public employees only.

both workers and employers. Part-time work enables many workers to handle other responsibilities and still earn some income. At the same time, because part-time workers usually do not receive benefits that are equivalent to those of full-time workers, they are less expensive to employ. In addition, the flexibility of part-time workers sometimes allows employers to schedule workloads more productively.

However, low wages and the lack of benefits are drawbacks for part-time workers. Also, for many employees, traditional part-time work does not provide enough time and/or flexibility to enable them to meet family caregiving responsibilities. To the extent that caregiving responsibilities force women to take part-time work, their incomes have been disproportionately reduced. In addition, part-time work is not always steady. New types of work schedules and work sharing must be developed, ones that do not require people to sacrifice pay and benefits to care for their family members.

Job sharing. When two part-time employees share one full-time job the practice is known as job sharing. Relatively rare until the late 1970s, job sharing has recently grown. In a 1985 survey of 500 large employers, between 11 percent and 17 percent were offering job sharing as an option. A 1986 survey of state personnel offices revealed that 35 to 50 states allowed public employees to share jobs (Olmstead and Smith 1986).

Unlike regular part-time work, job-sharing pay and benefits are equivalent to full-time employment by one person, except that the pay and benefits are shared by two workers. Employers find that job sharing allows them to keep experienced employees who would otherwise quit, including those who would leave employment to care for children or elderly relatives. Some employers have also reported that productivity improves with job sharing, citing the increase in experience gained through the use of two employees to perform one job (Olmstead and Smith 1986).

Voluntary reduced work time. These programs were introduced to blunt the effects of layoffs by asking workers to take voluntary cuts in their hours and pay. Later, employers found that workers were sometimes willing to reduce hours and pay for reasons of their own, especially for family-related activities. Voluntary reduced work-time policies can be effective when family responsibilities are episodic, or when a family crisis, such as the hospitalization of a family member, necessitates a short-term break from full-time work.

Phased and partial retirement. Retirement programs that allow individuals to retire gradually by reducing their work hours over a period of years can also be helpful for caregivers. Phased and partial retirement can allow, for example, one member of a couple to take time away from the job to care for another, even as he or she prepares for full retirement. Phased retirement also encourages workers to stay in the work force longer and reduces stress on them so that they can retain productive work habits. Phased retirement programs are now available in a significant number of companies—perhaps as many as one-fifth of companies with over 250 employees (Barocas and Lewis 1990).

Flextime. Although many restructuring programs require reduced work time, some simply allow employees to schedule their work flexibly within limits set by employers. In flextime programs, starting and quitting times are set by employees, although the total number of hours on the job are not usually negotiable. Flextime can cause some problems for employers, who may have difficulty ensuring work coverage, especially in service and manufacturing concerns. It is, however, highly popular with employees, and has been credited with substantial gains in productivity.

For family members who have dual work and family care responsibilities, flextime can be an important benefit. With flextime, for example, a working parent can schedule work around times when children must be taken to preschool or to school, and couples can use flextime so that together they can cover periods before and after school. Flextime also allows caregivers of elderly people to schedule informal care more effectively.

A more family-responsive workplace will help caregivers find more time to provide good care to their family members. However, unless public policies or private actions ensure that these options do not mean large losses in income, family caregivers will still not be able to afford many of the services that can help alleviate the physical, financial, and emotional stress of caregiving.

2. Expand the services available to caregivers. The problem of expanding choices for caregivers is really two-pronged: we must not only increase the range of services available but improve the ability of caregivers to organize, manage, and finance their choices. The types of services that are valuable to caregivers are well known, but we do not provide them very efficiently, in part because they are offered so sporadically in the community by government or nonprofit agencies. Here are some of the services suggested for inclusion on the caregiver's menu:

☐ Developmental child care. In our view, much needs to be done to expand the supply of developmental center care and to help family child care providers provide developmental care in home settings. A larger coalition to expand child-care services could be developed if intergenerational day care were provided as part of a more comprehensive approach.

☐ Intergenerational day care. Some companies, such as Stride Rite, have experimented with facilities in which elderly people who need care spend part of the day with children, in shared and separate activities.

☐ Adult day care. These services include activities that can keep the elderly healthier and prevent or delay the need for more extensive care, including nursing home care.

☐ After-school or "latchkey" services. The services provide a safe place for children before and after school and maintain a skilled labor force as shortages of younger workers continue.

☐ Home healthcare and "home help" services. Provided in conjunction with informal care, home healthcare could in many cases delay the need for institutional care, and be economically feasible.

☐ Respite care. Using one of the services just listed to give unpaid caregivers some time off from their responsibilities can be an important supportive service to caregivers.

☐ Institutional care. Nursing home care is the care of last resort for most families. There are also serious questions about whether the health care system can afford many more long-term care institutions. One way to limit the costs of long-term care would simply be not to build these facilities. This would further limit the choices of caregivers, but would also maintain considerable pressure on the society to find alternatives to institutional care for the frail elderly.

3. Finance caregiving differently to improve the range of choices for families. Caregiving is a multibillion dollar industry. The child care industry alone accounts for about $15 billion in revenues each year. Revenues for nursing homes amounted to over $40 billion in 1987, about 44 percent of which was paid by the Medicaid program (Rovner 1990). Roughly half of nursing home costs are paid by individuals and families. Less than 1 percent of nursing home costs are paid through private long-term care insurance. Home health services are financed primarily through Medicare and Medicaid with some private payments. Home care financing varies substantially among the states, depending on individual Medicaid policies. In 1988, Medicare paid about $2.3 billion for home health care (U.S. Department of Health and Human Services 1990). Adult day care, respite care, and other nonmedical services are financed primarily through the Older Americans Act of 1965 and through the Social Services Block Grant programs, and are generally funded at low levels.

If one of the most important goals of a national caregiving policy is to improve the choices of caregivers throughout the life cycle of the family, it may be useful to explore a financing option that utilizes the features of social insurance. The characteristics of such a system, if not the actual mechanism, can be envisioned as a new kind of credit account for care.

Caregiving accounts. A system of accounts set aside to finance care could be created through the Social Security system for every adult.

These accounts would be used to finance various caregiving services during the lifetime of the individual. Accounts would be drawn down when people had young children, and would be replenished during the years when children were in school and before caregiving responsibilities for the elderly were heavy. They could be used again to purchase eldercare services, such as home healthcare, when elderly family members became unable to care for themselves. Family members could apply caregiving "credits" to care for other members of the family. Unused credits could be transferred to other members of the family or could be converted into retirement benefits, if, for example, an elderly person died without needing care and his spouse lived on.

Caregiving accounts could be financed through a combination of a payroll tax and through designation of fringe benefits from employment to this purpose. A private employer who offered a caregiving benefit such as an allowance for child care or for eldercare as part of a cafeteria benefit plan, for example, could pay the benefit to the individual's caregiving account for current or future use. In addition, volunteer labor might accrue caregiving credits to a person's account. In several states, senior service "banks" have been created in which seniors volunteer caregiving services in return for future services of a similar kind. This system could be combined with a paid system through caregiving accounts.

Such a system would not be sufficient to pay for all the caregiving services potentially needed in our aging society. Current methods of payment for institutional caregiving would have to continue or be expanded. The purchase of long-term care insurance for nursing home care should also be encouraged. Long-term care could also be provided through a system such as the one proposed by Alice Rivlin and Joshua Wiener (1988), in which a new Part C of Medicare would finance long-term care benefits, including some noninstitutional care.

Caregiving accounts, or a similar mechanism, could be combined with long-term care financing to create a mechanism through which a broad range of noninstitutional caregiving services could be brought to bear on the caregiving crisis. Much more work needs to be done to explore this concept, however.

Fairness and Social Change

The system of caregiving in the United States today is unfair. Financial resources for caregiving are maldistributed. Low-income families—disproportionately minority families—have far fewer resources to care for children, the disabled, or the elderly. At all income levels, women bear the brunt of caregiving responsibilities, and are less able than men to finance alternatives to their own labor in providing care. For women, several features of the economic system make caregiving more difficult. Policies that redress these inequities are basic elements in the resolution of the caregiving crisis in our aging society. This chapter concludes with a brief discussion of three broad policy approaches to a fairer, and more effective, system of care.

1. Address pay equity as an issue in the caregiving crisis.   Of the many ill effects of the persistent wage differential between women and men, one of the most important is that it reinforces the tendency in nearly every married-couple family for the woman to be the one who takes time out from paid work to care for children or elderly parents. Since men make more money than women, on average, it would be irrational for most couples to decide that the man should take on the caregiving responsibilities by reducing time at work. As a result, women often find themselves primarily responsible for caring for their husband's parents, for example. If inequities in pay and career advancement can be ameliorated, at the very least the economic system would not give such a strong incentive for men to avoid caregiving responsibilities, even for their own parents. In addition, women's provision of unpaid care is partially responsible for the income gap. Caregivers who work full-time lose time at work, must periodically leave and reenter the labor force, and lose opportunities for advancement.

2. Enable and encourage men to take on more caregiving responsibilities.   Ultimately, men and women will have to share more fully in providing informal care—for children, the disabled, and the frail elderly. This will require sweeping changes in the ways men and women perceive their roles in family and society. Public policy changes cannot in themselves cause this rethinking, but they can reduce the barriers to social change. Undoubtedly, demographic trends will influence men's role in caregiving. As sons are more likely to be divorced, we may find employers more likely to offer family leave, and we may find more sons shouldering the caregiving burden.

3. Build coalitions to address caregiving comprehensively.   Social change and changes in public policy will not occur unless large numbers of people unite to influence government and private-sector actions. Until recently, the tendency of people to conceptualize different caregiving issues as belonging to separate categories of need has limited the ability of any one group to influence public policy on caregiving issues. Child-care advocates have steered a course separate from either advocates of greater services for the elderly or advocates for the disabled population. In many cases, these interest groups have been put in the position of competing for limited resources, rather than joining together.

Viewed as a single issue, however, the caregiving crisis provides an opportunity for people to unite to demand greater investment in prevention, more choices for caregivers, and increased fairness in the workplace. Since most caregivers are women, caregiving is certainly a women's issue, but it is a universal problem. Unlike many dilemmas facing America, the caregiving crisis cuts across the lines of income, class, and race. Although lower-income people and minorities are particularly hard-hit by the lack of caregiving choices, nearly every family in America is affected by the caregiving crisis. This means that broader coalitions can be formed to address the issue.

By offering more choices to families, we could also expand the paid caregiving industry and address many of the problems of people who now work in difficult and low-wage jobs. Both employers and unions have an interest in providing more options for families who must address the issue of caregiving, because worker productivity and welfare both depend in part upon solving the caregiving problem.

The aging of the U.S. population will intensify demand and make caregiving a more pressing issue for some time to come. Advocacy for both caregivers and those who need care at all stages in the family life cycle could become a powerful political and social dynamic. Virtually every family in America will face difficult caregiving responsibilities at one time or another. If the needs of all families can be expressed in the context of caregiving policy, the chances for positive change will be immeasurably strengthened.

References

Barocas, Victor S., and Deborah J. Lewis. 1990. "Elder Care: The Employee Benefit of the '90s?" *Human Resources Professional* 2(102) (Winter): 21–25.

Beck, Melinda, Barbara Kantrowitz, Lucille Beachy, Mary Hagar, Jeanne Gordon, Elizabeth Roberts, and Roxie Hamill. 1990. "Trading Places." *Newsweek,* July 16: 48–54.

Brody, Elaine M. 1985. "Parent Care as a Normative Family Stress." *Gerontologist* 25(1): 19–29.

Brody, Elaine M., Morton H. Kleban, Pauline T. Johnsen, Christine Hoffman, and Claire B. Schooner. 1987. "Work Status and Parent Care: A Comparison of Four Groups of Women." *Gerontologist* 27(2): 201–208.

Center for Policy Alternatives. 1992. "Family Leave Laws in the States." Washington, D.C.: Author.

Fernandez, John P. 1986. *Child Care and Corporate Productivity.* Lexington, Mass.: D.C. Heath and Co.

Friedman, Dana E. 1986. "Eldercare: The Employee Benefit of the 1900's?" *Across the Board* (June): 45–51.

Fullerton, Howard N, Jr. 1992. "Labor Force Projections: The Baby Boom Moves On." In *Outlook: 1990–2005. BLS Bulletin* 2402. Washington, D.C.: U.S. Department of Labor, May.

Gibeau, Janice L. 1989. *Adult Day Health Services as an Employee Benefit.* Washington, D.C.: National Association of Area Agencies on Aging.

Hodgkinson, Harold. 1989. *The Same Client: The Demographics of Education and Service Delivery Systems.* Washington, D.C.: Institute for Educational Leadership.

Johnston, William B., Arnold E. Packer, Matthew P. Jaffe, Marylin Chou, Philip Deluty, Maurice Ernst, Adrienne Kearney, Jane Newitt, David Reed, Ernest Schneider, John Thomas. 1987. *Workforce 2000: Work and Workers for the Twenty-First Century.* Indianapolis: Hudson Institute.

Leary, Warren E. 1989. "New Study Increases the Estimate of the Frequency of Alzheimer's." *New York Times*, November 11: A1.

Manuel, Ron C., ed. 1982. *Minority Aging: Sociological and Social Psychological Issues.* Westport, Conn.: Greenwood Press.

O'Connell, Martin, and Amara Bachu. 1990. *Who's Minding the Kids?* U.S. Department of Commerce, Bureau of the Census. CPR Ser. P-70, no. 20. Washington, D.C.: U.S. Bureau of the Census, July.

Odum, Maria. 1992. "If the GNP Counted Housework, Would Women Count for More?" *New York Times*, April 5.

Older Women's League. 1989. "Failing America's Caregivers: A Status Report on Women Who Care." In *Mother's Day Report, 1989.* Washington D.C.: Author.

Olmstead, Barney, and Suzanne Smith. 1986. *Creating a Flexible Workplace.* New York: American Management Association.

"People Patterns." 1990. *Wall Street Journal*, August 14: B2.

Quinlan, Alice. 1988. *Chronic Care Workers: Crisis among Paid Caregivers of the Elderly.* Washington, D.C.: Older Women's League and American Federation of State, County, and Municipal Employees.

Rivlin, Alice, and Joshua Wiener. 1988. *Caring for the Disabled Elderly: Who Will Pay?* Washington, D.C.: Brookings Institution.

Rovner, Julie. 1990. "No Help from Congress on a Near-Term Solution for Long-Term Care." *Governing* 3(9): 21–27.

Schwab, Teresa, ed. 1989. *Caring for an Aging World: International Models for Long-Term Care, Financing, and Delivery.* Washington, D.C.: McGraw Hill.

Select Committee on Aging, U.S. House of Representatives. 1988. *Exploding the Myths: Caregiving in America.* Washington, D.C.: U.S. Government Printing Office.

Silvestri, George, and John Lukasiewicz. 1992. "Occupational Employment Projections." In *Outlook: 1990–2005. BLS Bulletin* 2402. Washington, D.C.: U.S. Government Printing Office, May.

Sommers, Tish, and Laurie Shields. 1987. *Women Take Care. The Consequences of Caregiving in Today's Society.* Gainesville, Fla.: Triad Publishing Co.

Stone, Robyn, Gail Lee Cafferata, and Judith Sangl. 1987. "Caregivers of the Frail Elderly: A National Profile." *Gerontologist* 27: 616–26.

Stone, Robyn, and Peter Kemper. 1989. "Spouses and Children of Disabled Elders: How Large a Constituency for Long-term Care Reform?" *Milbank Quarterly* 67(3–4): 485–506.

U.S. Bureau of the Census. 1989. *Current Population Reports*, ser. P-25, no. 1018. Washington, D.C.: U.S. Government Printing Office.

U.S. Department of Health and Human Services. 1990. *Health United States: 1989*, DHHS Pub. No. (PHS) 90-1232. Washington, D.C.: U.S. Public Health Service.

U.S. Department of Labor. Bureau of Labor Statistics. 1989a. *Employment in Perspective: Women in the Labor Force.* Report 777, Third Quarter, 1989. Washington, D.C.: U.S. Government Printing Office.

————. 1989b. *Employment in Perspective: Women in the Labor Force.* Report 782, Fourth Quarter, 1989. Washington, D.C.: U.S. Government Printing Office.

————. 1989c. BLS Reports on Survey of Occupational Injuries and Illnesses in 1988. Washington, D.C.: U.S. Government Printing Office, Nov. 15, 1989.

U.S. Health Care Financing Administration. 1989. *Health Care Financing Review*, 1989. Washington, D.C.: U.S. Government Printing Office.

White-Means, Shelley I. 1990. "Long-term Care for the Black Elderly." In *Proceedings of the Second Annual IWPR Conference.* Washington, D.C.: Institute for Women's Policy Research.

Zedlewski, Sheila, R.O. Barnes, M.R. Burt, T.D. McBride, and J.A. Meyer. 1990. *The Needs of the Elderly in the 21st Century.* Urban Institute Report 90-5. Washington, D.C.: Urban Institute.

Chapter Four

YEARS GAINED AND OPPORTUNITIES LOST: WOMEN AND HEALTHCARE IN AN AGING AMERICA

Jo-Ann Lamphere-Thorpe and Robert J. Blendon

How will the aging of the U.S. population affect women both as healthcare providers and consumers? This is a critical question, given the difference in life expectancy between women and men, women's difficulty securing insurance for catastrophic medical expenses, and our society's continued reliance on women's unpaid long-term care. What will be the combined effects of women's changing social and economic status and the country's aging population on the availability of healthcare—especially for women of all ages and races—in the years ahead? What policy changes are needed now to ensure that all Americans have access to necessary healthcare as our society ages?

Americans' prospects for long, vigorous lives have never been better. However, though individuals can look forward to unprecedented good health as they age, our collectively aging society is facing a crisis in healthcare. Population aging is increasing the prevalence of chronic diseases—a trend that is expected to continue for the foreseeable future—and is shifting the provision of private and public health resources to costly long-term care. Without important changes in healthcare policy, the tremendous gains in life expectancy realized in the past century may come to represent not so much a gift of increased life as a burden of increased illness.

The intersection of the aging trend with the healthcare system affects all Americans, but it is primarily the domain of women, who suffer more chronic illness and use more long-term care services than do men. Women are also the main providers of healthcare—professionally, often as nurses, technicians, and aides, and, at home, as family caregivers. As both patients and providers, women stand to be disproportionately affected by changes that result from the aging trend and societal decisions about the allocation of scarce healthcare resources.

The aging of the U.S. population is accelerating at a time when the country is already experiencing a crisis in the cost and availability of healthcare. Spiraling healthcare costs and increasing consumer demand, especially for long-term care, have begun to devastate family savings, deplete federal and state treasuries, and threaten corporate competitiveness. By the year 2000, annual spending on healthcare is expected to average $5,551 for every man, woman, and child in the United States—in all likelihood reaching 15 percent of the country's gross national product (Health Care Financing Administration 1987).[1] At the same time, the benefits that our sophisticated healthcare system can offer are not equitably distributed. Nearly 14 percent of the nation's citizens lack basic health insurance coverage, and the infant mortality rates in many American cities rival those of Third World countries. Excess mortality for most diseases and lack of access to vital healthcare for black Americans, Hispanics, and American Indians have been well documented. Furthermore, it has become increasingly uncertain whether society is willing, or even able, to support an expanded medical sector to address such unmet needs.

This chapter highlights key trends affecting the demand for and delivery of healthcare—especially for women—in an aging society. We examine the relationship between population aging and women as both providers and users of healthcare. We begin with a discussion of factors affecting women's health status and their access to care. The impact of increased longevity on long-term care is a central theme. The second section of the paper addresses women's changing roles as healthcare providers in an aging society. Finally, we explore healthcare policy directions for an aging society. Such directions are important to consider *now:* the world of the future will be shaped by our values, investments, and choices today.

WOMEN'S HEALTH AND ACCESS TO CARE IN OUR AGING SOCIETY

The aging of the U.S. population is a significant demographic force that will have a serious and wide-ranging impact on women's healthcare needs and use in the years ahead, as demonstrated by Taeuber and Allen in chapter 2 in this volume. To assess the future effects of this aging trend, one must examine some of the indicators of women's health status today and assess their significance in an aging society.

Unequal Gains in Longevity

Although mortality rates for older Americans fell substantially during the 1970s and more slowly during the 1980s, these trends have not been uniform and are experienced unequally across age, race, and gender groups (Olshansky 1988). Reductions in mortality have been greater for women than for men, especially at older ages.[2] The total age-adjusted death rates for black women and men remain about 50 percent higher than those for whites, although the number of excess deaths, a primary indicator of the disparity in health status between minority and nonminority populations, has recently decreased. Despite dramatic gains in life expectancy for both blacks and whites, large differences remain between sexes and races, with black men continuing at particular risk.

Women are profoundly affected by the excess mortality of the men in their lives. The years of potential life lost before age 65 for men from death from heart disease, stroke, cancer, and homicide have a fundamental impact on women's healthcare needs and their use of services. Men's, especially black men's, excess mortality in an aging society contributes to women's premature widowhood, their increased probability of poverty in old age, and a diminished likelihood of spousal physical support and companionship as the disabilities associated with growing older are experienced.

Although women have a longer life expectancy than men, health statistics routinely display a higher use of health services for women. Women have greater overall rates of physical illness, disability days, physician visits, and prescription and nonprescription drug use than do men. Women are more frequently sick in the short run and have higher prevalence rates for numerous nonfatal chronic conditions in the long run. Women, at all advanced ages, suffer considerably higher rates of institutionalization. Thus, to the extent that longer life has been associated with deteriorating health, death of family, and resulting poverty, increased longevity may have been more of a burden for women than for men.

But what about the future? Many contemporary models of human mortality predict that life expectancy in the United States is unlikely to increase much beyond current levels, a view that has strongly influenced federal planning (Manton 1982). Some theorists have argued that mortality reductions and life expectancy increases will cease in the near future because of biological constraints on the length of the human life span (Fries 1980). At the same time, the average age of first serious infirmity could be raised so that most illness would be experienced during a relatively brief period before death—suggesting that society is entering an age in which people will be healthier longer. Thus, morbidity would be compressed into the shorter span between the higher age of onset of disability and the fixed occurrence of death.

Although the "compression of morbidity" theory paints a reassuring picture of a diminished burden of disability in an aged population, other authorities argue that the theory is undermined by common sense and clinical observation. Some predict that the prevalence of disease and disability will increase as life expectancy is increased, leading to a "pandemic of mental disorders and chronic disease" (Gruenberg 1977). The justification for this conclusion is the belief that life expectancy is increasing not by reducing the incidence of chronic diseases but by reducing their deadly effects. The successes of modern medical care have assured industrialized countries of an increase in the number of people who survive previously fatal illnesses only to be afflicted by chronic conditions for a prolonged period of time (Avorn 1986).

Many researchers, including ourselves, believe it is likely that both compression of morbidity and extended morbidity are occurring simultaneously. That is, there may be an increasing proportion of individuals in good health up to the point of death, as well as an increasing proportion with prolonged severe functional limitations (Rice and Feldman 1983). What is important for an assessment of women's health status in an aging society is the recognition that reductions in mortality could result in important changes in the surviving elderly population, with increased variation among individuals' health status at any given age (Poterba and Summers 1987). Medical progress is likely to make the best-off members of any aged population still better off in terms of health status, whereas marginal survivors would likely be in very poor health and less self-sufficient than the rest of the elderly population. Medical progress in reducing morbidity may be offset by increased survivorship among relatively unhealthy members of the population, and the pattern may not be gender-neutral. Compression of morbidity may be more characteristic of men and extended morbidity more applicable to women.

Whether or not one believes that older women (and men) will be healthier, on average, in the future depends in part upon one's interpretation of current mortality and morbidity trends. Past experience suggests, however, that great caution should be exercised in treating mortality projections as forecasts of future health status. National data on disability, restricted bed days, self-appraised health, rate of institutionalization at advanced ages, and selected clinical measures show no marked change in health status among those aged 65 and over, despite significant increases in life expectancy at advanced ages. As reductions in mortality do not seem to be associated with reductions in morbidity at any age, there may be little reason to assume that the typical elderly man or woman in the future will be better off than he or she is now (Poterba and Summers 1987). Yet, because some researchers have identified what seems to be a decrease in the severity of chronic diseases, many continue to believe that mortality reductions can extend the productive life span of individuals, not by eliminating chronic diseases but by reducing their severity at any given age (Manton 1982).

Projections about the future health status of women must consider many factors, including the extent to which women take responsibility for their own health, the presence of environmental and occupational risk factors, economic trends and disease patterns among different socioeconomic groups, the application of new technology, and society's conception of the value of life. These factors will interact, making it increasingly difficult to predict mortality levels among older people. What stands out as a primary health goal in our aging society is the control of chronic illness and its consequences among the elderly, not just further reductions in mortality.

Implications for Services

As people enter their last decades of life, their need for health services increases dramatically. The elderly use far more hospital care and physician and nonphysician services than do younger people. Their utilization of health services is not uniform, reflecting the heterogeneity of the aged population as well as medical practice patterns.

The high use of medical services by the elderly is of immediate and future concern to the U.S. government because of utilization's impact on federal expenditures, specifically for Medicare, the public insurance program providing coverage to about 97 percent of the U.S. aged population. Spending for Medicare has increased from $36.4 billion in 1980 to more than $108 billion projected for 1990 (Levit et al. 1991). Future cost estimates, affected by highly variable economic performance measures and demographic projections, indicate that annual Medicare expenditures could reach $302.8 billion by 2000 (Sonnefeld et al. 1991).

As the population ages, demographic changes, rather than more expensive medical treatments, are expected to increasingly influence

Medicare's expenditure growth. If, while the number of elderly people increases, average per capita cost also rises, annual growth in Medicare expenditures could exceed the rapid growth rates in the past (U.S. Congressional Research Service 1987). Concerns and controversy about the cost of Medicare benefits and the means used to finance them (currently, a combination of payroll tax, general revenues, and premiums) can be expected to increase during the next 20 years.

These financial projections alone are alarming, but they ignore the anticipated greater variance in health status of older persons and the increasing number and proportion with severe functional limitations. Because of these factors, population aging will have an even more dramatic effect on the utilization of long-term care services—almost none of it covered by Medicare.

Although nursing homes serve less than a fifth of the disabled elderly, they dominate long-term care financing.[3] Fully 82 percent of total expenditures for long-term care was allocated to nursing homes in 1988. Of that total cost ($43.1 billion), nearly 47 percent was paid by the public sector, primarily through the poverty-based Medicaid program (U.S. Bipartisan Commission 1990).

The importance of these costs is underscored by demographic projections, which show that the number of elderly in nursing homes could triple by 2030—an increase to 5.3 million persons—if current rates of disability persist along with projected improvements in mortality (Zedlewski et al. 1990).[4] Women's rate of institutionalization continues to be nearly double that for men. The need for long-term care services is expected to increase faster than the size of the elderly population between 1990 and 2030. New estimates predict that 43 percent of all those who turned 65 in 1990 will receive care in a nursing home, spending an average of 2.8 years there (Kemper, Spillman, and Murtaugh 1991). Clearly, large numbers of nursing home beds will be needed to meet the demand of the aging baby-boom population, forcing a reexamination of states' policies concerning nursing home bed supply.

It has been estimated that nearly three-quarters of severely disabled elders live in the community (U.S. Bipartisan Commission 1990). This disabled population is disproportionately female (67 percent), very old (aged 85 and over), of minority background, and poor, compared with the general elderly population (Rowland 1989). Despite the widespread need, home-care services are limited in supply and scope. The fact that only 25 percent of the disabled elderly in the community receive any paid home care underscores society's reliance on family members or other unpaid caregivers—usually women—as described by Foster and Brizius in chapter 3 of this volume. Less than $10 billion of the nation's total long-term care expenditures in 1988 supported home-care services.

More troublesome than the distribution of long-term care expenditures is the bizarre way in which such care is financed: initial out-of-pocket payments by patients, leading to poverty in about a quarter of all cases, at which time government absorbs through the Medicaid program the continuing expense for needed care. Thus the welfare-based Medicaid program has become the dominant source of public funding for long-term care, accounting for 71 percent of government spending for nursing home and home care in the period from 1986 to 1990 (Rivlin and Wiener 1988). Medicaid, enacted in 1965, was never intended to serve as a long-term care program for large numbers of disabled elderly persons (U.S. Congressional Research Service 1988). Their dependence on this program threatens the quality of care received and creates massive economic hardships for them and their families.

This perverse kind of public catastrophic insurance for long-term care has serious and growing consequences. For the elderly and their families, "spending down" lifelong assets to impoverishment is a dreaded process that carries catastrophic emotional as well as financial costs. In contrast with the shared risk for acute healthcare costs, the burden of payment for long-term care falls primarily on those unlucky enough to need it.

For federal and state governments, which share the cost of Medicaid, the economic burden is enormous. Public costs of the Medicaid program have been rising rapidly and are projected to reach $46 billion for nursing home services and $2.4 billion for home care (in 1987 dollars) annually between the years 2016 and 2020 (Rivlin and Wiener 1988). With no endorsement to increase taxes for the additional costs, states are now in the impossible position of allocating increasingly inadequate Medicaid funds between healthcare for poor women with children and long-term care for the disabled elderly, again primarily women. Poor women of all ages are thus increasingly feeling the impact and divisiveness of society's attempts to meet the chronic care needs of its aging population.

The future looks even more bleak: if the average age at which severe disabilities occur rises—which seems to be occurring—even fewer family resources may be available to ameliorate the public cost of long-term care, even as the proportion of frail very elderly people in our society continues to grow (Soldo and Manton 1985).

Health Insurance and Women's Access to Care

Private health insurance constitutes the single largest means by which nonelderly women and men secure healthcare for themselves and their families. Some coverage is nearly universal for full-time employees in private businesses with 100 or more employees or state and local governments. The breadth of job-based health insurance makes it all the more shocking that three out of four Americans without health insurance in 1987 were themselves workers or lived in families of workers (U.S. Bipartisan Commission 1990).

The link between full-time paid employment and health insurance is critical for women because they are less likely than men to obtain job-based coverage for themselves and their families. Women are more often in jobs offering no health insurance than are men for three reasons: women have higher rates of part-time work; they more frequently move in and out of the labor force; and they are more likely to work in occupations and for smaller employers where insurance is less often provided as a benefit. Women who are employed in private households or in the service sector have the highest probability of being uninsured. Women in only three industrial categories—transportation, manufacturing, and professional—have more than a 50 percent chance of obtaining insurance through their own employment plans. Women who do have health insurance through their employment group plan are a select group: two-thirds of them have yearly incomes over 500 percent of the poverty threshold; over 60 percent are relatively young (aged 18–44); and 85 percent of them are white (author's calculations from U.S. Bureau of the Census 1989b).

Women's access to health insurance is limited also by gender-assigned work-patterns and social roles outside the paid labor force. They may become uninsured when, to provide family care and perform unpaid housework, they accept part-time employment or leave the paid labor force altogether. Fully half of the uninsured adults not in the labor force described their major activity as "keeping house" in 1988 (Lewin/ICF 1990). Divorced women have been found to be twice as likely as married women to be uninsured (Berk and Taylor 1984). We believe that gender issues have interacted with changes in the group health insurance market to make health insurance a particular and growing problem for women.

Because of escalating costs, employers have reduced their contributions toward coverage of dependents (spouses and children) during the past 10 years and are expected to continue this direction in the absence of federal legislation and as medical costs rise. The scope of employee health benefits—such as family coverage, subsidized monthly premiums, and what services are insured—varies widely among employers. As employees are asked to pay more for dependent coverage, increasing numbers can be expected to drop this insurance, particularly low-wage workers with other pressing financial needs.

One demographic force that will continue to contribute to the growth of the uninsured population is the changing nature of American families. The proportion of households comprising "unrelated" individuals has been growing, and insurance policies generally do not allow such persons to be covered under family policies. This may be a particular problem for minority families, who have a long tradition of intergenerational support and shared housing (White-Means 1990).

Surprisingly, women are actually less likely to be uninsured than men—12.2 percent versus 14.4 percent—which has been partly attributed to the Medicaid program, as well as to the larger share of women among the elderly, who are almost universally covered by Medicare (Lewin/ICF 1990). Many low-income women are still uninsured, however. Because eligibility under the fiscally strapped Medicaid program has not kept pace with the increasing number of people with poverty-level incomes, only 41 percent of poor Americans were covered by Medicaid in 1986 (U.S. Congressional Research Service 1988). Fully 66 percent of uninsured women in 1988 fell below 200 percent of the poverty threshold and were not covered by Medicaid.

The major consequence of the lack of health insurance is reduced access to medical services. Numerous surveys indicate that the uninsured are indeed forgoing medical care. Lack of health insurance has important consequences for older women's health, a growing concern in an aging society. Uninsured women obtain fewer preventive services than the insured. A 1989 study reported that basic screening for four major illnesses was significantly less frequent for uninsured middle-aged women than for those who had insurance. The uninsured women studied were likely to have low incomes and to be at higher risk for the diseases these tests detect (Woolhandler and Himmelstein 1988). Yet, a focus on the prevention of disability can delay the need for costly long-term care services, three-quarters of which are delivered to women.

Women of all ages are about twice as likely to be *underinsured* as men. Women aged 55–64 are at greatest risk, because a larger proportion of privately insured individuals in this age group is enrolled in nongroup plans where coverage is less comprehensive. By limiting access to preventive healthcare, the lack of adequate insurance among midlife women may add to the costs of long-term care for these same women in old age.

For elderly women, inadequate long-term care financing remains the major gap in healthcare coverage (Rowland 1989). Although most women aged 65 and older are covered by the Medicare program, most spend a significant portion of their incomes on medical expenses. Women spend a higher percentage of their incomes than men, reflecting both gaps in coverage for women's chronic conditions and women's lower median income. Unmarried elderly women (aged 65 and over) spend an average of over 16 percent of their incomes on healthcare, compared with less than 9 percent for elderly married couples. Medicaid paid for 49 percent of the healthcare expenses of elderly unmarried men, but only 33 percent of the health expenditures of unmarried elderly women in 1986 (Older Women's League 1989).

Of growing concern in an aging society in which more and more women are working in the paid labor force is the issue of retiree health benefits. Some companies predict that by the year 2000 their biggest corporate challenge will be to meet the cost of providing healthcare to their retirees. This is not surprising, considering that per capita healthcare expenditures for Americans aged 65 and over averaged $5,360 in 1987 compared with $1,287 for those under age 65.

Because of rising costs and the implementation of new regulations by the Financial Accounting Standards Board (requiring employers to report future costs of postretirement benefits on an accrued basis), many businesses have begun to limit or eliminate their liability for retired workers' healthcare. Industry experts predict that retiree health benefits programs in the future will include larger retiree contributions for premiums, greater cost sharing, and the expanded use of managed care plans as well as tightened eligibility (DiCarlo et al. 1989). These changes, along with an expected continuing pattern of retirement before age 65 (when Medicare coverage begins), mean that gaps in healthcare coverage at later ages can be expected to grow (U.S. General Accounting Office 1990a).

The relationships among economic and social resources, marital status, and health are complex, and projections about the long-term effects of their interactions are difficult to make. Economic status is a strong predictor of women's health status, exposure to occupational and environmental risks, health behaviors, use of health services, and ability to purchase needed care. Poor and near-poor women are disproportionately represented among the uninsured. Low-income elderly women are also in poorer health, are more likely to suffer from chronic illness, and are more likely to be functionally impaired than higher-income elderly women (Parsons 1990). Of particular concern in an aging society are the long-term effects of economically generated health risks and inadequate healthcare for women at younger ages. Such risks threaten the health status of the large future population of elderly women.

Employment, too, is linked to economic status. The following section explores women's economic roles as healthcare providers in our aging society. The obstacles and opportunities women face as employees and caregivers will influence the nature of healthcare for everyone in the United States in the coming decades.

WOMEN AS HEALTHCARE PROVIDERS

The convergence of two major trends—women's increased labor-force participation and population aging—will powerfully affect the supply of healthcare providers. The aging trend is increasing demand for the unpaid family care that women continue to provide, despite their growing presence in the paid labor force. At the same time, population aging adds momentum to the rapid expansion of the healthcare labor force, which consists primarily of women. The aging trend creates both conflicts and opportunities for women as healthcare providers. The question of whether or not women will continue to provide the bulk of long-term care on an informal, unpaid basis—and at what personal cost—will profoundly affect the quality of life in our aging society. And considering that over three-quarters of the paid health-care sector is made up of women, the career and employment choices women make will profoundly affect both the availability and quality of health services for people of all ages well into the next century.

Healthcare is currently facing a labor shortage, the magnitude of which can be expected to increase in the future. Three trends are contributing to this shortage and are likely to obstruct all federal and corporate efforts to control both the utilization and cost of healthcare: society's expectation of ever-improving levels of health, the pace of technological change, and the aging of the U.S. population. A fundamental reason for today's labor shortage is that demand is increasing faster than supply. Future availability of health personnel is expected to remain inadequate to meet demand, given demographic changes and the structure of training, certification, and employment in the health sector.

Trends in Women's Healthcare Earnings

Past healthcare labor shortages have been generally attributed to wages that were noncompetitive with other sectors of the economy. In a more recent era where real wage gains have flattened overall, the hourly earnings of healthcare workers grew faster than the earnings of other American workers between 1979 and 1985. Reflecting demand, every major type of health establishment posted higher growth in wages (averaging over 6 percent) than was reported for the economy as a whole in 1988. One year after graduation, 93 percent of those with degrees in the health professions in 1987 were working in jobs related to their fields of study at an average annual salary of $22,900 (National Center for Education Statistics 1989). For young women interested in a health profession, all of this seems encouraging.

However, women continue to be concentrated in the lower-paying ranks of healthcare (Friedman 1989). Only 11 percent are in the six highest-paying professions, whereas 87 percent of those earning less than $20,000 are women. Even within a profession, women average less than men in earnings. Male nurses earned consistently higher wages than women from 1970 to 1984 (Link 1988). Women physician assistants annually earn nearly $8,000 less, women social workers nearly $5,000 less, and women physical therapists over $10,000 less than their male colleagues. Male physicians continue to earn about 30 percent more than female physicians, calculated on either a per-hour or per-patient-visit basis. Even though these income differentials are in part a consequence of specialty choice, years of experience, practice settings, and other variables, wide gaps in income have been found to persist throughout the 1980s and throughout women's medical careers.

Healthcare is an occupational sector that has relied overwhelmingly on the employment of women. In an era when women's overall labor-force participation continues to increase, healthcare employers will be compelled to reanalyze staff organization and financial structure if they are to meet the demands for quality healthcare delivery and, at the same time, remain competitive with other sectors of the economy.

Occupational Trends

Without a doubt, the total healthcare labor force is growing rapidly. The U.S. Department of Labor reported that employment in health services rose to 7.46 million in December 1988, a 41 percent spurt over the previous year's growth, despite systemwide cost containment efforts and a record number of hospital closings. Of the 18 million new payroll jobs the department predicts will be created between 1988 and 2000, 1 in 6 is expected to be in the private health services sector (Personick 1989). Healthcare employment continues to outpace the rest of the services sector, a well as the economy at large. Although rate of growth for the services sector overall is expected to be slower than in the past (averaging 2.5 percent annual growth between 1988 and 2000), jobs in the health professions are multiplying at a 4.6 percent annual rate. The explosion of jobs in the health sector indicates this sector's significance as a growing portion of the U.S. economy.

In new projections by The Bureau of Labor Statistics, half of the 30 occupations with the fastest projected growth rates from 1990 to 2005 are health service occupations (Silvestri and Lukasiewicz 1992). Topping the list are home health aides, with a growth rate of 92 percent. Other health occupations with rapid projected growth are the newly emerging and loosely defined allied health professions, especially radiologic technicians and technologists, physical therapists, surgical technologists, and occupational therapists, in addition to medical secretaries.

The nursing profession, long the backbone of healthcare delivery, experienced skyrocketing job vacancy rates in hospitals throughout the late 1980s, but not because women were deserting the nursing profession. In fact, nurses' participation in the work force had never been higher. Yet, the demand for registered nurses has significantly outpaced supply, owing to factors such as increased patient care needs, increased staffing requirements, and an increased need for specialist nurses. Specialty units, emergency rooms, 30 percent of urban hospitals, and 15 percent of rural hospitals all restricted admissions and temporarily closed beds in 1987 because of the nursing shortage.

Labor shortages have been emerging in several of the allied health professions, as well. Technologists and therapists are in greater demand, partly because of a growing reliance on medical technology. For all of the health fields, there are likely to be periods of greater or lesser imbalance in the 1990s, as well as local variations in supply and demand.

Among academic and policy experts, the issue of a projected physician surplus in the United States has been debated for years. The question is of increasing importance for women, who now make up 40 percent of all first-year enrollments in medical schools. The warning in the early 1980s of a future surplus of physicians seems incongruent with the experience of large numbers of American citizens, especially patients in poor communities, who currently find themselves without access to necessary medical care. Many relatively large cities are still expected to lack most types of subspecialists in the year 2000 (Schwartz, Williams, Newhouse, and Witsburger 1988). The need for more physicians to provide care to underserved urban and rural communities—populations that are disproportionately black and Hispanic—provides an impetus to increase the number of minority physicians (Hanft and White 1987). Yet, the enrollment of blacks in medical school has been declining. Women are now applying in greater numbers to medical schools than to nursing schools. Between 1986 and 2010, the number of women physicians will more than double, an increase of 166 percent, compared with a 14 percent increase for men (Marder 1988). More recent research has recognized an anticipated increase in the demand for physician services—due to factors such as technological advances, the aging of the population, the AIDS epidemic, greater availability of physicians in rural areas, and increases in real income—that could erase projections of a physician surplus in the years ahead (Schwartz, Sloan and Mendelson 1988).

The greatest healthcare labor shortages are expected to be experienced at the other end of the pay and status spectrum, in the homecare sector. At a time when the need for chronic care services is increasing, there is a growing shortage of adequately trained nurses aides and home healthcare workers. Turnover rates are high in these occupations (70–100 percent a year is not uncommon), with nursing homes and home health agencies scrambling to overcome new worker shortages (Quinlan 1988). Although there have been some experimental projects and demonstrations on local levels that have raised wage and benefit levels and reduced worker turnover, the marginal status of most of these workers shows no sign of improvement. This is especially true in financially strapped states where Medicaid cost growth is outstripping revenue increases. This is where women's— and men's—access to essential healthcare in an aging society may be most compromised.

Family Caregiving

Most of the long-term and supportive care in the United States is provided outside the labor market by family members, mostly women. One study estimated that more than 27 million unpaid days of informal care are provided each week (Rivlin and Wiener 1988). Despite women's increased participation in the paid work force, there is no evidence that they are abandoning the vital unpaid caregiving work they perform. But the expectation that women can "do it all" is on a collision course with profound social and economic changes and a dramatic increase in the number of chronically ill elderly persons who will require assistance in their daily lives.

The caregiving crisis and related issues of gender equity are analyzed in detail elsewhere in this volume and are therefore not discussed here. However, no comprehensive discussion of healthcare should ignore the enormous significance of unpaid care that families—mostly women—provide. As the U.S. population ages, the importance of this informal care will increase in the future.

The rising demand for supportive care to elderly family members, and provision of this care, may be the health sector development that most affects women in the future. Nowhere will conflicts between labor force and family responsibilities be more powerfully felt. Women, especially middle-aged women with moderate to low incomes, will be under increasing pressure to leave the labor force—including healthcare employment—or to take "lesser" jobs that may impair their careers or jeopardize their own retirement savings. This threatens women's own access to needed healthcare as they themselves age. In the following policy discussion, we explore some possible responses to this dilemma and to other effects of population aging on women's complex experiences with healthcare.

HEALTH POLICY DIRECTIONS FOR AN AGING SOCIETY

Universal Health Coverage for Life

Under active discussion throughout the nation are a series of proposals to provide healthcare coverage to over 35 million uninsured Americans. Strategies for revamping the nation's healthcare system are differentiated by their approach to financing and organizing health services and their definitions of "comprehensive benefits," as well as their attempts to achieve broader public health goals such as health promotion. Proposals are generally categorized as government-mandated benefits for employees, Medicaid expansion, national health insurance, market-based reforms, or a combination of these. Some of the proposed plans address long-term care coverage, as well.

Women have a great deal to gain or lose by the enactment of universal healthcare legislation. Legislative proposals would affect women differently depending on their age, health status, labor-force participation, and economic well-being. Modeling the effect of these legislative proposals on women is made more difficult because the nation's economy is undergoing change, as is the market for health insurance. We can only speculate as to how these changes will interact with the demographic force of an aging population to influence the delivery of healthcare into the next century.

The combined effect of current cutbacks in employer-sponsored health benefits (whether increased cost-sharing for employees or their families or reduced retiree benefits), a growth in self-insurance among larger firms, and the instability of the small-group market is increasing the number of uninsured in the United States. Without rapid and major changes in the nation's health insurance system, we can expect the number of uninsured women to grow. This trend is of special concern for women who work in small firms, those who are dependents of lower-wage workers, and those who fall into "high-risk" categories by virtue of their "preexisting conditions."

Aging escalates the risk of uninsurance in this environment because the probability of having a preexisting condition increases with age. During the next 20 years, baby-boom women will age, reaching the 45–64 age category by 2010. Enactment of some sort of employment-based reform—such as a "pay or play" system, mandated benefits for workers and their families, or small-group reform proposals—is necessary to protect older workers from the effects of discrimination in the work force due to increasing health risks and the harm caused by the costs of catastrophic illness. It is possible that the linking of health insurance reform to work-force activity may be a strategy of more value to men than women because of men's more extensive attachment to the work force. Whether or not this is a concern depends on a woman's risk of divorce or spousal death if a dependent, or unemployment, all events that could separate her from employment-based health insurance. Designers of work-based insurance reforms will need to attend to differences in women's marital status, employment patterns, and health histories in order to ensure equal coverage.

One might expect minority women to continue at a disadvantage with respect to insurance coverage so long as they are employed in positions that are less likely to offer health insurance. It is promising that (as Taeuber and Allen, in chapter 2 of this volume report) young minority workers are more likely than their parents to be employed in occupations covered by Social Security and pensions (and one would presume health insurance as well). At the same time, the rates of disability and of compromised health status are higher among blacks, both women and men. Health status and lower wages interact to increase the risk of uninsurance among minorities. As America ages, gaps in health insurance and private pensions can be expected to be particularly troublesome for minority women, owing to their lower wages. Current public policy recommendations for expanding private insurance coverage may exacerbate this situation unless market-based reform proposals are offset by benefit improvements and greater uniformity in coverage by public programs aimed at those with low income.

The recognition that fully one-third of the nation's uninsured have incomes below poverty level has fueled support in many sectors for immediate restructuring of the nation's Medicaid program. Suggested reforms include the establishment of national standards for eligibility, rates of payment, and a minimum benefit package. Individual support for this strategy as a way to provide improved health coverage is largely dependent on one's philosophy concerning the appropriate role of government or of charity in facilitating access to healthcare. A strong argument in favor of Medicaid expansion is that it is a highly effective targeting of scarce public resources.

In considering Medicaid expansion, one must take account of the emerging crisis in limited long-term care coverage. Our country's long-term care challenge is to graduate public assistance for care in a way that is more clearly targeted to need, without overcompensating the elderly as a group. In an aging society, any universal health insurance proposal should consider coverage for long-term care. Recall that both the private and public sectors play a role in financing long-term care. Few would call this an equitable partnership, however, because almost all the private share is fully paid for, without benefit of insurance, by the individuals who need care and their families. Attitudes differ as to how the responsibility should be divided between public and private efforts in the future, and the choice of emphasis depends upon one's political ideology and perceptions of what initiatives are feasible and affordable (Rivlin and Wiener 1988).

However, we would caution that if we create a universal health insurance program—either Canadian-style or through employer man-dates—that ignores the aging trend and the growing problem of long-term care, we could wind up with a situation where every American is "fully insured," yet lacks essential coverage for needed services. As the majority of those who use and provide long-term care, women have a big stake in the process and outcome of these debates. One proposal advanced by the U.S. Bipartisan Commission on Comprehensive Health Care in 1990 calls for the promotion of private long-term care insurance as well as a limited social insurance program to foster improved community-based care.

As policymakers search for an enactable compromise in the face of worsening budget crises, seemingly irreconcilable visions of the future of long-term care may be leading to common ground—the development of a workable public-private partnership. There is now an increasing realization by private employers, insurance carriers, healthcare providers, government, and labor unions that past piecemeal efforts to target resources and control overall costs cannot solve the nation's serious healthcare problems, and that a more radical and comprehensive approach is needed. Yet, there is still no consensus concerning the groups to which the additional costs of a reformed system should be assigned. Important interest groups do not seem willing to compromise their interests for the sake of a better overall system. At the same time, opinion polls suggest that the general public remains committed to a more-is-better health philosophy and is largely uninformed about the difficult policy choices ahead (Blendon 1988). We fear that an opportunity may be lost should no major universal health insurance legislation soon be enacted, especially considering the competing economic pressures that come with an aging society.

In the long run, only a universal health plan with nationally capped budgets can address the three most pressing issues for healthcare reform: insuring the uninsured, controlling healthcare costs, and reducing bureaucratic complexity in healthcare decision making. In their multiple roles as family caregivers and advocates, healthcare professionals, acute and long-term care users, and taxpayers, women must scrutinize these universal health plan proposals to ensure that their care and security objectives can be realized in an aging society.

Promoting a High-Quality Healthcare Labor Force

The future supply of healthcare personnel will be determined by a range of economic and social factors, including earnings expectations in relation to time and costs of training; working conditions; availability of training and jobs; geographic and occupational mobility; and intangible rewards such as status or the opportunity to do good. The future availability of healthcare workers will depend as well upon larger labor-force trends, such as participation rates.

With increased demand and the movement of women into many different occupational sectors, women can no longer be taken for granted by the healthcare industry as a readily available and cheap work force. The healthcare sector must offer competitive wages if it is to attract and retain the quality and quantity of labor needed.[5] In addition, previously overlooked labor pools, such as young men and mothers seeking part-time work, must be identified and offered necessary training in the health fields. With intensified competition among health providers for qualified candidates, it is conceivable that for those women committed to the health professions who have access to educational resources, opportunities may never have been brighter.

The sharp growth in employment of minority women in the U.S. work force is especially significant for the healthcare sector. Because minorities are least advantaged in terms of skill levels and educational backgrounds, the translation of skilled healthcare opportunities into actual jobs for women of color will be uncertain. Factors such as the commitment of medical schools and other professional programs to increase acceptance and retention rates for minority students, improved high-school and college preparation, a stable financial base for professional programs, and affordable student financing could all increase healthcare labor opportunities for minorities.

The levels of training for allied health professionals (including, among others, technologists and therapists) are as varied as the care they provide and the settings in which they work. In 1989 the Institute of Medicine recommended several measures to reduce shortages in the allied health professions, including more vigorous recruitment of potential students—especially minorities, older students, career changers, men, and those already employed in healthcare—as well as increased flexibility in state licensure statutes (allowing overlapping scopes of practice for some licensed professions as well as multiple paths to licensure).

Hospitals, nursing homes, and medical offices rely extensively on a locally generated labor force to fill lower-level administrative and patient-care positions. Entry-level positions in technology-dependent healthcare facilities require more abstract thought processes, literacy, computational skills, and computer facility than in the past. In the future, America's elderly will be turning to a labor force made up increasingly of minority workers, many of whom have been denied the kind of education needed to assume even entry-level positions in the workplace (Torres-Gil 1990). This public failure threatens to undermine the supply and quality of the nation's healthcare system, an increasingly complex sector of the economy. Because our society includes a diminishing proportion of households with children under 18 years of age, it is uncertain whether sufficient political pressure can be marshaled to provide school districts with the needed resources. The aging public needs to understand better how its future welfare is dependent upon improved educational opportunities for all citizens at younger ages.

Making a Commitment to Public Health and Research

Past significant reductions in mortality and morbidity have been attributed to public health interventions—such as clean water, sanitation, nutrition, and environmental and occupational safety—and to improvements in personal health habits. In the future, however, major overall improvements in life expectancy are considered unlikely because societal factors relevant to chronic disease risks have shown only marginal improvements (smoking rates) or actual deterioration (environmental toxicological hazards) (Manton 1982). This prediction masks the improvements that could yet be attained for significant numbers of Americans, especially those who are poor or live and work in areas threatened with environmental risks, if all members of society had the benefit of fundamental and proven public health interventions.

Influenced by public health education efforts, an individual's attention to good health habits clearly reduces the likelihood of illness and future development of many chronic diseases. Given greater health promotion efforts, it is possible that the elderly of the future may reach old age in better health than the elderly of the past (Rice and Feldman 1983). Twenty years into the fitness craze a growing body of evidence is challenging assumptions of what happens to people as they age, suggesting that an active life-style can dramatically retard physical decline. The oldest members of the baby boom will turn 50 in 1996, and they are taking an activist approach to the postponement of aging and the promotion of fitness. This trend is expected to continue in the future. The erosion of demeaning stereotypes of older people in the popular press, many of which concern women aged 40 and over, and the development of self-esteem and empowerment among older women are also broad public health interventions that foster feelings and behavior to increase vitality. These attitudes help change the very definition of aging. What it means to be 65 years old today is not the same as it was a generation ago or will be in the future.

Even while nonbiomedical factors should be emphasized in reducing mortality and morbidity in an aging society, medicine and technology are expected to play important roles, as well. Without substantial advances in the prevention and treatment of major disabling diseases, the aging of the U.S. population can be expected to increase future healthcare costs. It is hoped that in the future, both medical innovations in the management of chronic diseases and biomedical discoveries for slowing the rate of aging will yield some life expectancy gains. It is uncertain, however, that significant advances will be made toward the cure or prevention of chronic diseases unless there is a change in the focus and financial support of medical research.

Of the $145 billion spent annually on healthcare for the elderly in the United States today, less than one-half of 1 percent is invested in medical research. Nowhere is this lack of commitment more troubling than in the inadequate investigation of the aging process itself, a function of interacting and interdependent genetic, biological, psychological, environmental, and social forces. Some argue that it is primarily the neglect of this research area that limits society's ability today to foresee and control its future health status (Fries 1990).

Of great concern to women in an aging society is the recognition that they are still largely excluded as subjects in federally funded research. The National Institutes of Health (NIH) reported that it spent only 13.5 percent of its 1987 budget on women's health (Kong 1990). In 1990 the General Accounting Office testified to the continued exclusion of women from health research studies, despite official 1986 policy to include more women in research study populations. The underrepresentation of women in such studies and the omission of gender as an important variable "has resulted in significant gaps in knowledge" (U.S. General Accounting Office 1990b). Such omissions become ever more glaring and costly as the population ages, since women continue to greatly outnumber men in older age groups. As a result of pressure from the U.S. Congress, the NIH agreed to corrective measures, the effect of which should be monitored closely by those concerned with the nation's health.

Even with breakthroughs in medical research, it is unlikely that the cure or prevention of Alzheimer's disease, arthritis, stroke, diabetes, or any of the other chronic illnesses of old age will be realized any time soon. Barring such an unexpected set of discoveries, it is probable that, for the foreseeable future, the "armamentarium of moderately efficacious but extremely expensive procedures" (Rice and Feldman 1983) will grow and will be performed with increasing frequency for as long as the private and public sectors can support such medical treatment. These procedures raise critical ethical questions in an aging society.

CONFRONTING ETHICAL ISSUES UNDERLYING HEALTHCARE POLICY IN AN AGING SOCIETY

Death and Dying

The kinds of health services rendered to persons at the end of life, particularly the elderly with their high use of medical care, are of great concern, especially to the federal government because of the impact of these decisions on the Medicare program. Concern focuses on how these decisions should be made to protect those affected, the appropriateness of various medical procedures, and the distribution of resulting costs. In the future, will society have the economic means to provide all the medical interventions that are available to everyone who needs them?

In an aging society, the proportion of deaths that occur at older ages will continue to increase. By 2010, 30 percent of all deaths are expected to occur at age 85 and older, up from 10 percent in 1960 (U.S. Bureau of the Census 1989b, author's calculations). This fact, coupled with two additional trends—rising medical expenditures for the elderly and consumers' greater involvement in medical care decision making—is expected to lead to increased societal debate concerning the efficacy and ethics of medical treatment at the end of life.

Concern about the high cost of care for the elderly is heightened by evidence from several studies that a large part of these expenses is incurred in the last year or even the last month of life (Scitovsky 1984). One frequently cited study found that nearly 28 percent of Medicare expenditures in 1978 were on less than 6 percent of Medicare beneficiaries, all of whom died that same year (Lubitz and Prihoda 1984). Other economists have pointed out that the high medical expenses for conditions that ultimately result in death are the principal reason that medical care expenditures of the elderly rise with age (Fuchs 1984).

But do these studies support rationing of care by age or the limitation of care for certain conditions to the simple relief of pain and suffering? Many studies are limited to Medicare (hospital) costs and do not give a full picture of the total costs associated with care at the end of life. They also do not support the assumption that high medical expenses are the result of increasingly aggressive interventions. It is not surprising that medical expenses are highest at the end of life— the time when people are usually sickest and most in need of care. Finally, given the uncertainties of many medical interventions and of predictions in any given instance about who is clearly a terminal patient, it is difficult to fathom a public policy that singles out one group of patients for severe cost containment efforts.

Some ethicists argue against medical intervention to preserve life, once the "natural" life span has been achieved (Callahan 1990). But the implementation of such a point of view would give rise to the grave ethical problems of age-based rationing. First, there is the problem of discrimination. Is a given moment of life for a person older than the normal life span worth less than a comparable moment for a younger person? Second, there is the issue of heterogeneity. The fact that as people age their health histories and life histories increasingly diverge and become more individualized makes chronological age a poor basis for any decision to bar someone from medical care (Schneider and Guralnik 1990). Finally, and especially important for this chapter's discussion, there is the question of hidden sexism. Because of women's greater longevity, coupled with their greater use of chronic care, it is really women we are talking about when we speak of denying healthcare to the elderly (Butler 1989).

What is lost in many discussions about the allocation of medical care for the aged and dying is the fundamental importance of the preferences of the patient and of her or his family as well as the individual patient's health history and status. Considering the fear many people have of death in the hands of contemporary medicine, it is no wonder that patients have become more involved in making decisions about the end of life. Such involvement includes the execution of living wills, which express a person's desired treatment in terminal cases.

As the population ages, ethical problems in decision making about patients' medical care near the end of life are likely to grow more pronounced. Those elderly patients—frail, debilitated, very old, and mostly female—who, despite their poor health, are not clearly dying are likely to pose the most difficult problems for their physicians, families, and society in the years ahead. Quite possibly the dilemma will continue to be expressed as it is today: a question of the benefit of extending life with profoundly diminished quality at increasing cost.

Our understanding of illness and death is shaped by our understanding of the meaning of life and a recognition that we are all subject to aging, illness, and death. Of significance for women in an aging society is the recognition that their roles as relatives of the disabled, as patients, and as medical personnel will profoundly influence these perceptions as the future unfolds. Future public policies will also reflect society's perspectives on aging. Think about the different views of aging expressed by different individuals, and how their ideas might shape policy. Will society, for example, endorse the views of certain influential policymakers that the elderly cost the public too much and should somehow "move on"? Or will public sentiment come to embrace the view offered by Carl Jung: "A human being would certainly not grow to be 70 or 80 years old if this longevity had no meaning for the species. The afternoon of human life must also have significance of its own and cannot be merely a pitiful appendage to life's morning" (quoted in *Generations*, 1986).

From Whom and to Whom

Medical care spending—both as a percentage of GNP and per capita—is higher in the United States than in any other country in the world. If present health-status and healthcare-spending trends continue, our aging society will be faced with a series of difficult allocation choices, all of which hinge on the central problem that the United States can no longer afford to provide everything medicine has to offer. Women of all ages will be profoundly affected by these choices.

Age may become a more visible issue in controversies over healthcare resource allocations. Some health policy analysts have suggested that in an aging society it may be increasingly difficult to show the "cost-effectiveness" of increased spending to care for the elderly, as compared with the relative claims made on behalf of children. A healthcare equity issue that will grow in importance as society ages is the level of the country's infant mortality rate, a principal indicator of a nation's health status and well-being.

Since 1981, there has been a substantial and unprecedented slowdown in the improvement of the U.S. infant mortality rate. Currently ranked 22nd among industrial countries worldwide, the U.S. infant mortality rate is 9.9 deaths per 1,000 live births. Why should an aging society be concerned about infant death? First, the burden of preventable infant death and disability brings suffering to families, as well as unnecessary costs to the health sector. In addition, high infant mortality rates, especially the very high death rates among black infants, raise access and fairness issues in healthcare for women in an aging society. If excess infant mortality persists, it will be hard to argue, from a practical or an ethical basis, for the increasing allocation of public funds for expensive technology-intensive care to save individual lives among the elderly.

Although the healthcare needs of millions of children and young families remain unmet, many public opinion polls suggest that Americans believe that the nation should spend more of its resources on the healthcare needs of the elderly. With growing numbers and proportions of aged people in the population, there may be more political support for reducing hardships and inequities in healthcare for the elderly than for providing needed services for infants and children. The wide variation in payments among different groups of Medicaid beneficiaries would seem to support this position. Over the years, elderly Medicaid beneficiaries have accounted for a disproportionately large share of Medicaid payments for services.

It is ironic that the nation faces an apparent choice between meeting the healthcare needs of its youngest and its oldest members, considering that, as caregivers to both children and the disabled elderly, women's interests bridge the needs of the groups currently in competition for healthcare dollars. America has never seemed to have a problem raising funds for public purposes when a need was recognized as a social and political priority. Yet, healthcare has never had, and may never have, the raw political power of some other concerns, possibly because most Americans are generally satisfied with their own medical care at any given moment (Blendon and Donelan 1989). Solving the nation's pressing healthcare problems also requires increased government leadership and probably increased spending, thus running afoul of the public's prevailing aversion to government intervention and higher taxes.

The issue of universal health insurance coverage for young and aged Americans alike may have to percolate until the combination of a sympathetic public, erosion of stiff opposition from business and provider groups, and presidential leadership brings determined action to improve access to affordable healthcare. One thing is certain: such increased access must be coupled with cost control if healthcare is to achieve universal availability in an aging America. As consumers of healthcare, as caregivers, and as workers, women of all ages will profoundly influence, and be greatly affected by, the health policy choices made in our aging society.

Notes

The authors wish to express their appreciation to Kathleen Adams, Jessie Allen, Alan Pifer, and Kenneth E. Thorpe.

1. Medical care expenditures as a percentage of gross national product have grown because of increases in population and in average per capita cost of treatment.

2. Between 1980 and 2030 the population aged 85 and over—70 percent of whom are women—is expected to quadruple (U.S. Bureau of the Census, 1989b).

3. The nursing home industry is larger and more diverse than the hospital sector, and exceeded 1.6 million beds and 16,000 homes in 1986, according to the National Center for Health Statistics (1990).

4. Institutionalization rates are higher for whites than for blacks, with increasing rates of entry at the oldest ages for both sexes and races.

5. Salaries will continue to be a key enticement, but benefits oriented to women's needs, more on-the-job respect, better-defined career ladders and opportunities for advancement, and more innovative staffing can also be pursued by healthcare employers.

References

Amett, Ross H., III, David McKusick, Sally T. Sonnefeld, and Carol S. Cowell. 1986. "Projections of Health Care Spending to 1990." *Health Care Financing Review* 7(Spring): 1–35.

Avorn, Jerome L. 1986. "Medicine: The Life and Death of Oliver Shay." In *Our Aging Society. Paradox and Promise*, edited by Alan Pifer and Lydia Bronte. New York: W. W. Norton & Co.

Berk, Marc L., and Amy K. Taylor. 1984. "Women and Divorce: Health Insurance Coverage, Utilization, and Health Care Expenditures." *American Journal of Public Health* 74(11): 1276–78.

Blendon, Robert J. 1988. "The Public's View of the Future of Health Care." *Journal of the American Medical Association* 259(24): 3587–93.

Blendon, Robert J., and Karen Donelan. 1989. "The 1988 Election: How Important Was Health?" *Health Affairs* 8(3) (Fall): 6–15.

Butler, Robert N. 1989. "Dispelling Ageism: The Cross-Cutting Intervention." *Annals of the American Academy of Political and Social Science* 503(May): 138–47.

Callahan, Daniel. 1990. *What Kind of Life? The Limits of Medical Progress*. New York: Simon and Schuster.

Cowell, Daniel D. 1983. "Aging Research, Black Americans, and the National Institute on Aging." *Journal of the National Medical Association* 75(1): 99.

DiCarlo, Steven, John Gabel, Gregory de Lissovoy, and Judith Jasper. 1989. *Research Bulletin. Facing Up to Post-Retirement Health Benefits*. Washington, D.C.: Health Insurance Association of America.

Friedman, Emily. 1989. "A New Relationship." *Health Management Quarterly* 11(3): 2–7.

Fries, James F. 1980. "Aging, Natural Death, and the Compression of Morbidity." New England Journal of Medicine 303: 130–35.

————. 1990. "The Sunny Side of Aging." Journal of the American Medical Association 263(17): 2335–40.

Fuchs, Victor R. 1984. "Though Much Is Taken: Reflections on Aging, Health, Medical Care." Milbank Memorial Fund Quarterly 62(2): 143–66.

Gruenberg, E. M. 1977. "The Failures of Success." Milbank Memorial Fund Quarterly 55: 3–24.

Hanft, Ruth S., and Catherine C. White. 1987. "Constraining the Supply of Physicians: Effects on Black Physicians." Milbank Memorial Fund Quarterly 65(2): 249–69.

Health Care Financing Administration, Division of National Cost Estimates, Office of the Actuary. 1987. "National Health Expenditures, 1986–2000." Health Care Financing Review 8(4): 24.

Institute of Medicine. 1989. Allied Health Services. Avoiding Crisis. Washington, D.C.: National Academy Press.

Jung, Carl. Quoted on inside cover of Generations, journal of the American Society on Aging 10(1) (1986).

Kemper, Peter, Brenda Spillman, and Christopher M. Murtaugh. 1991. "A Lifetime Perspective on Proposals for Financing Nursing Home Care." Inquiry 28(4): 333–44.

Kong, Dolores. 1990. "Impatience Growing over Breast Cancer Research." Boston Globe, June 15.

Levit, Katharine R., Helen C. Lazenby, Cathy A. Cowan, and Suzanne W. Letsch. 1991. "National Health Expenditures, 1990." Health Care Financing Review 13(1): 29–54.

Lewin/ICF. 1990. The Health Care Financing System and The Uninsured. Washington, D.C.: Office of Research, Health Care Financing Administration.

Link, Charles R. 1988. "Returns to Nursing Education: 1970–84." Journal of Human Resources 23(3): 372–87.

Lubitz, J., and R. Prihoda. 1984. "The Uses and Costs of Medicare Services in the Last Two Years of Life." Health Care Financing Review 5: 117–31.

Manton, Kenneth. 1982. "Changing Concepts of Morbidity and Mortality in the Elderly Population." Milbank Memorial Fund Quarterly 60(2): 183–244.

Manton, Kenneth G., Clifford H. Patrick, and Katina W. Johnson. 1987. "Health Differentials between Blacks and Whites: Recent Trends in Mortality and Morbidity." Milbank Memorial Fund Quarterly 65(1): 129–99.

Marder, William D. 1988. Physician Supply and Utilization by Specialty: Trends and Predictions. Chicago: American Medical Association.

National Center for Education Statistics. 1989. Projections of Education Statistics to 2000. Pub. no. 89-648. Washington, D.C.: U.S. Department of Education.

National Center for Health Statistics. 1990. Health, United States, 1989. Hyattsville, Md.: U.S. Public Health Service.

Older Women's League. 1989. "The Picture of Health for Midlife and Older Women in America." In Women in the Later Years: Health, Social, and Cultural Perspectives, edited by Lois Grau. Binghamton, N.Y.: Harrington Park Press.

Olshansky, S. Jay. 1988. "On Forecasting Mortality." Milbank Memorial Fund Quarterly 66(3): 482–530.

Parsons, P. Ellen. 1990. "Health Coverage for Women." Paper presented at Second Annual Women's Policy Research Conference, sponsored by the Institute for Women's Policy Research, Washington, D.C., June 1–2.

Personick, Valerie A. 1989. "Industry Output and Employment: A Slower Trend for the Nineties." Monthly Labor Review (November): 25–41.

Poterba, James M., and Laurence H. Summers. 1987. "Public Policy Implications of Declining Old Age Mortality." In Work, Health, and Income among the Elderly, edited by Gary Burtless (19–58). Washington, D.C.: Brookings Institution.

Quinlan, Alice. 1988. Chronic Care Workers: Crisis among Paid Caregivers of the Elderly. Washington, D.C.: Older Women's League and American Federation of State, County, and Municipal Employees.

Rice, Dorothy P., and Jacob J. Feldman. 1983. "Living Longer in the United States: Demographic Changes and Health Needs of the Elderly." Milbank Memorial Fund Quarterly 61(3): 362–96.

Rivlin, Alice M., and Joshua M. Wiener. 1988. Caring for the Disabled Elderly. Who Will Pay? Washington, D.C.: Brookings Institution.

Robert Wood Johnson Foundation. 1987. Access to Health Care. Special Report #2. Princeton, N.J.: Author.

Rosenblatt, Robert A. 1990. "Abuse of the Elderly, Most Often by Family, Is Soaring, Panel Says." Boston Globe, May 1: 10.

Rowland, Diane. 1989. "Measuring the Elderly's Need for Home Care." Health Affairs 8(4) (Winter): 39–51.

Schneider, Edward L., and Jack M. Guralnik. 1990. "The Aging of America: Impact on Health Care Costs." Journal of the American Medical Association 263(17): 2335–40.

Schwartz, William B., Frank A. Sloan, and Daniel Mendelson. 1988. "Why There Will Be Little or No Physician Surplus between Now and the Year 2000?" New England Journal of Medicine 318(14): 892–97.

Schwartz, William B., Albert P. Williams, Joseph P. Newhouse, and Christina Witsberger. 1988. "Are We Training Too Many Medical Subspecialists?" Journal of the American Medical Association 259(2): 233–39.

Scitovsky, Anne A. 1984. "The High Cost of Dying: What Do the Data Show?" Milbank Memorial Fund Quarterly 62(4): 591–608.

Silvestri, George, and John Lukasiewicz. 1992. "Occupational Employment, Projections in Outlook, 1990–2005." BLS Bulletin, no. 2402. Washington, D.C.: U.S. Government Printing Office.

Soldo, Beth J. 1985. "In-Home Services for the Dependent Elderly." *Research on Aging* 7: 281–304.

Soldo, Beth J., and Kenneth G. Manton. 1985. "Changes in the Health Status and Service Needs of the Oldest Old: Current Patterns and Future Trends." *Milbank Memorial Fund Quarterly* 63(2): 286–319.

Sonnefeld, Sally T., Daniel R. Waldo, Jeffrey A. Lemieux, and David McKusick. 1991. "Projections of National Health Expenditures through the Year 2000." *HCFA Health Care Financing Review* 13(1): 1–27.

Spalter-Roth, Roberta M., and Heidi I. Hartmann. 1988. *Unnecessary Losses: Costs to Americans of the Lack of Family and Medical Leave. Executive Summary.* Washington, D.C.: Institute for Women's Policy Research.

Stone, Robyn, Gail Lee Cafferata, and Judith Sangl. 1987. "Caregivers of the Frail Elderly: A National Profile." *Gerontologist* 27(5): 616–26. (October).

"Ten Year Study Reports on Health Risks for Women." 1989. *Harvard University Gazette* 85 (Dec. 1).

Thorpe, Kenneth, Joanna Siegel, and Theresa Daily. 1989. "Including the Poor. The Fiscal Impacts of Medicaid Expansion." *Journal of the American Medical Association* 261(7): 1003–7.

Torres-Gil, Fernando. 1990. "Diversity in Aging: The Challenge of Pluralism." *Aging Connection* (April-May).

U.S. Bipartisan Commission on Comprehensive Health Care [Pepper Commission]. 1990. *A Call to Action: Final Report.* Washington, D.C.: U.S. Government Printing Office.

U.S. Bureau of the Census. 1989a. *Current Population Survey, March 1989.* Washington, D.C.: U.S. Government Printing Office.

———. 1989b. *Projections of the Population of the United States, by Age, Sex and Race: 1988 to 2080* by Gregory Spencer. Current Population Reports, ser. P-25, no. 1018. Washington, D.C.: U.S. Government Printing Office.

U.S. Congressional Budget Office. 1988. *Changes in the Living Arrangements of the Elderly, 1960–2030.* Washington, D.C.: U.S. Government Printing Office.

U.S. Congressional Research Service. 1987. *Retirement Income for an Aging Population.* Washington, D.C.: U.S. Government Printing Office.

———. 1988. *Medicaid Source Book: Background Data and Analysis.* Washington, D.C.: U.S. Government Printing Office.

U.S. General Accounting Office. 1990a. *Health Insurance: Cost Increases Lead to Coverage Limitations and Cost Shifting.* Washington, D.C.: U.S. Government Printing Office.

———. 1990b. "National Institutes of Health: Problems in Implementing Policy on Women in Study Populations." Testimony before Subcommittee on Health and the Environment of the U.S. House of Representatives. GAO/T-HRD-90-38. Washington, D.C.: U.S. Government Printing Office.

U.S. Senate Special Committee on Aging. 1988. *Aging America. Trends and Projections*. Washington, D.C.: U.S. Department of Health and Human Services.

White-Means, Shelley I. 1990. "Long Term Care for the Black Elderly." Paper presented at Second Annual Women's Policy Research Conference, sponsored by Institute for Women's Policy Research, Washington, D.C., June 1–2.

Wilkinson, Doris Y., and Gary King. 1987. "Conceptual and Methodology Issues in the Use of Race as a Variable: Policy Implications." *Milbank Memorial Fund Quarterly* 65(suppl. 1): 56–71.

Woolhandler, S., and D. U. Himmelstein. 1988. "Reverse Targeting of Preventive Care Due to Lack of Health Insurance." *Journal of the American Medical Association* 259(19): 2872–74.

Zedlewski, Sheila R., Roberta O. Burns, Martha R. Burt, Timothy D. McBride, and Jack A. Meyer. 1990. *The Needs of the Elderly in the 21st Century.* Urban Institute Report 90–5. Washington, D.C.: Urban Institute.

Chapter Five

PREVENTIVE MEDICAL CARE: TARGETING ELDERLY WOMEN IN AN AGING SOCIETY

Marianne C. Fahs

Current scientific belief among economists and health policy analysts holds that the long-term savings from preventive health services generally do not outweigh the short-term costs to society or private insurers (Russell 1986; Warner and Luce 1982; Weinstein and Statson 1977). However, it can be shown that preventive health initiatives for older women—especially high-risk groups within the population of women aged 65 and over—can save money as well as years of healthy life. With population aging and rapidly growing numbers of very elderly women in the United States, such targeted preventive measures are not only cost-effective; they are absolutely necessary if we are to avoid intolerably high rates of disability and soaring healthcare costs in the future. Yet, the United States currently allocates only 3.4 percent of its total healthcare budget to prevention, almost all of which is targeted to the prevention of acute disease among younger age groups.

Prevention activities do not have to save money to have value. They must, however, be effective to be worthwhile. If prevention activities are both effective and save money, obviously they should be undertaken. If they are effective but costly, then the opportunity costs of lost healthy years of life must be weighed against the financial costs of preventing such losses. The economic technique of cost-effectiveness analysis can be a useful aid in this decision-making process. However, as this chapter describes, cost-effectiveness analysis must undergo further methodological development, extension, and refinement if it is to serve as an unbiased tool in assessing the relative costs and benefits of prevention activities targeted to elderly women.

This chapter discusses issues affecting the economic analysis of preventive medical care for the elderly, focusing on the future consequences for older women and for society if our analytic techniques and our investment in prevention are allowed to remain at current levels. If present health and health policy trends continue, as the proportion of elderly Americans increases in our population the number of seriously disabled people will expand dramatically. This increase will be great enough to affect the quality of life not only for the elderly themselves but throughout the entire society that must support them.

PREVENTIVE CARE FOR ELDERLY POPULATIONS

Increasing evidence suggests that prevention programs for the elderly are indeed effective (German and Fried 1989; Larson 1988; Office of Technology Assessment 1985). Although it is clear that many chronic health impairments of older adults arise from their behavior during their younger years, it is also important to avoid the conclusion that prevention must begin early or not at all. As people live longer, there are more years for older people to benefit from prevention services. In many cases (as has been shown for smoking and lung impairment), the effects of risky behaviors in earlier years of life can be reversed by health promotion/disease prevention activities in later life (Omen 1990).

New concepts of normal aging are taking hold, leading us to expect enhanced social functioning, improved physical and mental well-being, prolonged independent living, and greater autonomy among the elderly. The phrases "successful aging," "productive aging," "active life expectancy," "preventive gerontology," and "compression of morbidity" all spring from the notions of health promotion and positive social value at older ages (Breslow and Somers 1977; Butler and Gleason 1985; Davis et al. 1988; Fries 1980; Hazzard 1983; Katz et al. 1983; Rowe and Kahn 1987; Somers 1984). Despite these conceptual advances, much health policy planning and practice continues to rest on outdated, negative concepts of aging: "chronic disease and disability are constant companions of the elderly and are likely to remain so, at least for the near term," intones a recent report from the Institute of Medicine (1990: 22–32). Such generalized pessimism fosters a lack of attention to prevention programs for older Americans that is more and more costly as the population ages.

Why Target Women?

There are many reasons for emphasizing preventive medical care for elderly women in our aging society, among them:

1. Women's greater longevity and the consequent disproportionate representation of women among the elderly;
2. The greater burdens of both disability and poverty among elderly women;
3. The economic consequences (such as higher medical care utilization and expenses) for the whole country associated with excess morbidity and disability among the expanding population of older women;
4. The social consequences (such as greater caregiving burdens for family members) of excess morbidity, disability, and premature mortality among older women;
5. The paradox that prior research and professional standards for prevention activities have often excluded both the elderly and women, focusing on younger men;
6. The difficulties currently encountered by women in achieving equity in our healthcare system; and
7. The potential benefit to women and men of all ages of increased prevention activities among elderly women, associated with lower indirect costs of illness for the daughters and spouses of elderly women and the continued productive contributions of older women to the society.

Despite the apparently strong case for increasing the availability of preventive health services for older women, current health policy has made little progress in this direction. To understand the obstacles to such a move, it is necessary to survey the background of preventive medical care in the U.S. today.

PREVENTIVE HEALTHCARE IN THE UNITED STATES: CURRENT STATUS

The structure of preventive care today rests on certain basic definitions of types of preventive care and classifications of the conditions such care is designed to prevent. Other important elements of preventive care include financing mechanisms and techniques for evaluating the results of prevention programs.

Defining Prevention

Healthcare in the United States has achieved undisputed excellence in diagnostic and treatment efforts once serious illnesses and injuries have occurred, while neglecting any significant investment in prevention (Omen 1990). Existing preventive services are generally defined using the following framework:

Primary preventive services are those intended to prevent or delay the onset of disease. Immunizations and counseling on life-style changes are classic examples of primary prevention.

Secondary preventive services are efforts to detect a disease or condition before it is symptomatic, or clinically recognizable, in order to avoid or delay its further progression. Screening procedures, such as mammography or Pap smears, fall into this category.

Tertiary preventive services attempt to reduce the impact of already-existing disease on the quality of a person's life by maintaining or improving her or his ability to function. Examples of such services would include self-care education for diabetic patients and rehabilitation for stroke victims.

However, the application of these traditional classifications of prevention to elderly women is not entirely adequate. In addition to disease prevention, there must be an increased focus on disability prevention. Numerous efforts have been made to develop uniform classifications of functional status as a step toward defining disability and identifying specific preventive approaches. However, the conceptual base for such efforts remains relatively undefined. Another significant problem is the lack of an accepted knowledge base regarding risk factors for elderly women (Institute of Medicine 1990). In addition, there is insufficient knowledge of the effects of various interventions aimed at reducing known risky situations or behaviors, due to the paucity of rigorous evaluations of prevention strategies among elderly women. Prevention of premature disability and mortality for elderly women will require a greater understanding of both the age-specific changes in risk factors affecting functional ability and the effect of interventions on risk factor change (Institute of Medicine 1990).

Improvements in the methods of prevention must also include improvements in the care and advice given by health professionals. A recent survey of expert geriatricians concerning the role of physicians providing primary care to the elderly emphasized the importance of prevention. These geriatricians stressed that the physician's treatment plan should include distinguishing between reversible and irreversible components of patients' problems, conducting multidimensional functional assessments, and collaborating with nonphysician personnel to address critical aspects of the elderly individual's environment (Fahs, Muller, and Schechter 1989). However, a follow-up survey of primary care physicians treating large numbers of elderly patients found very few who adhered to these recommendations (Fahs et al. 1989).

To be effective, prevention policy must also address the marked heterogeneity among older women, including the interactions among healthcare demand and availability, poverty, and the rapidly increasing numbers of "oldest-old" women. Research should be designed to examine the effects on elderly women of risk factors that include economic and social components. Results of such investigations may indicate that the detrimental effects of the lack of preventive services for women extend beyond the health of older individuals to broader social consequences, such as an increase in the female poverty rate (Muller 1990).

Financing Prevention

A serious impediment to progress in the delivery and evaluation of preventive services for elderly women is the current structure of Medicare reimbursement. The Medicare program, the primary source of health insurance for the nation's 31 million elderly people, reflects the national focus on treatment rather than prevention. Medicare is prohibited by law from offering benefits for preventive services, except for a small number of services that have been added following specific legislation amending the Medicare Act. Currently, vaccines for pneumococcal pneumonia and hepatitis B (primary prevention) and screening mammography and Pap smears (secondary prevention) comprise the whole package of preventive services covered by Medicare.

In recent years, there has been growing criticism of the wisdom of this blanket exclusion. The charge given to Medicare to pay for the consequences of *not* preventing episodes of illness or disability, without the obligation to pay for interventions that might prevent such episodes, appears shortsighted. However, for prevention to become part of public policy, economic concerns must be addressed.

The heart of the issue is that appropriate preventive care for the elderly and the structure of the reimbursement system are linked inseparably. Odd as it may seem, the current payment structure for Medicare was derived from acute-care services for younger populations. This is due, in large measure, to the historical importance of employment-based schemes, and to the high social value placed on one-time surgical interventions and advanced diagnostic procedures (Muller and Fahs 1990). Because physicians treating the elderly generally provide only those services for which they are reimbursed, these coverage limitations effectively restrict the clinical options available to patients (Fahs et al. 1989).

Evaluating the Effects of Preventive Care

Congressional approval of increased Medicare benefits for prevention services will be influenced by estimates of the costs of those services in relation to their expected benefits. The quantification of this relationship is called cost-effectiveness analysis (CEA). Many such analyses have concluded that providing preventive medical care services generally costs more money than it saves.

Yet, the widely accepted conclusion that prevention does not save money depends on the presence of several contributing conditions—conditions that often do not apply to elderly populations. For example, estimates of cost-effectiveness of prevention in younger population groups are negatively influenced by the long time lag, often 20–40 years, between expenditures and the expected realization of benefits. Another negative influence is the relatively low prevalence of disease in general populations. For the elderly, however, the time lag between expenditure and expected benefit is telescoped. Furthermore, the elderly have higher disease rates than do younger populations. Therefore, cost-effectiveness analyses that consider an average-risk young population may yield different results from targeted analyses of high-risk elderly populations (Fahs and Mandelblatt 1990).

The Significance of Particular Age-Related Factors

Clearly the application of cost-effectiveness analysis to geriatric clinical situations can lead to new discoveries. For example, in April 1988, the first cost-effectiveness analysis was published that specifically targeted a low-income elderly population for preventive care services. The finding that this group made a valid target for preventive services ran counter to the prevailing economic wisdom. Indeed, in this analysis of a Pap smear screening program for low-income women aged 65 and over, the results were notably different from those obtained in studies of other population groups. Overall, the analysis found that the preventive screening program (cervical cancer detection) both saved money and added years of life. These findings showed that the benefits from some prevention programs for the elderly can outweigh the costs (Mandelblatt and Fahs 1988).

This example also illustrates the importance of taking into account the heterogeneity of elderly women when considering costs and benefits of preventive programs. Blanket statements based on the results of cost-effectiveness analysis for general populations result in policies that effectively discriminate against vulnerable subgroups in the population. Many of the factors that crucially affect the results of cost-effectiveness analyses vary by age, race, and socioeconomic status.

The clinical experience of elderly women may be different from that of younger cohorts, which will affect the outcome of a preventive program. Examples include experience with nutrition, environmental and occupational exposures, and prior medical care that can differ from today's standards, perhaps because of technology advancement. Such differences may directly affect the healthcare needs of the elderly today and alter the cost-effectiveness of various treatment and prevention programs. For instance, many of today's elderly women went through their childbearing years prior to George Papanicolaou's development of the cervical smear. Consequently, many of them missed the opportunity to establish a schedule of regular screening. Previously unscreened elderly women will have a higher incidence of asymptomatic cervical cancer, increasing the cost-effectiveness of screening for this population (Mandelblatt et al. 1991).

Furthermore, the consistent use of preventive services by elderly women may be crucial for program effects, but factors affecting their utilization may differ from those operating in younger populations and even among different groups of the elderly. A woman's mobility problems, attachment to particular providers because of chronic problems, or expectation that burdensome expenditures will be initiated might reduce her use of preventive services. Realistic assessments of the costs and effectiveness of prevention programs need to identify such barriers to utilization and estimate the costs of removing them.

Which Results Are Being Measured?

There is a need for a balanced appraisal of the main issues affecting cost-effectiveness analyses of preventive services for the elderly, especially for elderly women, since these analyses carry significant weight among decision makers. The need is underscored by the tendency to question whether or not prevention for the elderly would benefit the macroeconomy, and the conflict that such a question heats up between goals stated in ethical terms versus goals defined economically.

On the one hand, a rational economic approach dictates that resource constraints be taken into account explicitly in deciding among prevention and treatment alternatives. Of particular concern is the likelihood that without direct objective appraisal, resource constraints will implicitly affect the selection of prevention and treatment programs for particular populations. Decisions based on implicit assumptions may be driven by a lack of information or awareness, or indeed by bias. Examples of biased assumptions held by some physicians that could affect treatment plans are the belief that the physician should not waste effort or money on old people who will die soon anyway, or that old people generally do not respond well to treatment, or that the elderly patient will just get another disease soon anyway.

On the other hand, ethicists from the formalist school believe that there are values, such as the preservation of life, that are absolute and should always be promoted, regardless of the outcome of any given situation. This line of thought often implies that cost can be neither ethically nor clinically relevant in deciding what treatment is appropriate. Here, for example, lies the justification for the extension of life "at all costs," without regard to patient or family burden or to the equitable allocation of limited resources.

The conflict is often characterized as one in which individual and social priorities are at odds. For instance, any preventive intervention is clearly valuable to the individual, so long as its benefits are not outweighed by adverse side effects. However, social priorities would suggest an inquiry into the question of whether or not these preventive services are economically feasible.

Individual priorities among the elderly, such as extension of life, are currently more clear-cut than social priorities for the elderly, which remain, like health policy in general in this country, rather ill-defined. This situation is reflected in the methodology of cost-effectiveness analysis. Certain outcomes, such as life extension, are more readily defined than others, such as relative freedom from disability. Thus, more easily measurable outcomes, that is, years of life saved, are often used over outcomes that are relatively difficult to measure but may be equally or more meaningful, that is, quality of life.

An important goal for the future development of cost-effectiveness analysis is to extend the analysis beyond how many years of life are saved, to how much improvement has been achieved in functional status, and to incorporate how people value those years. In the most limited sense, the quality of life that is lost or restored through treatment decisions affects the future of one particular elderly person, the direct beneficiary. In the broader sense, quality of life can also mean the impact on future generations to whom the elderly person contributes through the wisdom of his or her life experience, the indirect beneficiaries. Adding healthy years of life enhances that legacy. Yet, with no agreed-upon conceptual framework for the measurement of disability, the instruments needed to measure the worth and costs of different program designs and resource allocations remain underdeveloped.

Some of the indirect benefits of increased healthy years of life for older women are specific and well-documented. In particular, studies suggest that the premature death of a married elderly woman is associated with an increased likelihood of the premature death of her widowed husband (Rowe and Kahn 1987). Thus, not only are years lost from her life, but also from his. There are other examples of important indirect benefits that are currently ignored in cost-effectiveness analyses. These include an increase in productive time available for the adult, caregiving daughters of elderly women, and expanded grandparenting contributions, such as child care.

Cost-Effectiveness Analysis for an Aging Society

In summary, there are at least two kinds of problems with conventional cost-effectiveness analysis as it relates to preventive care for the elderly: (1) cost-effectiveness analysis of general populations ignores the particular circumstances of the elderly—especially of vulnerable subgroups—that could lead to new conclusions about costs and benefits; and (2) conventional cost-effectiveness analyses do not measure a program's impact on the quality of an individual's life or the indirect social-familial effects of preventive care for elderly women. These limitations suggest that a serious methodologic appraisal of cost-effectiveness analysis along these lines could contribute to more appropriate public policy choices and investments in program design, and to improving preventive service delivery for women. It is time to adjust our analytic techniques to be more in tune with social realities.

Such an adjustment is critically necessary because cost-effective prevention programs must be developed to meet the needs of our aging society. Otherwise, current health policies that fail to target preventable illness among aging women will lead to a heavy societal burden of disability as the population ages. In particular, programs must be designed to take into account the relationships in our society of sex, socioeconomic status, and age to vulnerability to preventable illness and disability. The section following reviews some aspects of the

burden of illness among elderly women that illustrate these relationships.

PREVENTABLE ILLNESS: RISK DIFFERENCES AMONG ELDERLY WOMEN

Healthcare delivery and financing systems for preventive services that
do not distinguish between sex or between income levels will have a
differential impact on women in general, and on some groups of
women more than others, because of their vulnerability to poverty
and their problems in obtaining medical and social support from
caregivers (Muller 1990). Yet, socioeconomic differentials in the relationship between aging and health have been surprisingly neglected
in policy discussions of the problems of health and aging in our
society (Black and Kapoor 1990). Understanding the heterogeneity of
risk can help focus prevention efforts both to help those most at risk
and to increase cost-effectiveness.

In a discussion of health risk differences, it would be instructive to
examine data on mortality and morbidity among older women categorized by socioeconomic status. However, this is not possible. The
United States is the only industrialized country that does not measure
the effect of social class on health. Instead, data are presented by race
and gender, categories that may be, in part, proxies for social class
and economic status. The data generally divide race simply into
whites and blacks. Thus, the data presented here reflect this distinc-
tion. However, because blacks have a higher rate of poverty than
whites, differences in health between blacks and whites may be due
less to race differences than to differences in social and economic
class.

Mortality Differences between Black and White Women

The age-adjusted mortality rates of black women are higher than those
of white women, for the three leading causes of death among elderly
women (National Center for Health Statistics 1990). The differences
in these rates represent the greater health risks experienced by black
women and the minimum excess (preventable) mortality among
blacks. This is a minimum estimate because the white rates may not
represent the lowest mortality achievable. One could, for example,
compare black rates in this country against countries with the lowest

rates globally. Another comparison would be against expert clinical judgment about what deaths are preventable given current medical science. Each of these measures of mortality risk differences is important, and each has different policy implications. The focus here is simply on describing some of the empirical differences by race found in the United States. In some cases, the data point to fairly large social and economic consequences of premature illness and death. Some examples of these consequences are presented.

Internationally, the United States has the 10th highest female life expectancy at age 65 (National Center for Health Statistics 1990). Black women have a shorter life expectancy than do white women, a difference at birth of 5.1 years. For women aged 65 and over, the life expectancy for white women is 83.7, versus 82.1 for elderly black women. That difference is significant: for black elderly women in the United States, the 1.6-year difference in life expectancy at age 65 translates to 245,000 years of potential life lost, a tremendous social cost.

Differences in Death Rates for Specific Diseases

There are also striking differences in age-specific death rates in the United States between white and black elderly women for specific diseases. The death rate for black women aged 65–74 for cerebrovascular diseases is double that for white women that age (Manton, Patrick, and Johnson 1987). Similarly, the young-elderly black woman has a 1.6 greater chance of dying from cardiac disease than the young-elderly white woman. Yet, black women have not been targeted as a high-risk group for premature mortality due to coronary disease, as men have, perhaps because the average rates for black and white women in general are lower than those for men.

Although the excess mortality among black women aged 65–74 may be due to the influence of behavioral and environmental factors prior to age 65, there are no studies yet on the potential effectiveness of reducing cardiac risk factors once women turn 65. Effective screening strategies to prevent coronary disease and cerebrovascular disease, as recommended by the U.S. Preventive Services Task Force (Goldbloom and Lawrence 1990), include measurement of blood pressure and serum cholesterol, and counseling of patients to stop smoking, lower dietary fat consumption, and increase physical activity levels. To date, with few exceptions, research on the effectiveness of strategies to prevent heart disease has been conducted only on younger men.

Death rates for malignant neoplasms tell a different story. This category of illness encompasses many different diseases—breast cancer, cervical cancer, uterine cancer, ovarian cancer, lung cancer, melanoma, to name but a few. Incidence rates for specific cancers like breast and cervical cancer increase dramatically with age.

Important Differences in Deaths from Breast Cancer

Average death rates for elderly black and white women across all cancers are remarkably similar. Such average rates can mask important variations within and between the different cancers. In particular, breast cancer dominates the average. The rates of death for breast cancer are, indeed, relatively similar. However, a narrow focus on mortality obscures a singularly important variation, that is, the stage of cancer at detection. Stage-specific data show that cancers are more advanced at detection for black women than for white women (U.S. Department of Health and Human Services 1991). One study suggests that only one-half of elderly black women are alive five years after diagnosis, compared with three-quarters of white elderly women (Bassett and Krieger 1986). The stage of breast and cervical cancer at diagnosis is related, in large part, to the utilization of prevention services.

Death rates for breast cancer for women prior to age 65 are markedly higher for blacks than whites. (Black women aged 45–54 have death rates that are 33 percent higher than their white counterparts.) Are lower death rates in later years for blacks a secondary effect of higher death rates in earlier years? It may be that more white women are dying of breast cancer in their 60s, 70s, and 80s, because they actually live longer with the disease. This may be because more white women benefit from preventive care that effectively postpones the disease's progression until a later age. Early screening for breast cancer will increase life expectancy following a diagnosis of asymptomatic disease, though definitive data from studies of long-term follow-up prognosis are not available. Differences in treatment for breast cancer have been documented for white and black women. It is also true that rates of breast cancer in elderly black women have been increasing over time.

In contrast to breast cancer, rates for cervical cancer mortality are distinctly higher for black elderly women. The elderly bear a disproportionate burden of this disease. Twenty-five percent of new cervical cancer cases and 41 percent of the deaths from this disease occur in women aged 65 and over. Here, all deaths are preventable, assuming early detection and current technology. The rate of death for black women aged 50 and over is almost three times the rate for white women aged 50 and over (Office of Technology Assessment 1990).

Disability Differences between Black and White Women

The disabling consequences of disease are particularly important for elderly women and for resource allocation in an aging society, because functional impairment can lead to an increased need for formal long-term care services. Disability is often measured by the number of activities of daily living (ADLs), such as bathing, dressing, and going to the toilet, or instrumental activities of daily living (IADLs), such as doing housework, preparing meals, and shopping, that the person is chronically limited in performing. Community-dwelling black women report higher disability rates than do whites.

Among elderly women, black women were more likely than white women to be disabled at all ages. In 1982, "young-old" (aged 65–74) black women had a disability rate of 22 percent, compared with 13 percent for white women that age. Among the oldest women, aged 85 and over, more than half (56 percent) of black women were disabled compared with slightly over a third (35 percent) of white women. Black women were also more likely to have more severe levels of disabilities at all ages. Eighteen percent of the oldest black women had five or six ADLs that they had limitations in performing, compared with only 8 percent of the oldest white women (Manton et al. 1987).

Risk Differences Are Critical for Cost-Effectiveness

The preceding examples illustrate two important insights into the prevention policy debate: first, that even for diseases generally considered "male," such as heart disease, there may be significant differences in risk among women from different socioeconomic backgrounds; and, second, that for diseases considered "female"—for example, breast cancer and cervical cancer—effective prevention policy must go beyond targeting "women." Attention must be paid to the identification of high-risk women and to the development of innovative models of care to screen and follow up women at high risk.

The Importance of Targeting

Even when funding for preventive services for general populations is approved, specific allocations for ensuring or enhancing utilization of the prevention program by high-risk members are often ignored. The irony is that without the utilization of those individuals at highest risk, the program will no longer be cost-effective. Often, this basic fact is not well-recognized at policy levels.

Mathematical models used by policymakers to predict the costs and effects of different prevention programs often depend on population simulations. These simulations incorporate a variety of epidemiologic, clinical, demographic, and economic data that characterize both high-risk and low-risk members of the population. Yet, final estimates of costs and effects usually combine the data from high- and low-risk groups and report "average" population estimates. It is critical to keep in mind, however, that even if these average results indicate that a program is cost-effective, that finding will be highly dependent on the inclusion of data from the high-risk populations. Furthermore, in many studies there is an association between lack of preventive care and barriers to access other than financing, such as provider availability and patient attitudes (American Cancer Society 1985; Baquet and Ringen 1987; McPhee and Schroeder 1987; Weintraub, Violi and Freedman 1987).

The impact of different levels of patient access and utilization on the estimated costs and effects of a preventive service can be illustrated by considering the mix of high- and low-risk elderly women involved in a given cervical cancer preventive program. Figures 5.1 and 5.2 depict an analysis of the relationships among utilization levels, risk-status mixes, screening effectiveness, and costs. For example, in figure 5.1, curves A and B show the differing combinations of high-risk and low-risk women users of the Pap smear that will result in the same number of life years saved. With a higher proportion of low-risk women, there must be more total utilization (80 percent at point A^0), than with a higher proportion of high-risk women (60 percent at point A^1). Figure 5.2 shows the resulting difference in costs (points A^0 and A^1) and cost-effectiveness ratios (lines R^0 and R^1).

Targeting the screening program to high-risk women increases its effectiveness by about 50 percent, as shown in figure 5.2. The figure shows that to save 30,000 life-years with a nontargeted program, the costs increase substantially—the difference on the graph between point Y_1 and point Y_0. Another way to interpret this difference is to say that for the same cost a targeted program with high proportions of high-risk women saves 30,000 life-years, compared with only 20,000 life-years saved by a nontargeted program.

Figures 5.1 and 5.2 illustrate an obvious imperative for the new screening programs financed by Medicare. High ratios of high-risk to

Figure 5.1 EFFECTS OF HIGH-RISK AND LOW-RISK USER RATIOS ON THE
SUCCESS OF THE MEDICARE PAP SMEAR BENEFIT

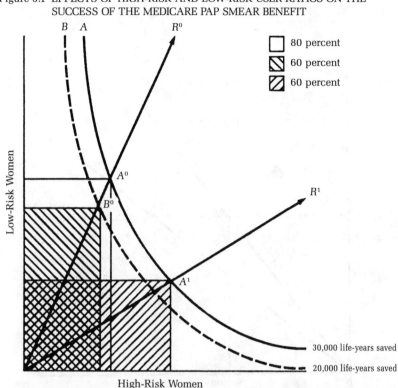

Notes: A is the curve showing the various combinations of high-risk and low-risk Pap smear users that result in 30,000 life-years saved; B is the curve showing the various combinations of high-risk and low-risk Pap smear users that result in 20,000 life-years saved; A^1 is the point denoting the number of high- and low-risk users where an efficient screening program will save 30,000 life-years, at 60 percent overall utilization; A^0 is the point denoting the number of high- and low-risk users where an efficient screening program will save 30,000 life-years, at 80 percent utilization; B^0 is the point denoting the number of high- and low-risk users where an efficient screening program will save 20,000 life-years, at 60 percent utilization; R^1 is a ray showing a high Pap smear user ratio of high-risk to low-risk women; R^0 is a ray showing a low Pap smear user ratio of high-risk to low-risk women.

low-risk women must be achieved to ensure successful outcomes of the new Medicare benefit—that is, saving the most lives at the most favorable cost. In the worst case, instead, a screening program would ultimately be used predominantly by low-risk women, resulting in excessive costs and low benefits in terms of life-years saved.

120 Women on the Front Lines

120   Women on the Front Lines

Figure 5.2 TOTAL COSTS, TOTAL EFFECTS, AND COST-EFFECTIVENESS RATIOS
FOR DIFFERENT PROPORTIONS OF HIGH-RISK AND LOW-RISK PAP
SMEAR USERS

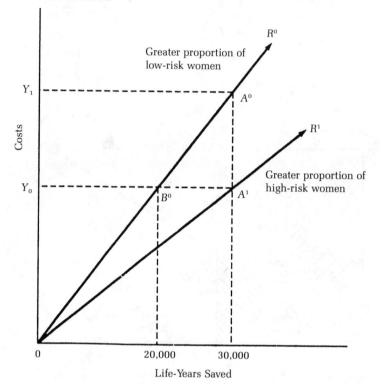

Notes: Cost-effectiveness ratios (CER) are shown by the slopes of R^0 and R^1, where CER
$= Y_1/20{,}000 > Y_0/30{,}000 > Y_1/30{,}000$. $Y_0 =$ total costs for: (a) 60 percent utilization
rate with high ratio of high-risk to low-risk users (i.e., point A^1 from figure 5.1, where
effects equal 30,000 life-years saved); and (b) 60 percent utilization rate with low ratio
of high-risk to low-risk users (i.e., point B^0 from figure 5.1, where effects equal 20,000
life-years saved). $Y_1 =$ total costs for 80 percent utilization rate with low ratio of high-
risk to low-risk users (i.e., point A^0 from figure 5.1, where effects equal 30,000 life-
years saved).

Of course, targeting efforts themselves will incur some amount of
additional costs, such as the costs of physician education or community outreach programs. The costs and effectiveness of alternative
targeting strategies should be taken into account in future cost-effectiveness analyses. Only with such enhanced models can we realisti-
cally evaluate alternative strategies for achieving the substantial im-

provements in the health of elderly women that are so crucial in our aging society.

Unfortunately, no solutions are appearing in the public policy debates to the problems of the health gap in the United States between whites and minorities (Foege 1991; Rice 1991) and of premature disability among elderly women. Yet the striking increase in racial and ethnic diversity among the elderly as projected by Taeuber and Allen in chapter 2 of this volume calls for immediate action if we are to avoid greatly increased rates of excess disability in the future. Without prevention, disparities in potential versus actual functional vitality will multiply the loss of productivity in our aging society, as we lose productivity among the elderly themselves and among their informal caregivers. This section examines some implications for the future, if current trends are allowed to continue. It offers some projections of the excess burden of illness (and cost) in the years ahead as more and more women enter the oldest age groups.

Heart Disease

Using the middle series of the U.S. Census (1989) population projections, and age-specific death rates presented by Manton et al. (1987), we can estimate that without increased prevention services, if present trends continue, there are likely to be 10,000 excess (preventable) deaths every year due to heart disease among black women aged 65–74 by the middle of the next century. These women dying from preventable heart disease will constitute .5 percent of young elderly black women. Add to this another 3,000 excess deaths every year among this age group due to cerebrovascular disease. If these deaths—and the huge societal burden of disability and healthcare costs they signify—are to be averted, preventive services must be targeted to the groups at greatest risk.

   A recent experimental cholesterol screening program in an urban black community in East Baltimore yielded a large number of people with previously undetected high cholesterol levels, as well as large numbers of people with coexisting hypertension and hypercholesterolemia. The screening sites included five churches, one public housing project, and two major grocery markets. Women and the elderly were more likely to come to be screened (Russell et al. 1991). There is a need for more such community-based screening programs, especially those focusing on the provision of follow-up care, given the scarcity of chronic disease prevention services in inner-city communities (Russell et al. 1991).

There have been few adequate cost-effectiveness analyses of the treatment of risk factors for heart disease and cerebrovascular diseases in women aged 65 and over. However, analyses of the results of the study by the European Working Party on Hypertension in the Elderly indicate a promising cost-effectiveness ratio (Amery et al. 1986). These analyses have measured the effects only in terms of years of life added. No analyses have been performed indicating the social costs of these excess deaths. In measuring the effectiveness of health services for the elderly, other variables besides the addition of years of life may mean a great deal. For instance, among the black population in this country, which is facing the devastating impact of AIDS on family life, the traditionally strong family and community roles that elderly black women have held in the past are particularly significant now and will continue to be so in the future. Without these women's contributions, already-overburdened formal social services would be taxed even further.

Tertiary prevention of disability related to heart disease has also been shown to be effective in elderly populations. In part because of concern about the allocation of high-cost medical technologies among a rapidly increasing elderly population, substantial data are available regarding one common and expensive technique in particular, that is, coronary artery bypass surgery. Data from the Coronary Artery Surgery Study (CASS), a multicenter study, show very favorable long-term results for elderly patients. Cumulative five-year survival was 83 percent in the elderly. Moreover, recurrent cardiac morbidity during that period was significantly lower in the elderly group (1,086 patients) than in the younger group (7,827 patients). As Rowe (1985: 834) pointed out in a review of physiologic studies of the elderly: "In view of the poorer initial status of the elderly, [the CASS] results are very encouraging and highlight the overriding importance of individual clinical characteristics, rather than age itself, in decisions about whether to perform bypass surgery in the elderly."

However, disturbing new evidence suggests that sex and race bias may affect physicians' treatment decisions for suspected or confirmed coronary artery disease. The likelihood that a woman will receive a cardiac catheterization or revascularization procedure is significantly lower than the likelihood that a man will receive such procedures, controlling for age and diagnosis (Ayanian and Epstein 1991; Foster et al. 1992). In addition, compared with whites, blacks are far less likely to be seen by a cardiologist, to have coronary angiography performed, or to undergo coronary artery bypass surgery (Maynard et al. 1986; National Center for Health Statistics 1979; Wenneker and Epstein 1989).

These data point to the need for increased efforts to reduce race and sex bias in the provision of medical services to prevent excess disability and mortality from heart disease. The adverse economic and social consequences for the nation as a whole will worsen in the future, if such bias is allowed to continue while there are growing percentages of minority women among the elderly. Policy guidance regarding minority initiatives in heart disease prevention, broadly defined, should be given increased attention and resources.

Hip Fractures

There are other examples of the excess social and economic costs we will face as a country if significant investment and progress are not made in treating many of the nonfatal diseases of aging. Hip fractures, for instance, contribute significantly to disability and institutionalization among women. Fifteen percent of white women, compared with 5 percent of men, will sustain a hip fracture during the course of their lives. The magnitude of this risk for women can be appreciated when one considers that it is equivalent to the combined lifetime risk of their developing breast, uterine, or ovarian cancer (Cummings et al. 1985). Many of these fractures result in disability or death. Hip fractures cost the nation an estimated $7 billion to $10 billion annually, costs that will rise as the population ages (Holbrook et al. 1988).

The devastating impact of this injury for women is not fully expressed by the 5–20 percent reduction in expected years of survival following a hip fracture (Cummings et al. 1985). Of those able to walk before sustaining a hip fracture, for example, fully half cannot walk independently afterward. The quality of life for these women is considerably compromised, and the risk of institutionalization is great. More than 60,000 nursing home admissions have been attributed to hip fractures annually (Phillips et al. 1988), as have more than 7 million restricted activity days among those not institutionalized. It is projected that in 30 years' time, there could be almost 350,000 hip fractures each year in the United States at an annual cost of between $31 billion and $62 billion (Cummings, Rubin, and Black, in press).

Many hip fractures are associated with osteoporosis. The alarming situation projected here can be at least partially avoided if methods to preserve bone mass can be refined, and environmental assessments can be promoted to identify and reduce the factors that precipitate serious falls.

Hip fractures among elderly women are also associated with high indirect costs due to the increased support necessary from family members or friends. No studies yet provide estimates of these indirect costs, although some research is underway (Strain et al. 1992, Fahs et al. 1992). The rising percentage of people who will have elderly relatives suggests the increased relevance for the future of developing cost-effectiveness measures that evaluate the benefits and costs to other family members of efforts to prevent hip fractures among elderly women.

Dementia

Dementia is another condition that will contribute significantly to huge increases in healthcare costs if current patterns of care persist. Today, less than 20 cents is spent on research into Alzheimer's disease for every dollar spent on its treatment. Such restricted spending today could lead to gigantic future expenditures. By 2040, the aging of the population could multiply the number of dementia patients three to five times, requiring as much as $150 billion per year for their care (Huang, Cartwright, and Hu 1988; Schneider and Guralnik 1990).

Again, the omission of indirect costs from these projections leads to an underestimate of the social and economic consequences of this major cause of disability among the elderly. Dorothy Rice collected primary data to estimate these costs and found that informal caregivers, usually middle-aged daughters, spent an average of 286 hours per month caring for a noninstitutionalized elderly person with Alzheimer's disease, and 36 hours per month on average for an institutionalized patient with Alzheimer's (Rice et al. 1991). Using replacement costs, that is, the costs of replacing the daughters' services with home care attendants, Rice estimates that the indirect costs associated with Alzheimer's constitute fully 65 percent of the economic costs to our society of this disease. Thus, the real annual costs (including indirect costs) of *not* preventing Alzheimer's disease would approach $230 billion by 2040.

These estimates once again point to the need for methodological refinement in cost-effectiveness analysis of prevention. The use of replacement costs to estimate the opportunity costs to the market of informal caregivers is controversial. Although market wages for women may underestimate the value of women's time because of gender disparities in income, replacement costs may also underestimate the true opportunity costs to society of losing the productivity of middle-aged women, a larger and larger proportion of whom are reaching their peak productivity levels in the labor market.

It has been estimated moreover, that delaying the onset of dementia for five years would reduce the incidence of dementia by one-half. The public policy debate on prevention should include an estimate of the increased economic productivity, particularly among women, that would be associated with an investment in basic sciences research that could lead to such a delay in dementia onset.

Elderly Women Living Alone

More elderly women with a need for services may be living alone. Some projections suggest that close to half (46 percent) of the elderly will live alone in 2030, compared with 38 percent in 1990 (Zedlewski et al. 1990). By age 85, the risk of disability approaches 50 percent. Today, much of the gap between needs and available services is being filled by informal caregivers. A recent report from the Institute of Medicine (1990) discussed the dangers of abdicating responsibility for care to individuals and informal caregivers, a situation that can result from current reimbursement systems that provide no other option. The relative number of offspring available to provide care to mothers will decrease in the decades ahead. Though the ratio of women older than 80 to children will peak in the year 2000 and decline somewhat over the next two decades, it will then soar to an even higher peak in the year 2030 (Institute of Medicine 1990). If elderly women living alone become increasingly disabled but lack support from family and friends, these women will have a greater need for paid, formal care.

PREVENTING THE BURDEN OF UNNECESSARY ILLNESS AND DISABILITY

The preceding section presents examples of consequences for our society if we do not invest money and energy in prevention and do not focus our health policies in the 21st century on "health expectancy"—maintaining quality of life during old age—rather than on simply adding years to an individual's life. To maximize the potential gain in healthy years of life for our elderly population, attention must be paid to the economic issues of distributional equity affecting women and minorities. Without direct targeting of healthcare resources to high-risk women, who are disproportionately members of minority groups, increased prevention budgets will not have the desired effect. That is, to actually achieve the reductions of excess illness, disability, and death that are possible, preventive programs must be aimed at high-risk populations.

Prevention Policy Objectives

The aging of the U.S. population will lead to a tremendous increase in the elderly population over the next 60 years and an even larger increase in the population aged 85 and over, most of whom are women. This unprecedented growth will have a profound impact on our society in the 21st century. Without a substantial increase in prevention efforts, both the disparity in mortality rates between socially advantaged and socially disadvantaged groups and the number of disabled elderly will expand dramatically. The associated costs of healthcare resources needed for this growing elderly population will increase exponentially.

Looking ahead, if we are to improve the quality of life for the elderly, and especially for the women who comprise a majority of the aged, we must modify the dominant goals of the medical community in the 20th century. The measurement of the success of healthcare policy in either ethical or economic terms must move away from its past focus on averting mortality. We need to shift the emphasis of healthcare in the United States from the biologic objective of increasing the duration of life up to a theoretical limit for the human species to the clinical and social objective of helping people maintain their functional competence for as long as their biologic life span permits. Major dividends could thus result in the form of the increased well-being associated with the reduction in functional disability, a shortened term of expensive medical care, and a postponement of long-term care (Institute of Medicine 1990).

What remains to be done? Public finance of cost-effective preventive care for vulnerable people is very much on the social agenda. However, public finance, while necessary, is not sufficient: research, public education, physician awareness, and outreach efforts also need to be involved for optimal program performance. Preventive healthcare efforts should focus on modifiable risky health behaviors and early diagnosis and be targeted to the most pressing health problems by functional status and age. A sizable gap still exists between recommendations made by leading experts and professional societies for prevention service delivery for elderly women and current prevention policy. There will be dire consequences for millions of older women and the entire society if the gap is allowed to remain as our population ages.

The compelling question for society thus becomes: Will the increase in longevity we have witnessed during the past decades represent a net gain in terms of healthy life, or are we merely prolonging the period of suffering and ill health, while adding to society's burden a greater number of sick, disabled, and institutionalized old people? The answer will depend on the prevention efforts we put in place now.

References

American Cancer Society. 1985. *Survey of Physicians' Attitudes and Practices in Cancer Detection*. Washington, D.C.: American Cancer Society.

Amery, A., et al. 1986. "Efficacy of Antihypertensive Drug Treatment According to Age, Sex, Blood Pressure, and Previous Cardiovascular Disease in Patients over the Age of 60." *Lancet* 2(8507): 589–92.

Ayanian, J. Z., and A. M. Epstein. 1991. "Differences in the Use of Procedures between Women and Men Hospitalized for Coronary Heart Disease." *New England Journal of Medicine* 325: 221–25.

Baquet, C., and K. Ringen. 1987. "Health Policy: Gaps in Access, Delivery, and Utilization of the Pap Smear in the United States." *Milbank Quarterly* 65(suppl. 2): 322–47.

Bassett, T., and N. Krieger. 1986. "Social Class and Black-White Differences in Breast Cancer Survival." *American Journal of Public Health* 76: 1400–3.

Black, J. S., and W. Kapoor. 1990. "Health Promotion and Disease Prevention in Older People: Our Current State of Ignorance." *Journal of the American Geriatrics Society* 38: 168–72.

Breslow, L., and A. R. Somers. 1977. "The Lifetime Health-Monitoring Program: A Practical Approach to Preventive Medicine." *New England Journal of Medicine* 292: 601–8.

Brody, E. M. 1981. "Women in the Middle and Family Help to Older People." *Gerontologist* 25: 19–29.

Butler, R. N., and H. P. Gleason. 1985, eds. *Productive Aging: Enhancing Vitality in Later Life.* New York: Springer-Verlag.

Cummings, S. R., J. L. Kelsey, M. C. Nevitt, and K. J. O'Dowd. 1985. "Epidemiology of Osteoporosis and Osteoporotic Fractures." *Epidemiological Review* 7: 178–208.

Cummings, S .R., S. M. Rubin, and D. Black. In press. "The Coming Epidemic of Hip Fractures in the United States." *Clinical Orthopaedics and Related Research.*

Davis, K., R. Bialek, et al. 1988. "Paying for Preventive Care under Public and Private Health Insurance: Moving the Debate Forward." Baltimore, Md.: Department of Health Policy and Management, School of Hygiene and Public Health, Johns Hopkins University.

Fahs, M. C., and J. Mandelblatt. 1990. "Cost Effectiveness of Cervical Cancer Screening among Elderly Low Income Women." In *Preventing Disease: Beyond the Rhetoric,* edited by R. B. Goldbloom and R. S. Lawrence. New York: Springer-Verlag.

Fahs, M. C., C. Muller, and M. Schechter. 1989. "Primary Medical Care for Elderly Patients, Part 2: Results of a Survey of Office Based Clinicians." *Journal of Community Health* 14: 89–99.

Fahs, M. C., J. Strain, J. Lyons, and J. Hammer. 1992. "Economic Methods in Cost Offset Measurements." *Proceedings of American Psychological Association:* 173.

Foege, W. H. 1991. "Preventive Medicine and Public Health." *Journal of the American Medical Association* 265: 3162–3.

Foster, D. A., M. K. Gillette, P. N. McNeill, and A. M. Collins. 1992. "Is There Sex Bias in the Management of Coronary Artery Disease?" *New England Journal of Medicine* 326: 570–71.

Fries, J. F. 1980. "Aging, Natural Death, and the Compression of Morbidity." *New England Journal of Medicine* 303: 130–6.

German, P. S., and L. P. Fried. 1980. "Prevention and the Elderly: Public Health Issues and Strategies." *Annual Review of Public Health* 10: 319–32.

Goldbloom, R. B., and R. F. Lawrence. 1990. *Preventing Disease: Beyond the Rhetoric.* New York: Springer-Verlag.

Haug, M. R., and S. J. Folman. 1986. "Longevity, Gender, and Life Quality." *Journal of Health and Social Behavior* 27: 332–345.

Hazzard, W. R. 1983. "Preventive Gerontology: Strategies for Successful Aging." *Postgraduate Medicine* 279–87.

Henderson, M. J., and D. D. Savage. 1986. "Prevalence and Incidence of Ischemic Heart Disease in United States' Black and White Populations." In *Report of the Secretary's Task Force on Black and Minority Health,* vol. 4. *Cardiovascular and Cerebrovascular Disease* (620–38). Washington, D.C.: U.S. Government Printing Office.

Holbrook, T. L., et al. 1984. *The Frequency of Occurrence, Impact, and Cost of Selected Musculoskeletal Conditions in the United States.* Chicago: American Academy of Orthopedic Surgeons.

House, J. S., R. C. Kessler, and R. A. Herzog. 1990. "Age, Socioeconomic Status, and Health." *Millbank Quarterly* 383–411.

Huang, L. F., W. S. Cartwright, and T. W. Hu. 1988. "The Economic Cost of Senile Dementia in the United States, 1985." *Public Health Reports* 103: 3–7.

Institute of Medicine, Division of Health Promotion and Disease Prevention. 1990. *The Second Fifty Years: Promoting Health and Preventing Disability.* Washington, D.C.: National Academy Press.

Katz, S., L. G. Branch, M. H. Branson, J. A. Papsidero, J. C. Beck, and D. S. Greer. 1983. "Active Life Expectancy." *New England Journal of Medicine* 309(20): 1218–24.

Larson, E. B. 1988. "Health Promotion and Disease Prevention in the Older Adult." *Geriatrics* 43 (suppl): 31–39.

Mandelblatt, J., and M. C. Fahs. 1988. "The Cost Effectiveness of Screening for Cervical Cancer among Elderly Low Income Women." *Journal of the American Medical Association* 259: 16.

Mandelblatt, J., H. Andrews, J. Kerner, A. Zauber, and W. Burnett. 1991. "Determinants of Late Stage Diagnosis of Breast and Cervical Cancer: The Impact of Age, Race, Social Class and Hospital Type." *American Journal of Public Health* 81: 646–9.

Manton, K. G., C. H. Patrick, and K. W. Johnson. 1987. "Health Differentials between Blacks and Whites: Report Trends in Mortality and Morbidity." *Milbank Memorial Fund* 65(Supp. 1): 129–99.

Maynard, C., L. D. Fisher, E. R. Passamani, and T. Pullum. 1986. "Blacks in the Coronary Artery Surgery Study (CASS): Race and Clinical Decision Making." *American Journal of Public Health* 76: 1446–48.

McKinlay, J., and S. Tennstedt. 1986. "Social Networks and the Care of Frail Elders." Final report to the National Institute on Aging. Boston: Boston University.

McPhee, S. J., and S. A. Schroeder. 1987. "Promoting Preventive Care: Changing Reimbursement Is Not Enough." *American Journal of Public Health* 77: 780–81.

Muller, C. 1990. *Health Care and Gender.* New York: Russell Sage Foundation.

Muller, C., and M. C. Fahs. 1990. "Medical Care for the Elderly." *Thesis: The Magazine of the Graduate and University Center* 4: 26–29.

Muller, C., M. C. Fahs, and M. Schechter. 1989. "Primary Medical Care for Elderly Patients, Part 1: Service Mix As Seen by an Expert Panel." *Journal of Community Health* 14: 79–89.

National Center for Health Statistics. 1979. *Office Visits for Diseases of the Circulatory System: The National Ambulatory Medical Care Survey, United States, 1975–76.* Vital and Health Statistics, ser. 13, no. 40. DHEW Pub. No. (PHS)79-1791. Washington, D.C.: U.S. Government Printing Office.

————. 1990. *Health, United States, 1989.* Hyattsville, Md.: U.S. Public Health Service.

Office of Technology Assessment. 1985. *Technology and Aging in America.* Washington, D.C.: Author.

————. 1990. "The Cost and Effectiveness of Screening for Cervical Cancer in Elderly Women." Pub. No. OTA-BP-H-65. Washington, D.C.: U.S. Government Printing Office.

Omen, G. S. 1990. "Prevention and the Elderly: Appropriate Policies." *Health Affairs* 9: 81–93.

Phillips, S., N. Fox, J. Jacobs, and W. E. Wright. 1988. "The Direct Medical Costs of Osteoporosis for American Women Aged 45 and Older." *Bone* 9: 271–79.

Rice, D. 1991. "Health Status and National Health Priorities." *Western Journal of Medicine* 154: 349.

Rice, D., and C. Estes. 1984. "Health of the Elderly: Policy Issues and Challenges." *Health Affairs* 3: 25–49.

Rice, D., P. J. Fox, W. W. Hanck, D. W. Lindeman, W. Max, T. Segura, and P. Webber. 1991. "The Burden of Caring For Alzheimers Disease Patients." *Proceedings* of the 1991 Public Health Conference on Records and Statistics. Washington, D.C.: U.S. Dept. of Health and Human Services, National Center for Health Statistics.

Rosenblum, R. 1985. "Medicare Revisited: A Look through the Past to the Future." *Journal of Health Politics, Policy and Law* 9: 669–81.

Rowe, J. W. 1985. "Health Care for the Elderly." *New England Journal of Medicine* 312: 827–35.

Rowe, J. W., and R. L. Kahn. 1987. "Human Aging: Usual and Successful." *Science* 327: 143–49.

Russell, L. B. 1986. *Is Prevention Better than Cure?* Washington, D.C.: Brookings Institution.

Russell, N. K., D. M. Becker, C. P. Finney, and H. Moses. 1991. "The Yield of Cholesterol Screening in an Urban Black Community." *American Journal of Public Health* 448–51.

Schneider, E. L., and J. M. Guralnik. 1990. "The Aging of America: Impact on Health Care Costs." *Journal of the American Medical Association* 263: 2335–40.

Somers, A. R. 1984. "Why Not Try Preventing Illness as a Way of Controlling Medicare Costs?" *New England Journal of Medicine* 853–56.

Stone, R. 1986. "The Feminization of Poverty and Older Women: An Update." Rockville, Md.: National Cancer for Health Services Research.

Strain, J., J. Lyons, J. Hummer, M. C. Fahs, A. Lebovits, P. Paddison, S. Snyder, and E. Strauss. 1991. "Cost Offset from a Psychiatric Liaison Intervention for Elderly Hip Fracture Patients." *Journal of the American Psychiatric Association* 148: 1044–49.

Strogatz, D. S. 1990. "Use of Medical Care for Chest Pain: Differences between Blacks and Whites." *American Journal of Public Health* 80: 290–94.

U.S. Bureau of the Census. 1984. *Current Population Reports,* ser. 952, no. 25. Washington, D.C.: U.S. Government Printing Office.

————. 1989. *Projections of the Population of the United States, by Age, Sex, and Race: 1988–2080*, prepared by G. Spencer. *Current Population Reports*, ser. P-25, no. 1018. Washington, D.C.: U.S. Government Printing Office.

U.S. Congress. House Select Committee on Aging. 1989. *Health Care Costs for America's Elderly, 1977–1988*. Comm. Pub. No. 101-712. Washington, D.C.: U.S. Government Printing Office.

U.S. Department of Health and Human Services. 1991. *National Institutes of Health, National Cancer Institute, SEER* [Surveillance Epidemiology and End Results]. Washington, D.C.: U.S. Government Printing Office.

Verbrugge, L. M. 1990. "The Twain Meet: Empirical Explanations of Sex Differences in Health and Mortality." In *Gender, Health, and Longevity*, edited by M. G. Ory and H. R. Warner. New York: Springer-Verlag.

Verbrugge, L. M., and D. L. Wingard. 1987. "Sex Differentials in Health and Mortality." *Women and Health* 12: 103–45.

Warner, K. E., and B. R. Luce. 1982. "Cost-Benefit and Cost-Effectiveness Analysis in Health Care: Principles, Practice, and Potential." Ann Arbor, Mich.: Health Administration Press.

Weinstein, M. C., and W. B. Statson. 1977. "Foundations of Cost-Effectiveness Analysis for Health and Medical Practices." *New England Journal of Medicine* 296: 716–21.

Weintraub, N. T., et al. 1987. "Cervical Cancer Screening in Women Aged 65 and Over." *JAGS* 35: 870–75.

Wenneker, M. B., and A. M. Epstein. 1989. "Racial Inequities in the Use of Procedures for Patients with Ischemic Heart Disease in Massachusetts." *Journal of the American Medical Association* 261: 253–57.

Zedlewski, S. R., R. O. Barnes, M. R. Burt, T. D. McBride, and J. A. Meyer. 1990. "The Needs of the Elderly in the 21st Century." Urban Institute Report 90-5. Washington, D.C.: Urban Institute Press.

Chapter Six

RESILIENCY AMIDST INEQUITY: OLDER WOMEN WORKERS IN AN AGING UNITED STATES

Paula Rayman, Kimberly Allshouse, and Jessie Allen

How is it that for years, many years, the same theme was always being repeated in my work? The premonition of sacrifice.
—Kaethe Kollwitz, age 47

Two social trends are converging as the United States moves toward a new century: Our population is growing steadily older, and women continue to enter the labor force in record numbers. Older workers, and in particular older women workers, will be an increasingly important ingredient in maintaining a strong economy and vital society. This chapter explores the employment options, workplace conditions, and work and retirement experiences facing a growing and increasingly diverse population of older women in the United States.

Recent projections suggest that most U.S. labor-force growth in the 1990s will come from increased participation by minorities and middle-aged and older women (Fullerton, Jr. 1992). Diversity among older women workers is also of growing importance. However, very few studies have examined the conditions and meaning of work for older women of color. The middle section of this chapter presents interview data from a series of focus groups that explore the diversity of experience among older women workers. The interviews focus on older women of color and provide rich stories of hope amidst hardship. The chapter's final section uses the common concerns voiced by the women we interviewed as a starting point for a consideration of policy changes that could improve conditions for older women workers in the future. As we discuss these issues, it is important to keep in mind their growing importance due to the demographic changes occurring.

COMING OF AGE

From 1975 to 1990, the U.S. labor force grew at an average rate of 1.9 percent annually. However, from 1990 to 2005 that rate is projected to decrease to only 1.3 percent a year (Kutscher 1992). Much of this growth will come from the greater participation of middle-aged and older women (Fullerton, Jr. 1992). The youth share of the labor force is dropping as the percentage of younger workers (aged 16–34) declines from a high of 50 percent in the late 1980s to a projected 37 percent in 2005. Simultaneously, workers aged 45 to 54, who made up only 16 percent of the labor force in 1990, will constitute 24 percent by 2005. The labor-force participation of men aged 55 to 64 was declining until recently, and is projected to remain virtually stable in the period from 1990 to 2005. In contrast, women in this age group have been rapidly increasing their participation rates. Though still less likely than men to be in the labor force, women aged 55 to 64 are projected to increase their participation by 9 percentage points between 1990 and 2005 (Fullerton, Jr. 1992). By 2005, 68 percent of men and 54 percent of women aged 55 to 64 are projected to be in the labor force, compared with 68 percent and 45 percent, respectively, in 1990. Work-force participation rates among older men and women are thus becoming more similar. However, in many other ways, older women workers face a strikingly different future. Not only do most women live longer than their male counterparts, but many can also expect to live their oldest years in poverty. Retirement benefits do not allow many older women to maintain a decent standard of living.

Most investigations of women and work have focused on career attainment and family and child-care issues for younger women. Perhaps this is a reflection of the age of the women undertaking the research (Shaw and Shaw 1987). Meanwhile, studies of older workers have concentrated on men's work lives, including questions of retirement, discrimination, and retraining. We cannot afford to continue overlooking older women in the work force. As more and more women work for pay for longer and longer periods, and as the work force continues to age, the fortunes of older women workers have increasingly profound consequences for the entire nation.

Who Are "Older Women Workers"?

The U.S. Department of Labor has sometimes used the term *older workers* to refer to those 55 years old and older, and at other times to refer to those approaching retirement. The baby-boom generation used to say that anyone over 30 was old, but as the baby boomers move up in age, so does their perception of what defines "old." This chapter's discussion focuses on women aged 40–65, because research has found that age discrimination is well established by age 40 for women, thus starting earlier than that directed at men, and because age 65 remains an endpoint for much of the statistical evidence available on older workers.[1] However, it is important to remember that many workers are retiring at age 62 or earlier, that others work well beyond age 65, and that age discrimination has been reported by women in their thirties.

Different Ages—Different Generations

We recognize that certain social, political, and economic circumstances that affected women now in their 60s are quite different from trends and events that have shaped the lives of women now in their 40s. The work lives of women are shaped by a mixture of personal and social factors, and it is important to distinguish which characteristics are specific to an age group at a particular time in history and which may be more general and thus applicable to succeeding generations.

The women we interviewed as part of the research for this chapter ranged in age from 45 to 71. When the oldest of these women was born in 1919, less than 2 million of the 8 million wage-earning women were married, and nearly one out of three women workers was employed in agriculture or domestic service (Kessler-Harris 1982). In contrast, by the time the youngest woman was born in 1945, 75 percent of women workers were married, and most of the newly created jobs were in clerical and manufacturing positions.

Today, more women are in the labor force more continuously than ever before. Changes in their labor force histories will affect older women's labor-force situation in the future. In addition, educational attainment has risen significantly for women during the last three decades, a factor that is bound to influence women's work experiences later in life.

What Does Work Mean for Older Women?

What do we know about the meaning of work for older women workers? Research has usually divided the subject into economic and noneconomic aspects of work. The few studies that have specifically focused on midlife and older women workers have concluded that factors influencing younger women's employment remain the same for the older group (Blau 1978; Cain and Dooley 1976; Gitter, Shaw, and Gagen 1986; Shaw 1983). Thus, lower family income will be likely to press married women of all ages into seeking employment. For most unmarried women, the lack of other household income results in their high labor-force participation rates.

A number of economic factors are likely to influence older women's future work-force participation. Because of the recent increase in women's labor-force participation, in the future more elderly women should have some pension income, which could decrease their need to work for pay. However, women's shorter average job tenure and overrepresentation in part-time jobs and small businesses means that without changes in pension structures, older women in the future would continue to receive fewer and smaller pensions than older men (Older Women's League 1990a). Even if coverage rates are leveling, it is likely that most women will continue to receive much lower pension benefits than men for a long time to come. That means that large numbers of the growing population of older women will have to continue to earn job income as long as they can.

In 1983, the federal government instituted changes in Social Security provisions that are meant to encourage older workers to delay retirement. In the period from 2000 to 2022, the age of full Social Security eligibility will rise from 65 to 67. The amendments reduce the rate of benefits available at age 62, and increase bonuses for delaying retirement beyond the age of full eligibility. Some analysts conclude, however, that it is unclear what long-term effect these reforms will have on the work activity of older persons (Herz and Rones 1989). The proliferation of Early Retirement Incentive Plans (ERIPS) as well as liberalized pension plan provisions have contributed to the increase of early labor market withdrawal. Thus, for Social Security changes to be effective, employers must be educated to value older workers and to promote policies that allow older workers to maintain their attachment to the labor force (Herz and Rones 1989).

Noneconomic factors influencing older women's employment that have attracted some research include the quality of jobs available to older women, and individual woman's level of satisfaction with housework, and attitudes toward the roles of women (i.e., family roles versus work roles). However, there are no large-scale studies of other noneconomic factors that may help explain why older women work. Qualitative studies by Rubin (1979) and Rayman (1987) suggest that in addition to economic needs, women seek work to achieve more independence, to have peer support, to activate skills and interests, and to maintain their self-esteem. Unemployed older women, many of whom experienced forced early retirement or on-the-job age discrimination, have reported the centrality of employment for their mental and physical health (Rayman, Forrest, and Kabria 1988). It is also possible that in the future, as more elderly women have higher education levels and continuous work-force histories more similar to those of men, their rates of participation will also approach those of men. More research is needed on the importance of noneconomic factors contributing to older women's employment.

STRUGGLE FOR DIGNITY

An older woman's status in the workplace is the accumulated result of a long history of choices and problems she will have faced throughout her working life. There has been much publicity concerning the movement of women into high-paying, male-dominated occupations. Undeniably, times are changing. Some young women have crossed barriers that have long limited women's employment. Those women whose attachment to the labor force will be continuous and who receive fair wages and benefits can look forward to spending their later years more comfortably than today's older women. However, the majority of women have not crossed the chasm between female- and male-dominated occupations. Despite the changing times, there are trends that remain ominously static, particularly for women of color.

Women's Occupations

Contrary to the popular myth, the majority of women, young and old, continue to work in traditionally female occupations and receive low earnings. In an analysis of population data, Deborah Figart (1988) concluded that, with few exceptions, the overall occupational distribution of women is the same for women of all ages.

Nearly 60 percent of women in the labor force were segregated into three occupations in 1989: sales, service, and clerical. Younger and older women's representation in these occupations was nearly identical—56.3 percent of women aged 20–44 and 56.9 percent of those aged 45–64 were in these three occupations. Executive, administrative, management, and professional specialties accounted for 27.8 percent of women aged 20–44 and 26.9 percent of women aged 45–64 (U.S. Department of Labor 1990). It is important to bear this point in mind when considering the future prospects of women currently in their 20s or 30s. Although there has been an increase in the percentage of women entering certain male-dominated professions, such as engineering, medicine, and law, the majority of professional workers (56 percent) are found in two lower-paying categories—teachers (except college and university) and registered nurses. Women in management positions are also crowded into low-paying categories, such as building managers, office managers, superintendents, and health administrators (Figart 1988).

Between 1950 and 1986, there was a major decline in the number of women employed in the manufacturing industry. Over one-quarter of all women (26 percent) were employed in manufacturing in 1950; by 1986 that number had dropped by almost half to 14 percent (Figart 1988). Part of this drop reflects the movement of textile and apparel manufacturing from the United States to overseas. Most of the decline was matched by increases in women's employment in service and trade occupations, both of which showed growth over the past four decades. These trends may have negative implications for older women workers in the future, since more of the manufacturing jobs were unionized and would have carried better pension and health benefit coverage than most of the service jobs that have replaced them.

A U.S. Bureau of Labor Statistics (BLS) analysis shows that women and minority workers are disproportionately employed in occupations that are projected to grow slowly or actually decline in the period from 1990 to 2005 and in jobs that pay relatively low wages, whatever their growth patterns. Black and Hispanic workers are clustered in fast-growing service occupations with below-average wages (Silvestri and Lukasiewicz 1992). The analysts conclude that unless these groups are used more efficiently in the labor force, there may be future labor shortages in the fast-growing, high-skill occupations. The fate of future older women workers—especially minority women—is also tied to this issue. The implication is that much more extensive occupational shifts are still needed if older women workers are to greatly improve their overall economic outlook.

TRENDS FOR WOMEN OF COLOR

There has been a considerable decline in the percentage of private household workers, a trend that has particularly affected young black women. In 1940, 70 percent of all black women workers were employed in domestic and personal service jobs; by 1981 that number had dropped to 6 percent (Malveaux 1985). Labor-force projections show further dramatic declines in these job categories in the near future (Silvestri and Lukasiewicz 1992). As Taeuber and Allen point out in chapter 2 of this book, young black women today are more likely to work in technical, sales, and administrative support occupations, which could mean some improvement in future older black women's Social Security and pension coverage, relative to that of white women. However, analyses by Julianne Malveaux (1987) have shown that black women continue to be crowded into not only typically female jobs but typically black female jobs. Malveaux compared the representation of black women in different occupations with their representation in the 1981 labor force. She defined jobs as "typically black female" if the percentage of workers in these jobs who are black women was between 50 percent and 150 percent of the proportion of black women in the labor force. Jobs in which black women are over-represented include dieticians, prekindergarten teachers, social workers, registered nurses, lab technicians, file clerks, typists, keypunch operators, calculating machine operators, social welfare clerical assistants, cleaning and health service workers, and private household workers.

The labor-force status of other minority women has rarely been studied. The Bureau of Labor Statistics has collected detailed labor-force data on blacks and whites since the 1960s, and it began to collect data on Hispanic workers in 1976. Accurate national data on Asian and American Indian women are unavailable; the size of these minority populations and the sampling technique used by the BLS limit researchers, because the cell sizes are often too small to make accurate analyses possible. However, research can be designed to overcome these sample-size limitations. For instance, some longitudinal surveys have begun to oversample for blacks, thus enabling rich research on labor-force behavior.

As the proportion of minority women in the work force increases, it becomes even more important to collect accurate data on their labor-force patterns. Malveaux and Wallace (1987) estimated the proportion of minority women in the labor force to be 20 percent of all women workers. The uncounted minority women in the labor force are likely to be those in jobs with the least status, least pay, and least possibility for promotion. Immigrant women, for example, who face not only cultural and language barriers but also sex and race discrimination, are easy targets for exploitation by employers.

Because minority populations themselves are aging, and because of the growing proportions of minority workers of all ages, there will be many more older women of color in the work force of the future. It is imperative that researchers endeavor to include minority women in their research and push for better national data collection on the labor-force behavior of these women.

Women's Earnings

It is important to view older women workers' earnings in the context of women's earning power at different ages and historically. Trends in younger women's earnings today can help project the future for older women's compensation.

WAGE GAP BETWEEN WOMEN AND MEN

In 1939, median annual earnings for full-time women workers in the labor force were 58 percent of the median earnings of men. More than half a century later, in 1990, that figure had risen by only 14 percentage points, to 72 percent (U.S. Bureau of the Census 1991). After a long period of relative stability, women's earnings have shown some relative improvement since 1980 (Marini 1989). However, women continue to be paid less than men, and the earnings ratio decreases with each age cohort until women reach their mid-50s.

The demographic overview in chapter 2 of this volume presents a wage ratio based on weekly earnings, and emphasizes the recent improvements in the wage gap, especially among younger cohorts. To what extent the increases in younger women's relative earnings will continue as these women age is open to question. The wage gap has historically been smaller at the youngest ages. The 1990 median weekly full-time earnings of women aged 25 and over were $370—72 percent of men's median weekly wages of $514. The median weekly earnings of women under age 25 are closer to men's earnings at that age, with a ratio of 90 percent (U.S. Department of Labor 1992). Both men and women engage in low-paying, entry-level positions at this age. The same trend was seen in 1979, when the ratio of women's to men's earnings in the group aged 20–24 was nearly 15 points higher than the ratio of those aged 25 and over. Women's earnings peak at ages 35–44, while men's earnings peak later in life, at ages 45–54 (Figart 1988). This may indicate that older women suffer "salary deceleration" in the form of smaller or fewer raises in salary than their younger counterparts (McConnell 1983).

The wage gap between men and women narrows to 75 percent (in 1990) after men and women reach age 65. However, the reason for this narrowing is due to men's lesser earnings rather than to an increase in women's earnings—median earnings for both women and men drop considerably after age 65 (U.S. Department of Labor 1992). As is the case in the youngest groups, similarities in wages among elderly men and women are due to men's lower earnings at this age.

EARNINGS BY RACE AND ETHNICITY

If you are a black or Hispanic woman, the statistics are grim. In 1991, black women aged 16 and over earned only 86 percent of white women's median weekly earnings; for Hispanic women, this figure was only 78 percent (U.S. Department of Labor 1992). A decade ago, in 1981, black women were actually faring better in relation to white women, earning 93 percent of the latter's median weekly pay (U.S. Department of Labor 1990). In 1991, black men had the same median weekly earnings as white women, and Hispanic men's median wages were about the same as those of black women (U.S. Department of Labor 1992). This reflects the reality that segregation into low-paying occupations is also a dilemma for men of color.

FUTURE EARNINGS OF OLDER WOMEN WORKERS

It is impossible to predict with certainty the earning power of older women in the future. However, we can highlight a number of factors that should affect that power. In some cases, the trends point in different directions. On the one hand, in the 1980s young women's earnings did show significant improvement relative to men's. On the other hand, as described earlier, as women age their earnings tend to stagnate, and apparently women's earnings are continuing to peak earlier than men's.

As the statistics in chapter 2 emphasize, the educational level of women is rising. Higher education is clearly associated with better jobs, more continuous careers, and higher earnings. Still, though education does raise women's earnings, it does not close the gender wage gap. When we compare earnings by education for men and women, the figures are familiar; a woman with four years of college earns only 70 percent of a male college graduate's median earnings—practically the same as the ratio for all workers. Here again, the gap is smaller for younger workers. Trends in the wage gap over the next decade will show whether or not improvements continue and spread to older workers.

For older women of color, the outlook is also uncertain. It is true that younger African-American women have moved out of the lowest-paid private household jobs and into broad occupational categories where most white women work. However, as already discussed, within these broad categories black women remain segregated in certain, usually lower-paying, occupations.

The number of black women who have completed high school has increased significantly among younger women, a trend that should enhance the wage-earning power of older black women in the future. In 1987, 80 percent of black women aged 25–34 had high school diplomas, compared with only 54 percent of those aged 45 to 64. However, a considerably smaller proportion of black women than white women complete college. In fact, the proportion of blacks among all women completing college is much *lower* in the 25–44 age group than it is among older women, because young white women have improved their college completion rates much more dramatically. Hispanic women continue to lag far behind both white and black women in both high school and college completion (U.S. Bureau of the Census 1988). If older women of color are to improve their earnings further in the future, better access to higher education will be a key factor.

Analysts disagree strongly on the role of women's relatively intermittent work-force attachment in the wage gap between men and women. The question is important for projecting older women's job earnings in the future, because women's patterns of work-force attachment are changing. In classic "human capital" theory, women's more frequent work interruptions to provide family care are thought to be an important reason they earn lower wages, because interruptions are presumed to decrease such "productivity factors" as women's educational and training levels, work-force experience, and job skills. But some studies have recently found either that work interruptions for family care have very little impact on a woman's earnings, or that earnings quickly rebound after an interruption (National Committee on Pay Equity 1989). Others find that work-force interruptions do significantly depress women's earnings, but that the negative effects cannot be entirely ascribed to resulting differences in productivity factors (Jacobsen and Levin 1992; Sorensen 1991).

Women are decreasing the length and number of their work-force interruptions, so if interruptions are a big factor in the wage gap, the gap should improve in the future as a result. However, very few women have no interruptions at all. One study found that in 1987, only 10 percent of women between the ages of 35 and 41 had worked continuously (Sorensen 1991). According to Social Security Administration (1985) projections, women who retire in 2000 will have spent an average of 54 percent of their adult lives in employment, and this figure will increase to 71 percent for women retiring in 2020. If this is so, the impact of work interruptions on women's earnings—whatever that impact is—should decrease significantly but persist to some extent so long as women continue to provide most of the family care.

There is the additional question of how the increased demand for eldercare will affect women's work patterns. As the numbers of disabled very elderly people increase, we may find women interrupting their paid employment more frequently to care for disabled parents and spouses. Such interruptions would occur at a later point in most women's work histories than interruptions for childbearing and child care and might have different wage effects.

Most studies of the earnings gap agree that at least some portion of it is unexplained by measurable differences between male and female workers. A review by a National Academy of Sciences panel showed that worker characteristics account for less than half of the female-male earnings gap (U.S. Department of Labor 1982). Aother explanation for the disparity in pay between men and women is sex discrimination, compounded for older women and women of color by race and age discrimination.

Age Discrimination

Discrimination, whether based on age, sex, or race, is one of the most difficult labor market influences to identify and quantify. Age discrimination is particularly elusive, because it is often subtle and subconscious; employers discriminating against older people may not be aware they are doing so, and even those being discriminated against can be incognizant of the situation. A further problem encountered in conducting research on age discrimination is that older people who can find no work or only poorly paid work may drop out of the labor force entirely. Thus, comparisons between younger and older workers within the labor market may not be representative of the true disadvantages older people confront. Research on age discrimination is scarce because of these limitations. Further, most of the research that is available has not included women, an omission that reflects the general view that women's work in the labor force is secondary.

A recent Louis Harris (1989) poll of discouraged workers overcame some of these problems by surveying both men and women not currently participating in the labor force. Findings from the survey of older Americans indicate that there are 1.1 million American men and women over age 50 who are ready and able to work but who are not participating in the labor force. Thirty-seven percent of these discouraged workers felt that employers would find them too old to hire. Nearly half of those polled (48 percent) indicated that a lack of suitable jobs within close proximity kept them from entering the paid labor force. In fact, older women were more likely to cite this as their primary reason for not working than were men. Those willing to work were flexible in their definition of suitable employment: they would be willing to take a part-time job (83 percent); do seasonal work (75 percent); work alone (63 percent); work standing for most of the day (49 percent); and work in the evenings and on weekends (44 percent).

Other research has queried employers on their views and practices related to age discrimination. A survey of more than 500 employers in 1981 found that 61 percent agreed that systematic age discrimination occurs in the workplace; 22 percent claimed that it was unlikely that the company would hire someone over age 50 for a position other than one in senior management without the presence of legal requirements; 20 percent said that older workers have fewer opportunities for promotions or training; and 12 percent acknowledged that older workers' pay raises are not as large as those of younger workers in the same category (McConnell 1983). Rosen and Jerdee (1985) conducted research into the hiring and promotion decisions of managers who were given hypothetical workers whose qualifications differed only by age. In most cases, respondents consistently made different hiring, promotion, training, and discipline decisions based solely on the age of the workers.

In spite of federal legislation banning age discrimination, employers continue to perceive older workers as a group unfit for certain jobs because of declining mental and physical capacities, an inability to learn, a lack of creativity, and inflexibility (McConnell 1983). These myths continue despite strong evidence to the contrary. In a survey of the literature, Meier and Kerr (1976) found at least 20 studies showing that vocabulary, general information, and judgment either rise or never fall before age 60. Further, they cited studies showing that older workers have greater stability on the job, fewer accidents, and less time lost from work than younger workers.

In an aging society, negative stereotypes about older people could be detrimental not just to older workers but to overall job quality. If employers believe that the capacities of available workers are limited (and older women are forming an increasing proportion of that pool), they may react not by investing in training to improve worker productivity but instead by creating more low-productivity, high-turnover, low-wage jobs.

AGE DISCRIMINATION AND WOMEN'S CHANGING WORK PATTERNS

Although age discrimination affects both men and women, it does so differently. This is because of a combination of women's work patterns and the hiring and promotion policies of many employers. As previously discussed, women historically have had a pattern of discontinuous participation in the paid labor force—both exits and reentrances are common. Because many women have reentered the work force when they are older, they have faced age discrimination at the point of hiring more often than men. This is reflected in the fact that more women in their 40s report cases of age discrimination than do men. A 1984 study of age discrimination lawsuits revealed that women were more likely to sue for discrimination in hiring, promotion, wages, and fringe benefits, whereas men more frequently filed owing to involuntary retirement or termination (Schuster and Miller 1984).

As younger women develop more continuous work histories, we might expect that fewer women in their 40s would face age discrimination at the hiring point, and that women's experiences of age discrimination in the work force would become more similar to those of men. However, more women are delaying childbearing to older ages. As a result, employers' negative attitudes about hiring women who are likely to have children could combine with societal attitudes that define women in their 40s as "over the hill," thereby creating more virulent combinations of sex and age discrimination for middle-aged women. Then again, as more older women workers contend with their families' eldercare needs, they may be forced to leave the labor force periodically at later stages in their careers and so may face age discrimination in hiring more frequently at still later ages, when it may be even stronger. Older women of color would face the added problem of race discrimination in all these situations.

DIVERSITY AND OLDER WOMENS' LIVES

In this chapter's discussion of the trends affecting the status of older women workers, we have tried to emphasize the diversity of their experiences. However, we were initially stymied by the lack of information specifically on the employment experiences of older minority women. We therefore decided to undertake a small qualitative study on this subject.

In spring 1990, we conducted a series of focus groups in the Greater Boston area. Participants completed a brief background questionnaire concerning individual demographics, work histories, and household patterns. The heart of the focus groups were partially structured discussions on the meaning of work for the women, discriminatory practices found in their workplaces, identification of social support networks, and hopes and fears regarding work and aging.[2]

The focus groups were designed to reach out to different minority populations in the Boston Metropolitan Area. Community organizations with a history of serving older women of color were asked to cooperate in forming the focus groups, which met at the various organizations.

Statistical Portrait

Although not a random or representative sample, the 29 women who participated in the focus groups provide insight into the work experiences common to black, Hispanic, and Asian women. Our sample included 19 blacks, 3 Chinese, 2 Hispanics, 2 whites, 1 woman from India, 1 woman from Haiti, and 1 woman who described herself as multiracial. They ranged in age from 45 to 71. The average salary of the women was $11,500, whereas their average household income was $19,500. In terms of education, 4 of the women reported less than 11 years of schooling; 11 women had completed high school; and the remaining 12 women indicated that they had taken courses beyond high school, including 5 women who had completed college.

One of the most important aspects of our portrait of this group of older women workers is that most of them headed their households. Only 9 of the women were married with a husband present; 7 were widowed, 11 were divorced or separated; and the rest were single. Some of the women had children, elderly parents, or other relatives who either lived with them or for whom they were financially responsible. For example, Marcy, who came to Boston from Guyana four years earlier and was separated from her husband, was supporting her three children and four grandchildren from her $16,000-a-year job as a hospital housekeeper.

All of the women in the focus groups were workers in the service sector of the economy in what have become known as "women's jobs." Twelve of the women had been in their present jobs for 3–10 years, 8 for less than 3 years, and 5 for over 19 years. Four of the women considered themselves retired but doing volunteer jobs. In describing their family histories, the majority listed their mother's occupation as homemaker (17), while their fathers primarily worked in lower-income positions as janitors (3), carpenters (3), farm workers (2), and workers in small businesses (4). Therefore, many of the women broke new ground in finding employment outside of the home, with the majority having to support themselves without other sources of income.

Telling Their Stories

What was striking about the focus group discussions was the common set of obstacles the women have had to face in trying to achieve economic stability while preserving their dignity. Their stories varied regarding specific jobs, family composition, and original cultures. Regarding the latter, differences emerged both among racial and ethnic groups and within groups. For example, all the Chinese women faced the added burden of not having English as a native language. Some black women felt strongly connected to their families, but others felt it "would take a miracle" for their children to be there to help them. However, common themes did thread their way through the group interviews, and primary patterns of continuity and differentiation are presented in the descriptions that follow.

JOB SATISFACTION AND DISSATISFACTION

At the time of the focus group interviews (1990), some of the women held full-time jobs, some held part-time positions, and some were retired but had returned to do voluntary or paid part-time work. All the women reported a lifetime history of paid work that had been satisfying in many ways. There was uniform agreement that there was no question about working—you worked to support yourself and your family. There was also a shared sentiment that what made a job good was having good coworkers, a place to use your abilities, and an environment in which you were treated fairly. The Chinese women spoke with pride about their years in the garment industry, about the skill required, for example, to sew a collar onto a shirt or measure a pattern. A Hispanic hospital housekeeper reported her pride in keeping rooms clean for patients, while the black supervisor of a day-care center felt "good about my work" because she liked the children, the support she received from the teachers, and the positive feedback she got from her supervisor. Women who had been retired, even those who managed to have small pensions to count on, told of the importance of keeping busy and of still wanting to use their skills and help others.

Although some of the women, particularly those from the black community, found themselves raising their grandchildren and in one case even great-grandchildren, they still wanted independence and the chance to get out of the house. For these women, there were strong intergenerational ties. They reported how their parents and older relatives had helped them raise their children and how they were now doing it for their daughters (and granddaughters). But they were very worried that this pattern would not continue. One woman stated, "The microwave has caused the death of the family." She felt that families no longer ate together, went to church together, or spent time together; and although she took care of the young in her family, she was not so sure that when she needed them they would be there for her.

In contrast to many published interviews with middle-income and professional women, these women did not speak of "balancing" work and family roles. They assumed that they would have to work to make a living, many relying on family and neighborhood friends to help raise the children. When reporting their difficulties, they focused instead on the low pay, the hard physical demands of their jobs, and, in some cases, their experience with race or age discrimination.

The single most-reported dissatisfaction with jobs was the low pay. Even the women who worked in a unionized setting and were among the higher-paid service-sector workers had difficulty advancing into better jobs because of functional illiteracy, lack of access to retraining programs, and/or insufficient self-confidence and external support. For the women who were home healthcare workers or hospital workers, the union's fight for higher wages and better benefits was key to their union loyalty.

Difficulty with the hard physical demands of the job was also commonly reported by the women. Two of the Chinese women, for instance, had lost the jobs that they had held for many years in the garment industry during plant shutdowns. They were unemployed for a year before eventually finding work as a cafeteria worker and as a laundry worker. Both of these new positions required many hours of standing while doing manual labor. Here are brief descriptions of the jobs given by the women, ages 56 and 59, respectively:

> I stand eight hours a day serving food, not allowed to sit down except for one 10-minute break in the A.M., the other in P.M., and one half-hour lunch. There are no other Chinese, and the younger black and Hispanic workers in the kitchen do not speak to me.

> I work eight hours a day cleaning and folding sheets in a badly ventilated room. I am not allowed to sit on a stool while I fold, although I have said it would help me, and I could still do a good job. I get two 15-minute breaks a day, and no paid lunch time. There are 28 people where I work in the laundry, seven other Chinese women, the other black and Hispanic. I travel almost one hour to work each way on public transportation that sometimes doesn't work.

Both of these women missed being able to use their garment worker skills and were worried about how long they could continue in their present jobs, which they needed to support themselves. A number of the women who worked in a hospital reported the onset of various physical disabilities, including a recent heart attack and arm muscle tremors, which were jeopardizing their ability to perform the jobs they depended upon for economic survival.

Finally, there were a variety of ways in which focus group participants discussed their experiences of alienation and discrimination at work. The Chinese women acutely felt the multiple burdens of not knowing English well, of not being in communication with their co-workers, and of facing age discrimination by younger supervisors. One black woman who had retired but needed to find new work described how "seniors are hit upon for volunteer work," rather than being given paid employment possibilities. She said that the "younger generation does not understand what is going on, what the older generation needs." Another woman described how she had been fired from the job she had held for 29 years as director of a day-care center because the new younger white male supervisor felt she was no longer qualified. It took her 18 months to find new employment after facing race, sex, and age discrimination during her job search. A woman who currently supervises a day-care center in the black community stated that "older people in day care deserve more respect. We are expected to do the training of the younger people, but we are not compensated for it." There were other more subtle ways that many of the women felt discrimination. They said they were never thanked for doing a good job—whether neatly folding sheets or serving cafeteria food. They often felt invisible and that their skills and years of training went unrecognized. In spite of this, the women's attachment to their jobs and the pride in continuing to do a "good job" stood out clearly during the interviews and seems remarkable.

PATTERNS OF SUPPORT

The older women workers we interviewed responded to the question, "Where do you get support?" with a complex picture of institutional and individual networks. Within the work setting, women most often spoke of the support of coworkers, although for some, such as the isolated Chinese women, this did not exist. The person who acted as a supervisor or boss in some cases was a positive, supportive individual, but in many cases, especially when the supervisor was considerably younger, male, or of a different racial or ethnic background, discrimination rather than support prevailed. A sympathetic union leader or steward was credited by the women as really making a difference when having troubles at work.

The focus group women worked in different settings, from doing individual home-care services on a one-to-one basis to working for a large firm. In the smaller settings, feelings of support came from having a good relationship with a home healthcare client or with a day-care child. In the larger workplaces, there was less opportunity for intimate contact, and the women never reported feeling that an employer was on their side. Even in a public hospital where the city of Boston had agreed to provide literacy and training programs, the women did not experience a supportive institution. Because of the unstable nature of the city's economy, the literacy and training programs were continually being cut back or canceled. As the union president remarked, "I just about convince a worker to take the risk and enter a class, when it no longer is available." Her comment also reveals that many of the hospital workers feel hesitant, even ashamed, to admit they are not literate. Further, many have had prior negative experiences in school. To successfully enter education and training programs, these older women need special support and encouragement.

There was a range of experience concerning family support. Only a few of the older women had husbands, and those who did never mentioned them as an important part of their supportive networks. Instead, children, sisters, and other relatives were mentioned, with Chinese and Hispanic women likely to mention family, and black women more divided. Black women were the group most often mentioning the church as an institutional support, sometimes viewing it as the center for social and spiritual life. Some of the black women also spoke of the importance of the "movement" in their lives as a source of support—the strength they felt from being a part of the civil rights and social justice struggle. They remembered days when the black community was united and they did not have to lock their doors. They worried about the loss of this type of community and the lack of a sense of "freedom movement" among the younger generations. One woman, who was supporting her 19-year-old nephew, spoke of being afraid to let him out of the house with the rising drug abuse and street violence.

Women also mentioned support from other women. There were stories of women's groups that had been meeting for years, of a collective housing situation that allowed women to live decently despite marginal incomes, and the importance of just getting together with other women because "when we get together, we hear one chord."

Although the women reported sources of support that clearly played a significant role in their lives and "kept them going at work," many felt that they were quite alone in managing to get by. There were statements like "I take care of myself, I have always taken care of myself"; "I stand on my own two feet"; and "All our lives we have had pride, we go without, we put one foot in front of the other with never quite enough to get by." An important ingredient of living day by day was the ethic of caring—almost all the women spoke of caring about doing a good job, of not letting others down, and of wanting to help others less fortunate than themselves. They sustained themselves by seeing themselves as part of a larger whole, connected in some way to others.

Focusing on the Future

The women who participated in our focus groups are not a representative sample of older women workers today, and they cannot be said to mirror a future group of older women who will have lived their youth in different circumstances. Nevertheless, there are interesting parallels between the characteristics of the women in the focus groups and the projected characteristics of tomorrow's older women workers. First, as women of diverse ethnic and racial backgrounds, they reflect the increasing diversity in the labor force of the future. Second, most are household heads—a growing trend among older women. Third, all are workers in service occupations, an expanding sector where the majority of young women still work and where a majority of older women workers are likely to remain for some time. Fourth, several are healthcare workers—one of the fastest growing occupational categories in our aging society.

Interestingly, all of the women reported a lifetime history of paid work, a characteristic likely to be more typical of older women in the future than it is today. Most of the women were managing the competing demands of caring for family members and paid employment, a situation likely to remain common for older women in coming decades. The women we interviewed spent their youth in a world very different from the one in which young women work today. Still, many of the same problems they face as workers are likely to continue to confront future generations of older women workers unless policies and practices are changed.

HOPES AND FEARS FOR THE FUTURE: FRAMING A POLICY AGENDA

When the women we interviewed were asked about their hopes and fears for the future regarding work, a number of common themes arose, many with implications for public policy. The final section of this chapter highlights these themes, speculates about their continuing relevance for older women workers in the future, and considers some broad policy approaches to these issues.

Healthcare

The largest and most widespread fear of the focus group participants concerned their health. Without universal healthcare coverage, the women feared what would happen if they became ill, disabled, and unable to care for themselves. Some women felt they could count on family members for support, but many did not. The specter of becoming dependent or left alone in illness was clearly frightening. A number of women were already taking care of ill relatives and friends. We know that population aging will increase the incidence of disability in our society, and that the overwhelming majority of unpaid care for the elderly disabled is provided by women. If more and more women are themselves elderly and in need of care, and if fewer able-bodied women have the "leisure" time in which to provide unpaid care, the fears of the women we interviewed appear quite realistic.

Because of the labor segregation of women and the lack of benefits for most part-time work, many women workers are ineligible for healthcare coverage. Further, women's work lives are sometimes broken up by periods of unpaid caregiving labor, so women are especially vulnerable in any system where healthcare coverage is linked to employment status. With more frequent health problems than younger male workers, older women are greatly disadvantaged by health plans that penalize "preexisting conditions." The reform of the nation's healthcare system is an extensive policy area outside the focus of this chapter. Clearly, however, whatever system of healthcare provision is ultimately adopted must take account of the situation of older women workers in order to ensure that they have full access to the adequate healthcare that is their right.

Job Training

A number of women in the focus groups said they wished they could enter retraining programs to develop old skills or start new ones. The idea of lifelong learning was attractive to them. Other women spoke of vocational changes: a woman who had been a clerk in a bank spoke of wanting to be trained to work with teenage mothers; another woman who had worked in the civil service wanted to care for babies who had AIDS: a Hispanic woman, reflecting the reality of those not born in the United States, felt her biggest challenge would be to enter a work education program to improve her literacy skills. As a group, older women workers in the future will have higher levels of education than they do today. Still, many of them—especially minority women and immigrants—will continue to need basic literacy and skills training.

Older women of the future will be better equipped to move into jobs requiring computer skills, as training in computer-based technologies becomes a component of the standard educational curriculum. However, technologies develop and change rapidly, and unless employers develop strategies for in-house training, retraining, and skill-updating of their employees, the skills of older workers will continue to obsolesce.

Unfortunately, there is a pervasive view that older workers, particularly older women, are resistant to learning new skills required by technological transformations. The "you can't teach an old dog new tricks" mentality is too often adopted by employers. However, older workers are eager to update their skills. In a survey conducted by the American Association of Retired Persons (1986), four out of five employees expressed a wish for training opportunities. Older women's access to knowledge that allows them to control and implement emerging technologies will continue to be a critical factor in their work-force status.

Some may argue that it is only rational to use the limited resources that are available to train younger workers, because they will be employed longer than their elder counterparts. However, there is evidence that turnover and absenteeism among older workers are much lower (Birren, Robinson, and Livingston 1986; McClelland 1973). Further, workers aged 45 to 55 still have 10 to 20 years of service ahead. The argument that money for training is always better spent on younger workers reflects a lack of understanding of the need to utilize the full productive potential of older workers in an aging work force. Older women who do participate in training programs face additional barriers: they generally receive fewer permanent job placements than their male counterparts, and the job placements they do receive are in traditional female, minimum-wage occupations, such as health, clerical, and service jobs (Older Women's League 1990b).

Public- and private-sector employers, as well as policymakers, must realize that job-training opportunities must be extended to older women in the future, to maintain work-force skill levels. Women will constitute an increasing proportion of the older work force. Constant changes in workplace technologies escalate the demand for training programs, and in the future employers will be unable to rely upon a cushion of young employees already trained in new technological skills. Questions concerning who will bear the cost of basic education training, training in new skills, and skill-updating for older workers must be addressed.

Employment Options

Several of the women in our focus groups worked part-time, and others expressed the hope that they would be able to in the future. For many older women, it was not a question of wanting to have more leisure time but of being unable to work a full 35-hour week because of family care duties or their own health problems.

Part-time work has been increasing recently, but almost entirely because of increases in involuntary part-time workers (Callaghan and Hartmann 1991). The BLS defines an involuntary part-time worker as someone who works fewer than 35 hours a week because she or he cannot find a full-time job (Callaghan and Hartmann 1991). All other part-time work for any reason is classified as voluntary. However, even when women are said to "choose" part-time employment, it may be because there are no alternatives.[3]

With the aging of the work force, we may see future increases in so-called voluntary part-time employment. In 1990, 37 percent of male and female workers aged 55 and over worked part-time, and of these fully 85 percent did so "voluntarily." In contrast, 66 percent of the 26 percent of all women workers who worked part-time were classified as voluntary. Among black women of prime working age (ages 20–54), the percentages were even lower: 18 percent worked part-time and only 60 percent of those did so voluntarily.

Employers are increasingly turning to part-time workers to fill job vacancies. Over 44 percent of employers now use part-time help, and three out of four began the practice within the last eight years (Older Women's League 1990a). The growth of part-time employment has paralleled the growth of service and retail trade industries. Part-time workers' hourly wages are low even if measured against equivalent full-time work, and the costs of fringe benefits for the part-time worker, including health coverage and pensions, are usually shifted from the employer to the employee.

Women of all ages are more likely to work part-time than men— they constitute two-thirds of all part-time workers. Currently, over a quarter (26 percent) of all women workers work on a part-time basis

(Callaghan and Hartmann 1991), and the majority (60 percent) of women workers over the age of 65 work part-time (American Association of Retired Persons 1988).

It is possible to imagine a future scenario in which employers take advantage of the pressures of family care and personal health felt by older women workers to marginalize a growing proportion of the work force in poorly compensated jobs. On the other hand, the aging of large numbers of women workers who have had longer and more continuous work-force careers could increase pressure to improve the status of part-time work, to ensure that part-time workers receive the same hourly wages and fringe benefits as full-time workers in comparable jobs and that they are eligible for unemployment insurance.

Hilda Kahne (1985) has argued for "new concept" part-time employment, where wages for part-time workers are prorated, benefits offered, channels for job mobility opened, and training provided. The benefits to older women workers of such a configuration are obvious. In the future, expanding attractive part-time work and scheduling options may also benefit employers facing a shrinking pool of young workers. Employers will have to seek ways to retain older, skilled workers, many of whom now opt to retire early, and to maximize the productivity of the growing number of women workers, many of whom must combine paid work with unpaid family care. Other innovative work options that could help maintain high productivity in an older, feminized work force are documented in various sources (Buchmann 1983; Jessup and Greenberg 1989; Kahne 1985; Moore 1982). These options include: job sharing, phased retirement, and various forms of flexible scheduling (i.e., flextime, variable day and week, and a compressed work week). Employers who seek creative ways to redesign jobs today should have an edge in tomorrow's economy.

Pay Equity

The focus group women were united in their concern for their future economic security. For these women, a lifetime of employment in low-paying work did not allow them to build up a cushion of savings or a pension income. Women of all ages continue to be clustered in female-dominated occupations where earnings are low. As a consequence, many younger women workers today face a future of inadequate income as they age.

Given that the occupational patterns of women's work are not changing dramatically, pay equity, or comparable-worth, initiatives should be undertaken to raise the economic position and future prospects of women in the labor force. Available research shows that the costs of implementing pay equity have been overestimated and the benefits underestimated (Hill and Killingsworth 1989; Kelly and Bayes 1988). The costs of implementing comparable worth, although high on a national level, are manageable to certain employers; implementation has been successful in Minnesota, in San Jose, California and in the state of Washington.[4] In a recent review of the literature, Ronald Ehrenburg concluded that comparable-worth wage setting reduces the gender wage gap from 25 percent to 10 percent, and that disemployment effects are minimal (Ehrenburg 1989).

It is difficult to estimate the amount that poverty among tomorrow's elderly women would be reduced if pay equity policies were implemented to increase wages during their working years. The implementation of pay equity is very new and its long-term benefits still to be realized. Nevertheless, given the burgeoning older female population, the potential savings from pay equity implementation in terms of lower poverty rates among older women, and thus lower public assistance costs, could be significant.

Retirement

Most of the focus group women spoke of working until they died. The idea of a leisurely retirement was not in their vision of the future, although projected patterns of work varied and included images of part-time work and volunteer efforts as well as full-time employment. Obsolete and unfair Social Security practices and inadequate pension coverage and personal savings contribute to the lack of retirement security for older women workers today.

As mentioned earlier, younger women's work patterns have changed significantly in recent decades, which will lead to some differences in their likely retirement scenarios. Women's pension coverage rates are rising. However, although more women have some pension income in the future, it will continue to be far less than that received by men for a long time to come. Women's continued lower earnings are a factor, as is their tendency to change jobs more often than men. Unless some changes are made in retirement policy, today's younger working women will still be likely to end up with inadequate retirement incomes.

Social Security Inequities

Social Security is projected to remain by far the largest component of single older women's income, declining only three points—from 71 percent in 1990 to 68 percent in 2030—according to the Urban Institute DYNASIM models (Zedlewski et al. 1990). Social Security benefits are wage-based, so women's continued lower earnings translate into low benefits at retirement. In 1990, retired women workers received only 76 percent ($519) of men's monthly benefits (Smith 1992).

Lower earnings are not the only reason why women's Social Security income is so low. Social Security benefits are calculated by averaging a worker's annual earnings over a period of 35 years. Workers who have less than 35 years of covered earnings have a zero averaged into their record for each missing year, lowering their benefit base. In this way, earnings losses for women who take time out of the work force to engage in family care are actually compounded by further reductions in their Social Security income.

Women are increasing their years of covered employment, but they continue to spend time out of the work force for family care. The DYNASIM projections show that in the year 2010, only 12 percent of women aged 62 and over would have been in the work force for 35 years or more, and only 22 percent of the youngest retired women, aged 62–69, would meet that standard. Even by 2030, only about 1 in 3 women aged 62–69 would have 35 years or more of work experience (Fierst and Campbell 1988).

Women's Work and Marriage Patterns and Benefit Calculations A person aged 65 or older who is married to a retired worker is eligible for a dependent benefit of 50 percent of the retired spouse's worker benefit. The dependent benefit was conceived to provide an adequate income for older couples composed of one retired full-time wage earner and one full-time homemaker. Protection for widows has been increasing over the years; they are now eligible to receive 100 percent of the working spouse's retirement benefit.

The problem is that the life patterns on which this system is based are becoming less and less common among older Americans. Women, in particular, are losing out as a result of the poor fit between retirement policy and reality. Fewer and fewer women reaching retirement age have spent their entire adult lives providing unpaid family care while being supported by an income-earning husband. Yet, for many women the "zero years" averaged into their benefits base mean that their own worker benefits would actually be lower than the dependent benefits they would receive on their husband's work record. Such women are classified as "dually entitled" by the Social Security Administration. However, they can not collect both of their benefits. Instead, a woman can receive only the amount of one or the other, whichever is higher. The usual result is that a dually entitled woman receives only the equivalent of her dependent spouse benefit despite years in the paid labor force; her own contributions to the Social Security fund count for nothing. The numbers of women who are dually entitled are projected to increase in the future (Fierst and Campbell 1988).

Besides being more likely to have spent substantial time in the paid labor force, more older women in the future are expected to be divorced—14 percent of women aged 65 and over in the year 2020, compared with only 5 percent in 1990, according to the projections given by Taeuber and Allen in chapter 2 of this volume. Divorced women who were married for fewer than 10 years are not eligible for any spouse benefit. A woman who had a longer marriage faces the same options as married women—if her own worker benefit is less than 50 percent of her ex-husband's benefit, she is dually entitled and will receive the dependent-benefit amount, receiving no return on her own years of Social Security contributions. However, she faces the additional problem of how to get along on the small spouse benefit (50 percent of the worker benefit) by herself, whereas a still-married couple has a shared income three times as great (150 percent of the worker benefit).

Combining Social Security with Paid Employment   Many elderly women, particularly if they live alone, must engage in paid labor in order to get by. The most important predictors of employment past retirement age for women are being single and not receiving any other pension in addition to Social Security. In the future, more women will receive some small pension income. The demographics chapter projects that the proportion of single elderly women will remain fairly stable in the coming decades, but that there will be fewer widows and more divorcées among them. This could tend to reduce the Social Security benefits received by single women, since widows receive 100 percent of their spouse's worker benefit but divorcées get only 50 percent for as long as their ex-husband is alive.

Social Security policies set a very low limit on the amount that can be earned before benefits are reduced. In 1991, those younger than age 65 could earn up to $7,080, and those between the ages of 65 and 69, $9,720. Beyond these limits, Social Security benefits are reduced $1 for every $2 earned for those under age 65 and $1 for every $3 earned for those aged 65 to 69. These universal limits ignore the fact that the average woman receives 25 percent less in her Social Security check than does the average man and that she is less likely to have personal savings or significant pension income. The result of such a low ceiling for earnings is that many women are forced to work part-time in low-paying positions or to be paid "under the table" (Rones and Herz 1989).

POLICY CHANGES FOR RETIREMENT EQUITY

Changes must be made so that the Social Security system does not continue to amplify the inequities older women face. To accomplish this, a commission should be appointed to construct a policy reform package that will more fairly and accurately reflect the life patterns and retirement needs of its beneficiaries, the majority of whom are women. Here are some promising policy approaches to consider:

☐ *Dependent Care Credits:* Provide benefit credits for each year a worker (woman or man) spends caring for a young child or disabled relative without income covered by Social Security that exceeds some base amount (Glasse 1992).

☐ *Dropout Years for Caregiving:* Exclude from the benefits formula some of the years a worker spends out of the work force while providing family care. This would eliminate or reduce the "zero years" that are averaged into many women's benefit base today (King 1992). A targeted, low-cost version of this approach would provide dropout years for caregiving only to those workers who qualify for the special minimum benefit—workers who have had long-term employment at low earnings (Smith 1992).

☐ *Earnings Sharing:* Do away entirely with the worker/dependent benefit structure and instead have married couples pool their earned worker Social Security credits and split them equally at retirement, death, divorce, or disability. This would be a profound structural change with widespread consequences. Various modifications of the basic plan have been devised, but essentially all versions would tend to benefit dual-earner couples and divorced women. Single-earner couples, many divorced men, and some widows would receive reduced benefits. The earnings sharing approach certainly better reflects the current realities of most families' lives today. However, the fact that implementing earnings sharing would either cut some Americans' benefits or generate large additional costs makes it politically unviable at this time. Nevertheless, as growing numbers of retired women workers recognize that they are paying into the system for years and getting no additional benefits in return, the political balance may shift toward some version of the earnings sharing plan.

☐ *Benefit Equity for Widows:* A much smaller reform based on an earnings-sharing approach would be to change the amount of all survivor benefits to two-thirds of the couple's previous benefit. This is the amount a widow currently receives if she was previously collecting a dependent benefit—because she and her husband received 150 percent of his worker benefit, and as a widow she would get 100 percent. However, if a couple had been receiving benefits on both of their work records, the survivor receives only his or her own benefit, which may be as little as 50 percent of the couple's previous income.

☐ *Optional Increased Widow's Benefit:* Another approach to providing better income for long-lived widows would be to allow retired workers to voluntarily accept lower retirement benefits in order to provide a higher benefit for their survivors. Many private pensions now offer this option.

☐ *Earnings Limit Adjustment:* Studies have shown that eliminating the limit on work earnings for Social Security beneficiaries would primarily benefit affluent older Americans (Families USA 1990). A relatively small proportion of people with low incomes have work earnings above the limit. Still, raising the earnings ceiling from its current very low levels to, say, $12,000 or $15,000 would allow those elderly people who must earn income to keep their hard-earned modest salaries and Social Security benefits. If it is true that few people would be affected, then the cost of this adjustment would be minimal. Alternatively, the earnings test could be waived for Social Security recipients who have little or no previous work record, often because of family care responsibilities, and who are working late in life to build up some small savings.

OTHER RETIREMENT POLICIES

So long as women's earnings and pension income are lower than those of men, Social Security policy cannot equalize women's and men's retirement income. To bring about greater income equality, the private pension system will need restructuring so that employer-contributing, portable pensions are standard. Employers will need to offer a flexible pension plan package, with a selection of widely accepted plans to choose from, so that a woman's future economic security is not threatened if she moves from one job to another.

Finally, women need to be educated about their retirement benefits and the consequences of the options available to them. For too long, women have been shocked to find themselves living in poverty at the end of a lifetime of hard work. It is our responsibility to change this pattern for future generations.

The Role of Unions

For the women we interviewed, unions, where they existed, were viewed as an institutional part of women's support network. For the future, questions exist about the extent of unionization among women workers and the ability and willingness of unions to focus on women workers' needs. A recent report on the union movement in the United States has stated that union membership is still declining, with only about 17 percent of the labor force now unionized (U.S. Department of Labor 1990). According to the Bureau of Labor Statistics (U.S. Department of Labor 1989), about 13 percent of all women workers are currently unionized, but the percentage climbs for older women, with 17 percent of women workers aged 45–54 unionized and 16 percent of those aged 55–64 union members. This indicates that the percentage of women under age 45 who are union members is very low.

Historically, the labor movement has not been attuned to the specific needs of women workers. Family–work issues have not been the bread and butter issues of unions, which have often preferred to stick to traditional wage structure and seniority issues at the bargaining table. However, recent victories by the Harvard University Union of Technical and Clerical Workers and other service-sector unions have demonstrated the importance of organizing around issues of significance to women workers in general and older women workers specifically. During the Harvard Union organizing drive, child care and job security for older women workers were among the concerns that successfully engaged the attention and support of the workers. Given the new labor force demographics, unions should be increasingly taking up the challenge of meeting the needs of older women workers.

THE FUTURE FOR OLDER WOMEN WORKERS

The trends in earnings, occupational distribution, and work-force and retirement status of older women in the United States, as well as the accounts of the women we interviewed, reveal major problems—low pay, lack of access to retraining programs, difficulty advancing into better jobs, and age and sex discrimination. The stories recounted to us by women workers were diverse but connected by common problems and coping strategies. Together, they form a "quilt" of these women's working lives, a cloth of resiliency in the midst of inequality. In each focus group, there was a strong shared sense of pride in doing good work and in acting in a caring way. One wonders if future generations of older women workers will bring the same commitment and values into their aging years.

Older women workers in the future will certainly have different characteristics than older women workers of today, and they will face different social and economic circumstances that we cannot entirely foresee. As a group, they will have higher educational levels and longer careers than today's older women workers. They may also be less tolerant of the unfair caregiving burden our society continues to place on women's shoulders, an anachronistic retirement system, and the second-class status accorded all women's work. One thing is certain: unless we create better work opportunities for the growing numbers of older women, we will be creating a large group of economic bystanders at a time when our aging nation should be building economic strength on a foundation of mature, productive workers.

Older women workers, who constitute a growing share of the American labor force, struggle daily to maintain their dignity. Although their struggle is a personal one, the forces that shape it reflect our larger social, political, and economic institutions and values. Population aging in the United States should increase our recognition and respect for that struggle and its growing impact on the economy. Increasingly, the welfare of the whole nation will be linked with the welfare of older women workers.

Notes

1. Kathleen Allen, a commissioner of the Massachusetts Commission Against Discrimination (MCAD), has reported that, according to MCAD statistics, women in the workplace face age discrimination earlier than men. She cited records kept by the Equal Employment Opportunities Commission (EEOC) that portray a similar picture (Presentations to Older Worker Task, Mass. Job Council, Sept. 1988–June 1989).

2. For more information regarding the focus groups and questionnaire, contact Paula Rayman at the Center for Research on Women, Wellesley College, Wellesley, MA 02181.

3. This is the case for many mothers who work part-time because they cannot find affordable child care. A national study of mothers who had a child under the age of five found that 1 in 4 was prevented from working more than part-time because of a lack

of suitable, affordable day care (Presser and Baldwin 1980). It is estimated that there is only 1 day-care slot open for every 10 children who need placement (Appelbaum 1987).

4. For instance, the Minnesota legislature approved pay equity adjustments in 1982 for 9,000 of 29,000 state employees. Since that time, the state's payroll has risen by only 3 percent and the state budget by under 2 percent (see also Kelly and Bayes 1988 and Rix 1990).

References

American Association of Retired Persons. 1986. *Work and Retirement: Employees over 40 and Their Views.* Washington, D.C.: Author.

_____. 1988. *America's Changing Work Force.* Washington, D.C.: Author.

Appelbaum, Eileen. 1987. "Restructuring Work: Temporary, Part-time, and At-home Employment." In *Computer Chips and Paper Clips: Technology and Women's Employment*, edited by Heidi I. Hartmann (268–310). Washington, D.C.: National Academy Press.

Birren, James E., Pauline K. Robinson, and Judy E. Livingston, eds. 1986. *Age, Health, and Employment.* Englewood Cliffs, N.J.: Prentice-Hall.

Blau, Francine D. 1978. "The Impact of the Unemployment Rate on Labor Force Entries and Exits." In *Women's Changing Roles at Home and on the Job* (263–86). Special Report 26, U.S. Department of Labor, Employment and Training Administration. Washington, D.C.: U.S. Government Printing Office.

Buchmann, Anna Marie. 1983. "Maximizing Post-Retirement Labor Market Opportunities." In *Policy Issues in Work and Retirement*, edited by Herbert S. Parnes (109–29). Kalamazoo, Mich.: W. E. Upjohn Institute for Employment Research.

Cain, Glen G., and Martin D. Dooley. 1976. "Estimation of a Model of Labor Supply, Fertility, and Wages of Married Women." *Journal of Political Economy* 84 (Aug.): S176–S200.

Callaghan, Polly, and Heidi Hartmann. 1991. *Contingent Work: A Chart Book on Part-Time and Temporary Employment.* Washington, D.C.: Economic Policy Institute.

Ehrenburg, Ronald G. 1989. "Empirical Consequences of Comparable Worth." In *Comparable Worth: Analyses and Evidence*, edited by Anne M. Hill and Mark R. Killingsworth (90–106). Ithaca, N.Y.: ILR Press.

Families USA. 1990. "The Social Security Retirement Test: Should It Be Changed?" Washington, D.C.: Author.

Fierst, Edith U., and Nancy Duff Campbell, eds. 1988. *Earnings Sharing in Social Security: A Model for Reform.* Washington, D.C.: Center for Women Policy Studies.

Figart, Deborah M. 1988. *Economic Status of Women in the Labor Market and Prospects for Pay Equity over the Life Cycle.* Washington, D.C.: American Association of Retired Persons.

Fullerton, Jr., Howard N. 1992. "Labor Force Projections: The Baby Boom Moves On." In *Outlook: 1990–2005. BLS Bulletin* 2402. Washington, D.C.: U.S. Government Printing Office, May.

Gitter, Robert J., Lois B. Shaw, and Mary G. Gagen. 1986. "Early Labor Market Withdrawal." In *Midlife Women at Work: A Fifteen-Year Perspective,* edited by Louis B. Shaw (87–98). Lexington, Mass.: Lexington Books.

Glasse, Lou. 1992. "Women and Social Security: Families Are Changing, the Workplace Is Changing. Should Social Security Change Too?" Testimony, before House Subcommittee on Social Security, Committee on Ways and Means, Apr. 8. Washington, D.C.: Older Women's League.

Herz, Diane E., and Philip L. Rones. 1989. "Institutional Barriers to Employment of Older Workers." *Monthly Labor Review* (Aug.): 14–21.

Hill, Anne M., and Mark R. Killingsworth, eds. 1989. *Comparable Worth: Analyses and Evidence.* Ithaca, N.Y.: ILR Press.

Jacobsen, Joyce P., and Laurence M. Levin. 1992. "The Effects of Intermittent Labor Force Attachment on Female Earnings." Paper presented at the American Economic Association Conference, New Orleans, Jan. 3–5.

Jessup, Denise, and Barbara Greenberg, 1989. "Innovative Older-Worker Programs." *Generations* (Summer): 23–27.

Kahne, Hilda. 1985. *Reconceiving Part-Time Work: New Perspectives for Older Women Workers.* Totowa, N.J.: Rowman and Allanheld.

Kelly, Rita Mae, and Jane Bayes. 1988. *Comparable Worth, Pay Equity, and Public Policy.* New York: Greenwood Press.

Kessler-Harris, Alice, 1982. *Out to Work.* New York: Oxford University Press.

King, Gwendolyn S. 1992. "Statement by Commissioner of Social Security." Testimony before House Subcommittee on Social Security, Committee on Ways and Means, Apr. 8. Washington, D.C.: Social Security Administration.

Kollwitz, Hans, ed. 1988. *The Diary and Letters of Kaethe Kollwitz.* Evanston, Ill.: Northwestern University Press.

Kutscher, Ronald E. 1992. "New BLS Projections: Findings and Implications." In *Outlook: 1990–2005. BLS Bulletin* 2402, Washington, D.C.: U.S. Government Printing Office, May.

Louis Harris and Associates. 1989. *Older Americans: Ready and Able to Work.* New York: Author.

Malveaux, Julianne. 1985. "The Economic Interests of Black and White Women: Are They Similar?" *Review of Black Political Economy* (Summer): 5–27.

_____. 1987. "Comparable Worth and Its Impact on Black Women." In *Slipping through the Cracks: The Status of Black Women,* edited by

Margaret C. Simms and Julianne Malveaux (47–62). New Brunswick: Transaction Books.

Malveaux, Julianne, and Phyllis Wallace. 1987. "Minority Women in the Workplace." In *Working Women: Past, Present, Future*, edited by Karen S. Koziara, Michael H. Moskow, and Lucretia D. Tanner (265–98). Washington, D.C.: Bureau of National Affairs.

Marini, Margaret Mooney. 1989. "Sex Differences in Earnings in the United States." *Annual Review of Sociology* 15: 343–80.

McConnell, Stephen R. 1983. "Age Discrimination in Employment." In *Policy Issues in Work and Retirement*, edited by Herbert S. Parnes (159–96). Kalamazoo, Mich.: W.E. Upjohn Institute for Employment Research.

McClelland, Diana. 1973. "Opening Job Doors for Mature Women." *Manpower* (August): 8–12.

Meier, Elizabeth L., and Elizabeth A. Kerr. 1976. "Capabilities of Middle-Aged and Older Workers: A Survey of the Literature." *Industrial Gerontology* (Summer): 147–56.

Moore, Shelley L., ed. 1982. *32 Million Older Americans*. New York: National Urban League.

National Committee on Pay Equity. 1989. "Briefing Paper #1: The Wage Gap." Washington, D.C.: National Committee on Pay Equity.

Older Women's League. 1990a. *Heading for Hardship: Retirement Income for American Women in the Next Century*. Washington, D.C.: Author.

————. 1990b. *Making Ends Meet: Midlife and Older Women's Search for Economic Self-Sufficiency through Job Training and Employment*. Washington, D.C.: Author.

Presser, Harriet B., and Wendy Baldwin. 1980. "Child Care as a Constraint on Employment: Prevalence, Correlates, and Bearing on the Work and Fertility Nexus." *American Journal of Sociology* 85(7): 1202–13.

Rayman, Paula. 1987. "Women and Unemployment." *Social Research* 54(2): 355–76.

Rayman, Paula, C. Forrest, and K. Kabria. 1988. *Unemployment, Women, and Mental Health*. Stone Center, Wellesley College, Wellesley, Mass.: Photocopy.

Reskin, Barbara F., and Heidi I. Hartmann, eds. 1986. *Women's Work, Men's Work: Sex Segregation on the Job*. Washington, D.C.: National Academy Press.

Rix, Sara E., ed. 1990. *The American Woman, 1990–91: A Status Report*. New York: W.W. Norton & Co.

Rones, Philip L., and Diane E. Herz. 1989. *Labor Market Problems of Older Workers*. Washington, D.C.: U.S. Department of Labor.

Rosen, Benson, and Thomas H. Jerdee. 1985. *Older Employees: New Roles for Valued Resources*. Homewood, Ill.: Dow Jones-Irwin.

Rubin, Lillian B. 1979. *Women of a Certain Age: The Midlife Search for Self*. New York: Harper & Row.

Schuster, Michael, and Christopher S. Miller. 1984. "An Empirical Assessment of the Age Discrimination in Employment Act." *Industrial and Labor Relations Review* 38: 64–74.

Shaw, Lois B. 1983. *Unplanned Careers: The Working Lives of Middle-Aged Women.* Lexington, Mass.: Lexington Books.

Shaw, Lois B., and Rachel Shaw. 1987. "From Midlife to Retirement: The Middle-Aged Woman Worker." In *Working Women: Past, Present, Future,* edited by Karen S. Koziara, Michael H. Moskow, and Lucretia D. Tanner (299–331). Washington, D.C.: Bureau of National Affairs.

Silvestri, George, and John Lukasiewicz. 1992. "Occupational Employment Projections." In *Outlook: 1990–2005. BLS Bulletin* 2402. Washington, D.C.: U.S. Government Printing Office, May.

Smith, Marie. 1992. *Statement of the American Association of Retired Persons on Women and Social Security before the Subcommittee on Social Security, Committee on Ways and Means, U.S. House of Representatives, Apr. 8.* Washington, D.C.: American Association of Retired Persons.

Sorensen, Elaine. 1991. *Exploring the Reasons behind the Narrowing Gender Gap in Earnings.* Washington, D.C.: Urban Institute Press.

U.S. Bureau of the Census. 1988. *Educational Attainment in the United States: March 1987 and 1986. Current Population Reports,* ser. P-20, no. 428. Washington, D.C.: U.S. Government Printing Office.

_____. 1991. *Money Income and Poverty Status in the United States: 1990 (Advance Data from the March 1990 Current Population Survey). Current Population Reports,* ser. P-60, no. 174. Washington, D.C.: U.S. Government Printing Office.

U.S. Department of Labor, Bureau of Labor Statistics. 1982. *The Female/Male Earnings Gap: A Review of Employment and Earnings Issues.* Report No. 673. September. Washington, D.C.: Author.

_____. 1990. *Unpublished Tabulations from the Current Population Survey: 1989 Annual Averages.* Washington, D.C.: Author.

_____. 1992. *Employment and Earnings, 1991.* Washington, D.C.: Author, January.

U.S. Social Security Administration. 1985. *Social Security Bulletin* 48(2, Feb.): 24.

Zedlewski, Sheila R., Roberta O. Barnes, Martha R. Burt, Timothy D. McBride, and Jack A Meyer. 1990. *The Needs of the Elderly in the 21st Century.* Washington, D.C.: Urban Institute Press.

Chapter Seven

RACE, POVERTY, AND WOMEN'S AGING

Julianne Malveaux

The woman is almost sixty and it shows. She wears the starched white uniform of a nurse or home health aide, and carries herself with the stiff dignity of someone used to working hard for a living. Her cracked knuckles and rough skin suggest that she is not afraid of using elbow grease or of getting down on her knees and scrubbing floors to survive. Her cushioned white shoes suggest that many of her years have been spent standing on her feet. Today, she accompanies a wheelchair-bound woman down a city street, a woman not 15 years older than herself. Women like this pair are often separated by race. They are tenuously connected by their age (one is "old-old," the other "young-old"), bound by their gender, separated by their economic status, connected by their predicament of being old and alone, and separated by the way they survive this predicament.

It takes little to establish that the woman navigating the wheelchair has always worked in low-wage jobs like this one, as a home health worker, cleaning service worker, private household worker, or nurse's aide, earning an hourly wage that puts her at the bottom of the pay distribution. At the same time, it is obvious that her charge is protected by her economic past. Perhaps her spouse died recently, leaving her a pension. Perhaps she was a single career woman who put 40 years into the labor market and left having built up a pension history for herself. Even though she is being cared for, though, her position is far from secure. If the insurance company that invested her pension funds chose junk bonds, her ability to afford the help she gets may be jeopardized. If her certificates of deposit exceed $100,000 and they are held by a bank that faltered, her income is also at risk. For that matter, if her disability persists or worsens so that she requires full-time care, even a generous pension income will not be adequate. She will then be forced to "spend down" her savings to qualify for public assistance with which to pay nursing home fees.

In what year are we observing these women? It could be 1950, when more than half of all black women worked as private household workers, when the typical black woman could be found in some caretaking role. It could also be 1990, when, despite changed occupational status, black and brown women were far more likely to be home health aides and other service workers. Will racial differences in economic status persist until 2030? Will the woman in the wheelchair still be white, her caregiver a woman of color? Will both continue to face an uncertain economic future? The answers depend on policy decisions we make today.

We avert our eyes from the women on the sidewalk because we hope that their fate is one we will be spared—working into old age with no pension to come, or being in faltering health, dependent on a stranger, worrying that the money will run out and poverty will follow. Although most older women have not met this fate—more than two-thirds have incomes of at least 150 percent of poverty level—the possibility of poverty is ever-present for many women who have not contemplated it before.

The economic status of older women is a map or mirror of their past lives, reflecting their education, employment history, and marital status. The economic problems that older women face are extensions of the problems and choices they faced earlier in their lives. Those who were underemployed as adults have this status reflected by continued underemployment and low retirement incomes in their older years. Those who spent years out of the work force providing family care may be devastated by the loss of pension income when a spouse dies. Half of all women aged 65 and over who live alone have incomes below 150 percent of the poverty line ($6,268 a year for an elderly person living alone in 1990), compared with 39 percent of similarly situated men. Of these poor and near-poor older women, more than one in four (27 percent) are African-American or Latina.

Because economic status reflects past experiences, it is difficult to address elder poverty through social policy targeted strictly to the elderly. Poverty is reflective of low pay and occupational segregation during women's working lives, as well as the key assumption society makes about the focus of women's lives—that they will bear responsibility for caregiving in families, whether they are mothers, daughters, sisters, nieces, or wives, without social support for child care or eldercare.

Is this situation likely to change in the future? Today's young and middle-aged women have an advantage that older women do not. They have higher education levels and time before old age to improve their economic histories and, thus, the likelihood that their later years will offer more economic options. Some will not have children, and so will take less time from the paid labor force for caregiving. Others will work at firms whose parental leave policies will not force them to choose between work and family. Does this differ for women of color? In general, the labor market profile of women of color has changed along with that of white women. As is the case with white women, an increasing number of African-American women and Latinas are likely to have continuous work histories. But because many minority women still lack opportunities for higher education and fewer will work in high-paying professions and management (Sokoloff 1992), fewer women of color than white women will escape poverty.

If changes in workplace demographics are not accompanied by changes in labor market and family policy, younger women's greater work-force attachment may not be enough to protect them from the plight of today's older women. In some cases, structural changes in the labor market may put some women of color at increasing risk of poverty. In particular, the economic status of African-American men, and their lower rates of labor-force participation (than those of white men) suggest differences in family economics between this group and others.

Even the best prepared older women, regardless of race, are often unable to protect themselves from poverty. The high cost of nursing homes, or of continuous home health care, and the requirement of depleting assets before public (Medicaid) assistance is available for long-term care, mean that women whose spouses have had lengthy illnesses face widowhood with few financial resources. Other widows may not inherit their spouse's pensions. Still others have annuities jeopardized by the uncertain financial status (if not outright failure) of some life insurance companies. Despite the best intentions and preparations, for many older women poverty is an accident waiting to happen, a function of the death or disability of a spouse or adult child, or of life's other uncertainties.

Furthermore, the current fiscal and regulatory climate provides older people with less, not more, government protection, and as governments grapple with issues of limited resources, this is likely to get worse. Because the elderly are not the only ones facing economic uncertainty, legislators have begun to question how much health and social insurance should be provided exclusively for older people. But social spending has clearly made a difference in the economic status of this group. Eighty-six percent of those seniors who would be poor without federal programs are lifted out of poverty by government tax and transfer programs (Taylor 1991).

In 1990, there were some 2.7 million women aged 65 and over who lived in poverty. Some of them accompanied wheelchairs; others rode in them because government subsidies provided them with home health care. A disproportionate number of them were women of color. This chapter discusses the economic status and poverty levels of minority women in the present and future.

Issues of race and gender equity have dominated political discourse in the latter part of this century and have been pivotal in the life experience of the baby-boom generation. These issues will continue to play themselves out as our population ages and as the members of the baby boom enter retirement in the first decades of the next century. Although women of color have experienced some labor market progress in the past two decades that is likely to pay off in the future, this progress must be balanced by the current, stagnant economy and the social indifference to racial economic gaps. It is entirely possible that the debates about equity and distribution that shaped the adolescence and adulthood of baby-boom women will also affect them in old age.

POVERTY, INCOME, AND THE FAMILY STATUS OF OLDER WOMEN

The elderly poor are not a large group today—in 1990 at about 3.7 million, they were 12 percent of the total elderly population. But poverty is not evenly distributed among the elderly. It hits women harder than men, and people of color harder than whites. In 1990 women were 58 percent of the population aged 65 and over, but almost 74 percent of the poor population for that age group (see table 7.1).

Table 7.1 ELDERLY (AGED 65 AND OVER) POPULATION AND PERCENTAGE IN POVERTY IN THE UNITED STATES, 1990

	Elderly		Poor Elderly	
	# (thousands)	Percentage of Total Elderly	# (thousands)	Percentage of Poor Elderly
Total	30,093	—	3,658	
Men	12,547	41.69	959	26.22
Women	17,546	58.31	2,699	73.78
White men	11,235	37.33	634	17.33
White women	15,663	52.05	2,073	56.67
Black men	1,031	3.43	286	7.82
Black women	1,516	5.04	574	15.69
Hispanic men	461	1.53	86	2.35
Hispanic women	631	2.10	159	4.35

Source: U.S. Bureau of the Census (1991a).

Among older women, poverty is disproportionately concentrated among women who live alone and women of color. In 1990, black women constituted 8.6 percent of women aged 65 and over, but 21 percent of the female poor in that age group. (In contrast, white women made up 89 percent of all elderly women, and 77 percent of the female elderly poor; Hispanic women[1] constituted about 4 percent of the elderly female population and about 6 percent of poor elderly women) (U.S. Bureau of the Census 1991a.)

Although the majority of older women are not poor, the average older woman is within poverty's reach. In 1990, there were more than 17.5 million women aged 65 and over. These women had a median annual income of $8,044, an amount that was a scant 28 percent above the poverty line of $6,268 for an individual aged 65 and over living alone in that year (U.S. Bureau of Census 1991b). Women of color had lower median incomes than white women—elderly black women had a median annual income of $5,617, which was 66.4 percent of white women's income; Hispanic women had a median annual income of $5,373, or 63.5 percent of white women's income. These income gaps are consistent with income gaps that women of color experience during their working lives, as well as with differences in the labor market status of minority men that affect the pensions women of color receive as widows and survivors.

More than 15 percent of all older women (aged 65 and over), or 2.7 million women, had incomes below the 1990 poverty line (table 7.1). In general, older women have a lower incidence of poverty than do young women (aged 18–24) and girls (under age 18), but a higher incidence of poverty than women of other ages (table 7.2). Poverty

Table 7.2 POVERTY RATES FOR WOMEN IN THE UNITED STATES, BY AGE, RACE, AND HISPANIC ORIGIN 1989

Age	Total (%)	Black (%)	Hispanic (%)	White (%)
Total	14.4	34.0	28.3	11.3
Under 18	19.8	44.8	35.6	14.7
18–24	18.2	34.5	29.1	15.2
25–34	13.9	31.5	26.0	11.0
35–44	9.6	22.8	23.0	7.6
45–54	8.9	19.0	20.9	7.4
55–59	11.4	33.3	18.9	8.8
60–64	10.5	29.2	21.6	8.4
65 and over	13.9	36.5	22.4	11.8
65–74	10.6	32.7	19.1	8.3
75 and over	18.5	42.0	29.2	16.4

Source: U.S. Bureau of the Census (1991b).

rates rise sharply after age 75: the incidence of poverty among women aged 75 and over is 75 percent higher than that for women aged 65 to 74. The rise is sharpest among white women, but rates in this oldest group are about 10 percentage points higher for both black and Hispanic women, as well. This sharp increase in poverty among the oldest, most vulnerable women reflects, perhaps, the dwindling resources on which many women rely as they age.

How is this likely to change in the future? The occupational profile of African-American and Hispanic women has improved, and more work in jobs that qualify for pensions. Based on current data, it is likely that poverty will continue to be unequally distributed among older women by race; still some women of color, especially those with continuous work histories, will escape poverty.

The Prevalence of Near Poverty

Poverty data understate the economic predicament of many older women. Although older women's poverty incidence in 1990 was 15.4 percent, nearly a third of all women had incomes within 150 percent of the poverty line (see table 7.3). This was the condition for the majority (57.7 percent) of black older women, for nearly half (47.1 percent) of all elderly Latinas, and nearly 3 in 10 (29 percent) white older women. In contrast, just over half (55.2 percent) of all women could be considered "out of the woods" economically, with incomes higher than twice the poverty line. Fewer than a third of all black women could be so described. Indeed, 6 percent of all older black women had incomes only half as high as the poverty line or less.

In contrast, few women conform to the image of the wealthy elderly. Fewer than 1 in 12 women aged 65 and older had incomes of $25,000 or more in 1990. Fewer than 2 percent of black and Hispanic women had incomes at that level (U.S. Bureau of the Census, 1991b). To be

Table 7.3 POVERTY AND NEAR POVERTY FOR OLDER WOMEN (AGED 65 AND OVER) IN THE UNITED STATES, BY RACE AND HISPANIC ORIGIN, 1990

Income[a]	Total (%)	Black (%)	Hispanic (%)	White (%)
Half poverty line	**2.4**	**6.0**	**2.4**	**2.0**
At the poverty line	**15.4**	**37.9**	**25.3**	**13.2**
125 percent of poverty	23.4	49.6	38.2	20.9
150 percent of poverty	31.5	57.7	47.1	29.0
175 percent of poverty	38.7	64.2	54.5	36.3
Twice the poverty line	44.8	68.4	61.7	42.6

Source: U.S. Bureau of the Census (1991a).
a. Each entry represents those who earn that income level or less.

sure, some 1.4 million women did have incomes in that range, but depending on their marital status, health, and age, these income levels may not be secure. Far more older women live in poverty (2.7 million), at poverty's periphery as "near poor" (2.8 million), and at risk because their incomes are between 150 percent and 200 percent of the poverty line (2.3 million). Nearly half of all older women fit into one of these three categories.

Annual poverty data are most commonly released by the U.S. Department of Commerce, and provide information for blacks, whites, and Hispanics. Data on Asian poverty are only released with decennial census data. Although Asians have often been portrayed as the "model minority," with median income higher than that of whites, experts indicate that there is a significant incidence of poverty among Asians. In particular, poverty among Vietnamese-Americans is estimated at 36 percent, and at 25 percent among Filipino-Americans (Bergman 1991). Many Asian working-class men have little education, are concentrated in agricultural employment, and have life expectancies similar to those of black men. As a result, their widows are at higher risk for poverty. These women, many of whom are not facile with English, sometimes face discrimination in applying for federal income supplements like Supplemental Security Income (SSI) (see the section following for further discussion of this income source). Only a portion of those eligible receive this assistance, partly because they have difficulty dealing with the bureaucracy (Bergman 1991). Some of this is likely to change in the future. The assimilation of immigrant populations makes it easier for them to deal with the bureaucracy, as does the rise of advocacy groups (like San Francisco's Chinese-American group, Self Help for the Elderly) that target their efforts to minority elders.

The Significance of Family Status

When poverty incidence is viewed by family status and living arrangement, the highest concentration of poverty is among older women living alone (i.e., those widowed, separated, divorced, or never married who are not living with other family members). Nearly 1 in 4 elderly women living alone is poor, compared with 1 in 8 older women heading households, and 1 in 20 older women living in married-couple families (right-hand column of table 7.4). When the composition of poverty by living arrangement is examined, one finds that those living alone represent the vast majority—nearly three quarters—of older poor women (middle column of table 7.4).

Table 7.4 POVERTY AMONG WOMEN AGED 65 AND OVER IN THE UNITED STATES BY SELECTED FAMILY/LIVING STATUS, 1989

Race/Ethnicity Family/Living Status	Poor Women Aged 65 and over		Poor Women as Percentage of all Women Aged 65 and Over in Family/Living Status Category
	Number (thousands)	Percent Distribution	
All Races			
In all family/living status categories[a]	2,398	100.0	13.9
In married couples	367	15.3	5.4
Household heads	180	7.5	12.2
Living alone	1,698	70.8	23.2
Black			
In all family/living status categories[a]	541	100.0	36.5
In married couples	56	10.4	15.0
Household heads	93	17.2	30.9
Living alone	350	64.7	60.6
Latina			
In all family/living status categories[a]	124	100.0	22.3
In married couples	29	23.4	13.8
Household heads	16	12.9	17.6
Living alone	62	50.0	41.9

Source: U.S. Bureau of the Census (1991b).
a. Includes women living in household relationships other than those listed separately below.

The pattern of high concentration of poverty among women living alone cuts across racial lines, though it is less strong among elderly black and Hispanic women than among all elderly women. The slogan often used by women organizers, "a woman is only a husband away from poverty," is less true for women of color than for white women. Fifteen percent of older black women in married-couple families are poor; 31 percent of all older black women who head households live in poverty (right-hand column of table 7.4). But consistent with the overall pattern, the majority of black poor women, 64.7 percent, live alone (middle column of table 7.4).

Hispanics have different family patterns than the other groups studied here. Hispanic poor women aged 65 and over are more likely than their black or white counterparts to live in families, especially married-couple families (table 7.4). Even so, the overall pattern of single women's poverty prevails among Hispanics, too. The incidence of poverty among Hispanic women living alone is much higher than among those who live in families (right-hand column of table 7.4). And women living alone are the largest group of the elderly Hispanic poor (left-hand column of table 7.4).

The information in table 7.4 suggests that policy directed toward relieving poverty among older women must focus on women who live alone. This may be as true in the future as in the present, especially for women of color. Demographers project that the proportion of married women aged 65 and older will rise only slightly, from 31 percent to 33 percent, between 1990 and 2030 (Zedlewski et al. 1990), and current life expectancies for black and Hispanic men are lower than those of white men. Further, the projected rise in the proportion of never-married women (from 4.5 percent in 1990 to 8.2 percent in 2030) is likely to be greater among women of color. If current data, which show an increase in the number of black never-married women under age 35, hold, there will be more, not fewer, black women living alone in the future. In chapter 2 of this volume, Taeuber and Allen estimate that there will be 4.4 million black women aged 65 and over by 2030. If present trends hold, 1.7 million of them would be poor and another .9 million would have incomes between 100 percent and 150 percent of the poverty level.

SOURCES OF INCOME AND POLICY

The race/gender income gap (which compares the earnings of black, Latina, and white women to those of white men) is more pronounced for women over age 45 than for their younger counterparts. If current income is a proxy for future economic well-being, extrapolating this information might suggest that the disproportionate incidence of minority women in poverty would decline in 20 years.

But the data still do not suggest future parity between men and women. Further, although black and Latina baby boomers (i.e., the 35–44-year-old cohort) earn more than both older and younger minority women, there are continuing gaps between minority women and their white women counterparts at younger ages. The earnings gap is smallest between black and white women aged 35–54. Indeed, black women aged 35–44 have slightly higher earnings (about 3 percent more) than white women of their age group. Much of this difference relates to the greater work effort required of African-American women, given differences in family status (Malveaux 1990).

Current income data are likely to tell only part of the story. Another way to understand the poverty that many elderly minority women face today, and the chance of elderly women of color facing such poverty in the future, is to examine the sources of income available to them and the ways that their life circumstances may have influenced their access to these income sources. Then we can address the relationships between the sources of minority women's income and their disproportionate poverty.

Social Security

Social Security benefits are the major source of income for the elderly. More than 90 percent of all seniors, including 19.4 million women aged 62 and over, receive Social Security income (Sidel 1986). Social Security contributes about 42.5 percent of the income that individuals aged 65 and over receive, as well as 28.5 percent of the income that families with householders in that age group receive. The contrast between the jobs that the poor and nonpoor hold in their working years results in a different set of opportunities to accumulate wealth and to invest in other income-producing assets. Chapter 6 in this volume, by Rayman, Allshouse, and Allen, addresses issues of women's employment income and Social Security benefits. Poor and near-poor individuals and families are far more reliant on Social Security income than are the nonpoor, with the average elderly poor individual receiving nearly 80 percent of her or his total income from Social Security, and the average poor family receiving nearly three-quarters of total income from Social Security. For about a third of older unmarried women, Social Security provides about 90 percent of income

(Muller 1983: 23–31), and 60 percent of all older women depend on Social Security as their only source of income (Older Women's League 1991a).

There is no direct race bias in the Social Security program. Retirees' benefits are based on the number of quarters they work, earned income, and spousal income. However, differences in work patterns yield differences in Social Security benefits by race, as do differences in life expectancy and family status. These differences have an impact on the poverty status of older women of color today and will continue to do so in the future.

Some of the differences include:

☐ A higher incidence of female-headed households among blacks.
☐ A lower male life expectancy among minorities (66 years for black men, compared with white men's 73).
☐ Differences in pension-earning income. Women of color are still more likely to be employed "off the books" where benefits do not accrue.

In general, although there have been many reforms to the Social Security system in the past decade, women fare less well than men, and black and Hispanic women fare less well than white women. These differences both reflect lifetime differences in earnings and are a function of ignoring differences in the family responsibilities shouldered by women—differences that are likely to persist in the future.

How could the Social Security system be changed to minimize the amount of older women's poverty? One way would be to allow women credit for caregiving responsibilities. At a minimum, a woman should not be penalized for the time she spends out of the labor force doing family care. Perhaps women's earnings should be calculated on the basis of 25, not 35, years of paid work to allow for the greater number of years a woman spends out of the labor force on her family responsibilities. Indeed, the estimated value of women's unpaid work ranges from $700 billion to $1.4 trillion (Prescod 1991). Crediting that unremunerated work would certainly close the gap between men's and women's Social Security, and thus reduce the prevalence of older women's poverty. Congresswoman Barbara-Rose Collins, of Michigan, plans to develop legislation on crediting unpaid work. However, such legislation is not likely to be passed in the near future, mostly because the belief that unremunerated work should be rewarded is far from universal. Still, it represents a basis for the development of a more equitable Social Security system, and a pivot from which to look at women's poverty issues.

Whatever the flaws in the Social Security system, it is important to note the progressive income redistribution inherent in this program, and its effectiveness in moving elderly Americans out of poverty. "If Social Security benefits payments were excluded from after-tax income, the poverty rate in 1986 among the elderly would have been about 45.9% rather than 12.4%" (Hurd 1990: 581). The challenge in changing this progressive income redistribution system is to structure it to allow for differences in family type, so that all benefits are not calculated as though the norm is working husband and stay-at-home wife, a badly outmoded family stereotype that now describes just one-tenth of all American families.

Means-Tested Cash Assistance

The needy elderly qualify for the Supplemental Security Income program, a joint federal-state program that guarantees a minimum level of income to financially hard-pressed individuals who are aged 65 and over or blind or disabled. About 2 million elderly individuals and families received SSI in 1989, with slightly more individuals than families receiving the benefit. Seventy-five percent of those receiving SSI aged benefits were women (U.S. Department of Health and Human Services 1990: 33). Although about 10 percent of the elderly received SSI, only 30 percent of all poor elderly individuals and a third of all poor elderly families received this benefit. Why do so few poor seniors qualify for SSI? This low participation is not fully understood, but one factor is the assets test. Seniors must be extremely poor and own few assets to qualify for SSI. Except for the value of a home and car, some personal property, and a small life insurance policy, assets must be worth no more than $3,000 per couple. In addition, monthly income must be less than a minimum, which varies by state, although some types of income (e.g., part of earned income, food stamps, and some gifts) are not counted.

The base SSI benefit amount was $422 a month for an individual in 1992, with a larger amount available for couples. States supplemented the base amount by a variable sum, depending on other income and need—$28 in Washington State and $223 in California in 1991. Many older persons and families receive only a fraction of the SSI amount, because they have income from other sources.

The Politics of Future SSI Policy

The fact that states may supplement SSI payments by variable amounts raises questions about the future size and stability of these payments.

Although at the federal level the political strength of older Americans has made it almost impossible to cut senior programs, most states are unable to run budget deficits from year to year. Issues of competing need among age groups that are only hinted at on the federal level are the source of heated discussion at the state level, and few programs have been left intact in the recent round of state budget cuts.

The black and Hispanic aged, with a history of low-paying jobs and intermittent work histories, bear a heavier burden when SSI is cut than do others (Torres-Gil 1990). SSI programs are not a political sacred cow like Social Security, and pressure to keep Social Security intact or to minimize cuts to that program does not protect the SSI program, which clearly addresses the needier elderly. Future support for SSI programs will depend on both the politics and economics of the future. Should elderly individuals and families have an income floor? How can we pay for this, given state budget shortfalls? The answers that legislators provide to these questions will determine the fate of the SSI-dependent elderly, a disproportionate number of whom are black and brown women.

Wages and Salaries

It is tempting to think that though older women's past labor market experiences affect their present economic circumstances, current labor market problems have little impact on them. However, this is not the case. More than 1 in 6 older (aged 65 and over) Americans continue to work. Older white men are most likely to work, followed by black men, black women, and white women (data in this category were not available for Hispanics), and participation rates fall off with age (U.S. Department of Labor 1992). The poor and near poor are much less likely to work, and earnings account for a lower percentage of total income for them. There is a similar pattern for families with householders aged 65 and over (although the higher percentage receiving wage income may be a function of the number of under-65-year-olds in the household) (U.S. Bureau of the Census 1991a).

Where do older women work? Private household workers are among the most likely to stay in the labor market, reflecting both their low income and the fact that such jobs do not provide pensions (Shaw 1988). In addition, private household workers can work "off the books" and receive small amounts of SSI or Social Security income. Note that this income would not be reflected in data showing older people's income sources. It may be that poor and near-poor women work for pay more often than is reported. Unlike many of the white men who stay in the labor market because they enjoy their work, or because their prestigious managerial and professional jobs have no mandatory retirement provisions (in constrast to most manufacturing and clerical jobs), the private household workers in the labor market are there because they need the income. According to Shaw (1988), elderly women with only Social Security or SSI income had poverty rates, in 1984, of 25 percent. But those who were either employed or had a pension in addition to Social Security had poverty rates of 5 percent.

Shaw (1988) also noted that women who work often do so without jeopardizing their Social Security benefits. Social Security recipients face an earnings test; those aged 65–69 must forfeit $1 of every $3 of their earnings above the exempt amount of $9,720 (in 1991). However, that amount is more than half the average earnings ($13,500) of a female clerical worker. In other words, a woman working half time as a secretary would not jeopardize her Social Security income. Thus, although some economists suggest that the structure of the Social Security system dampens the work incentive for those subject to a means test, especially over age 65 (Herz and Rones 1989), women's wages may be so low that the question of work incentive is irrelevant.

Pensions

In 1940, pension coverage was rare, and only 15 percent of all private wage and salary workers were covered by pension plans (Turner and Beller 1989). But private pension coverage grew rapidly in the 20 years that followed 1950, so that by 1970, 46 percent of all workers were covered by pension plans. Until very recently, these numbers have remained steady—in 1988, 46 percent of all private-sector workers were covered by pension plans, as were 83 percent of all public-sector workers (Hurd 1990).

In chapter 2 of this volume, Taeuber and Allen describe the increasing likelihood that a young minority woman will work in a job covered by a pension. However, pensions have been structured to reflect male employment patterns, and to reward continuous employment. Despite some reforms, biases against women in pension policy persist. Women have greater childcare and eldercare responsibilities, which mean that they work fewer years and less continuously than do men. And women's pay is lower than men's pay. When women switch jobs or move because of family responsibilities, it affects their access to pensions (most pensions vest at 5 or 10 years, and the median job tenure for women is 3.7 years, compared with 5.1 years for men) (Older Women's League 1990). Further, women's concentration in part-time work, and as employees of small businesses, means that fewer women than men will, in the future, have access to pensions. Finally, as women have moved into self-employment and business ownership, often to avoid work-family conflicts, they have removed themselves from the very jobs that provide pension coverage.

PENSIONS IN A SHIFTING ECONOMY

The role of government in regulating and insuring pension funds is important, especially as workers have been encouraged not to rely fully on Social Security for their retirement income. Even though pensions are safeguarded by government regulation, the 1980s were an unstable financial period, in which the words "junk" and "bonds" were ironically used in the same sentence. For those pension funds whose viability depended on the type of investment, the 1980s were a period where some defined contribution plans yielded low, if any, returns.

The case of Executive Life, in California, although extreme, illustrates the danger. Retirees bought annuities in an insurance company that went on to invest in junk bonds, speculative real estate, and other shaky investments. As a result, thousands of individuals who had purchased annuities received less than they were promised as a return (Willis 1990: 137). More significantly, large corporate pension funds that put money into annuities at Executive Life have jeopardized the incomes of their retirees. Under the provisions of the Employee Retirement Income Security Act of 1974, the U.S. Department of Labor sued the Pacific Lumber company for violating its fiduciary responsibility by buying annuities from Executive Life (Lucas 1991).

There has also been concern about the effects of mergers and acquisitions on pension payments, especially as overfunded pension plans have been described as a lure for corporate raiders (Mitchell and Mulherin 1989). The Pension Protection Act of 1987 was passed to protect pensions from the acquisition process, and although economists see this law as perhaps inhibiting the corporate acquisition process, its passage indicates legislators' concern about the viability and integrity of pension plans. On the other hand, during the 1990–91 recession, at least 18 states considered delaying or reducing their contributions to their pension funds. Further, growing numbers of state and local governments began to see funds accumulated in pension funds as possible loan sources (Stevenson 1991). Public employee pension coverage is far more comprehensive than private employee coverage, with 83 percent of all public-sector workers having coverage (Andrews 1985). Although public-sector occupational distributions reflect the race and gender bias of private-sector occupational status, it is interesting to note that women and minorities are disproportionately represented in the public sector (Malveaux and Wallace 1987). Experts in pension accounting disagree about whether or not withdrawals and deferred contributions imperil pension funds in the long run—in most states, no short-term consequences are predicted for one-time borrowing. But public employee unions say that borrowing on a one-time basis sets a bad precedent, and it is ironic that government is protecting private-sector pension funds on the one hand and using public-sector pension funds to bridge budget gaps on the other.

PENSION COVERAGE AND OLDER WOMEN'S POVERTY

The pension issue is important to older women, because those receiving pensions, or some income source other than Social Security, are less likely than others to live in poverty, and because the transition to widowhood seems to induce poverty for some older women, simply because of the assets lost upon the death of a spouse. Hurd (1990: 583) has stated that the average increase in poverty following widowhood is 30 percent, due to permanent changes in economic resources.

There was a slight decline in pension coverage during the 1980s, and those not covered were more likely to be women than men. With 46 percent of all full-time workers participating in employer-funded pension programs, 49 percent of men and 43 percent of women were covered. Low rates of coverage were found among those working less than five years and among those employed in very small companies (less than 10 employees), where only 11 percent of employees were covered (Social Security Bulletin 1990).

Will these trends continue into the future? And will there be a special impact on women of color? To the extent that women of color hold the least advantaged positions in the labor market, they will continue to have less access to pension coverage, and erosions in the pension fund structure will affect them. Women of color are disproportionately employed in the public sector, so borrowing on public pension funds has a greater impact on them. On the other hand, to the extent that women of color have employment profiles that begin to resemble those of white men, their pension coverage rates and income should improve.

PRIVATE RESOURCES: INTEREST, DIVIDENDS, AND PERSONAL WEALTH

Although income is a snapshot of monies received during a year, wealth and net worth measure assets accumulated over a lifetime. The way this wealth has been used, in buying a home or in investing in interest-bearing securities, affects the way older people, especially elderly retirees with low incomes, are able to live. Wealth also measures consumption opportunities, flexibility, and mobility. For example, if most net worth is tied up in a home, then the homeowner may have much less choice and flexibility than if wealth is distributed among an array of assets.

Home Equity and "House Poverty"

When the value of home equity is subtracted from the median net worth ($25,088) of the lowest income quintile of households aged 65 and over in 1988, remaining assets are valued at about $3,200, hardly enough to invest in interest-producing assets. Households in the lowest income quintile represented 37 percent of all families with householders aged 65 and over in 1988 (U.S. Bureau of the Census 1990). When home equity is subtracted from net worth, it is easy to see why so many elderly women are house-poor, and have little mobility. NBC's situation comedy "The Golden Girls" suggests that this house-poverty can be dealt with by finding a few friendly roommates, but in a weak housing market, when the option is unavailable, too many older people, especially older women, are stuck in homes too large for them and with incomes insufficient to maintain them.

This lack of mobility may be exacerbated for black and Latino seniors by depressed housing values in inner cities. For many, housing appreciation is a key method of wealth accumulation, but those whose property values have been constrained by redlining may be strangled both by high property taxes and urban decay. Stanford (1990: 47) suggests that housing policy is an area with a special impact on the black aged. Since a greater portion of black wealth is concentrated in home value (67 percent, compared with 42 percent for whites and 58 percent for Hispanics), the housing issues that Stanford raises are especially important to blacks.

Wealth data reflect the same pattern of differences among the elderly by race that appears in data on income, unemployment, and poverty. White families in which the householder was aged 65 or over had a median net worth of $81,600, compared with $22,210 for black families with elderly householders and $40,371 for Hispanic families in 1988 (U.S. Bureau of the Census 1990). There may be intergenerational consequences to the low net worth of elderly black and Hispanic households. Those with few assets are likely to depend more on their children who, based on their own occupational options, may have less than others to give.

When aging baby boomers boost the elderly portion of the black population from 8.2 percent in 1990 to 17.5 percent in 2030, the ratio of the black retirement age population (aged 65 and over) to the black working-age population (aged 20 to 64) will rise from about 15 per 100 to about 31 per 100 (U.S. Bureau of the Census 1989). If policy changes are not made to prepare the minority members of the baby boom economically for old age, their children may have to take on more responsibility than the baby boomers are assuming for their own parents.

Wealth, Poverty, and Women of Color

Two factors are important in explaining how private income sources affect the poverty status of older women of color. First, what wealth has a woman amassed during her working lifetime? Second, are her children in a position to contribute to her well-being after she retires? Older women of color today, who earned less in their lifetimes, are likely to have less wealth upon retirement. Depending upon the way the private labor market closes racial wage gaps, the children of these women are also likely to have less to spend on supporting their mothers. The stark difference between the status of middle-income minorities and poor minorities may mean that in the future there will be both a larger group of elderly minority women who are financially secure and a continued high incidence of poverty. In 1990, 14 percent of all black families had earnings that exceeded $50,000, while about a third lived below the poverty line (U.S. Bureau of the Census 1991a, b). Twenty years from now, these differences will be reflected among the black elderly.

THE LOW-INCOME ELDERLY IN A STAGNANT ECONOMY

In the 1980s, cities and states followed the federal government in cutting social welfare programs because of budget pressures. In some cases, a reduction of block grants from the federal government was directly responsible for program cuts at the city and state level. The multiyear economic recovery that followed the 1981–83 recession was accompanied by corporate downsizing, lower wages for workers, and other erosions of the economic status of ordinary people. Indeed, in 1979, a quarter of all workers earned less than $12,000, about the poverty rate for a family of four. By 1988, that proportion had risen to 31.7 percent (Mishel and Frankel 1991). This erosion of worker status was compounded by the recession of 1990–92, when unemployment rates reached 7.5 percent.

The short-term attention accorded cyclical issues of recession and recovery mask long-term structural changes in the economy and society. The labor market currently provides less job security than it has in a decade, with those, like women and minorities, at the periphery especially affected. If current wages affect future economic status, then the displacement of thousands of workers, as well as the increase in part-time jobs and self-employment, have implications for the elderly minority women of the future.

Structural change in our economy has rendered a larger portion of our population more vulnerable and insecure. Some families have struggled to maintain their economic position by moving from a one-earner to a two-earner base. Those families with only one earner, meanwhile, have watched their standard of living erode as the "family wage" has lost value. These are adults who will have fewer resources to share with aged parents and fewer resources to set aside for their own retirement. Workers who have moved from manufacturing to service jobs may have experienced not only a drop in their standard of living; if they faced long periods of unemployment, they may have been forced to cash out any accumulated retirement benefits. In the past, federal employment and training programs might have eased the transition between sectors, but between 1980 and 1990, federal spending on employment and training was cut by 70 percent. In the 1990s, with a large budget deficit, a political climate hostile to public spending for social programs, and no explicit labor policy, workers have little assistance in making the sectoral transition.

Many economists assessing the current situation agree that there must be some coordinated response to current structural shifts. Absent a response, only a few American workers can look forward to the "good jobs" that offer pensions, benefits, and perquisites (Reich 1991). The economic insecurity that workers face today will be reflected in their economic status as seniors in the future. The insecurity workers face may also make them less willing to allocate resources to ease the plight of the elderly poor, especially a disproportionately minority and female group, with whom they are least willing to identify.

CONCLUSION: PREVENTING OLDER WOMEN'S POVERTY

In the future the over-65 population will be older, and more black and brown than it is today, while continuing to be disproportionately female, especially at the oldest ages. Because elder poverty is concentrated among women and minorities and the very old, these demographic trends suggest that unless corrective policies are instituted, the incidence of poverty will increase in the future. Younger women's educational levels have improved, to be sure, and they are working more continuously. However, the fact that social policy has not been modified to deal with women's dual responsibilities in the workplace and the household, as well as the fact that there is no family policy in the United States, exacerbates the tendency toward older women's poverty. Educational access and occupational shifts may protect some women, but young minority women still lag behind white women in higher education, and many others will be disadvantaged by their need to take time out of the labor force for caregiving. Older women's poverty, then, is not a cohort effect that only affects today's older women, but a necessary outcome of the absence of social, family, and health policies that would support women's dual roles as family caregivers and members of the work force.

Among older women of color, especially black women, poverty seems less a function of marital status than of past work experience. But in 1990, fewer then 1 percent of black women earned more than $50,000 per year (compared with about 2 percent of white women and 11 percent of white men) (U.S. Bureau of the Census 1991b). By 2030, there will be a much greater minority representation among the aged population. From a policy perspective, this fact should draw our attention to labor market policies that currently affect the employment status of minorities, especially minority women, who are more likely to survive into very old age than minority men. The poverty of older women—black and white—can be avoided in the future if labor market policies generate access to good jobs and pensions in the present.

The years that women spend outside the labor market for caregiving responsibilities, the unequal pay women receive even when they are working, the peripheral work that many minority women accept that reduces their access to pensions and Social Security, and the likelihood that women will spend part of their old age alone all contribute to high poverty rates among elderly women of color. Certain policy initiatives, affecting both older women and those who are preparing for old age, could help young minority women avoid the predicament of older women's poverty. Included among these initiatives are:

☐ *Pay equity and other equal pay policies* that would assist women in building pension credit for retirement. Women are still heavily concentrated in low-paying occupations, and the long-term consequence of their low pay is low retirement benefits.

☐ *Enforcement of age and race discrimination laws,* which would enable those women who choose to work past age 65 to find employment. It is especially important to note that age discrimination sometimes combines with race discrimination to create a dual hardship for older blacks.

☐ *More equitable retirement policies,* which could ensure that higher proportions of older women have retirement income from sources other than Social Security. Such policies include those that would reflect women's unpaid work, that would allow workers to begin vesting retirement benefits sooner, and that would make it easier for workers to invest in vehicles like individual retirement accounts (IRAs). As more women work part-time, it also makes sense to mandate that employers allow part-time workers to accumulate retirement credits on a proportional basis.

Older minority women follow many paths to poverty. Following demographic and social trends, some of those paths will narrow or even disappear, but others may widen in the future. Clearly, some women will be protected because of more continuous work histories and improved labor market profiles; but others who have not had the benefit of higher education and good jobs, or who have worked sporadically because of family responsibilities, poor health, and other factors, will face some of the same risks that women face today. It will take some policy intervention to change this outcome, and the challenge will be to create policies that affect not only minority women who are already over age 65 but the women who are approaching their older years with limited means to protect themselves from future economic hardship and dependency.

Note

1. The U.S. Bureau of the Census uses the term "Hispanic" to refer to a group of people of diverse cultural backgrounds. Mexican Americans make up the largest segment of

this population, followed by Puerto Ricans and Cuban Americans. The Hispanic population also includes people of Central and South American origin or descent.

References

Andrews, Emily. 1985. *The Changing Profile of Pensions in America.* Washington, D.C.: Employee Benefit Research Institute.

Bergman, Gregory. 1991. "Aging Confab Focuses on Older Women of Color." *Sun Reporter,* Apr. 17.

Herz, Diane, and Philip L. Rones. 1989. "Institutional Barriers to Employment of Older Workers." *Monthly Labor Review* (April): 14–21.

Hurd, Michael D. 1990. "Research on the Elderly: Economic Status, Retirement, and Consumption and Savings." *Journal of Economic Literature* (June): 565–637.

Lucas, Charlotte Ann. 1991. "U.S. Sues Firms Over Pensions." *San Francisco Examiner,* June 13.

Malveaux, Julianne. 1990. "Women in the Labour Market: The Choices Women Have." In *Enterprising Women,* edited by Julia Parzen and Sara Gould. Paris: Organization for European Cooperation and Development.

Malveaux, Julianne, and Phyllis Wallace. 1987. "Minority Women in the Workplace." In *Working Women: Past, Present, Future,* edited by Karen Koziara, Michael Moskow, and Lucretia Tanner. Washington, D.C.: Bureau of National Affairs Press.

Mishel, Lawrence, and David Frankel. 1991. *The State of Working America.* Economic Policy Institute. New York: M.E. Sharpe.

Mitchell, Mark, and J. Harold Mulherin. 1989. "Pensions and Mergers." In *Trends in Pensions,* edited by John A. Turner and Daniel J. Beller (211–34). Washington, D.C.: U.S. Department of Labor.

Muller, Charlotte. 1983. "Income Supports for Older Women." *Social Policy* (Fall).

Older Women's League. 1987. *The Picture of Health for Midlife and Older Women in America.* Washington, D.C.: Author.

———. 1988. *The Road to Poverty: A Report on the Economic Status of Midlife and Older Women in America.* Washington, D.C.: Author.

———. 1990. *Heading for Hardship: Retirement Income for American Women in the Next Century.* Washington, D.C.: Author.

———. 1991a. *Fact Sheet.* San Francisco: Author.

———. 1991b. *Paying for Prejudice: A Report on Midlife and Older Women in America's Labor Force.* Washington, D.C.: Author.

Prescod, Margaret. 1991. "Count Women's Work: Implementing the Action Plans and Strategies of Houston and Nairobi." Los Angeles: International Wages for Housework Campaign.

Reich, Robert. 1991. *The Work of Nations*. New York: Knopf.

Shaw, Lois. 1988. "Special Problems of Older Women Workers." In *The Older Worker*, edited by Michael Borus, Herbert Parnes, Steven Sandell, and Bert Seidman. Madison, Wis.: Industrial Relations Research Association.

Sidel, Ruth. 1986. *Women and Children Last*. New York: Penguin Books.

Social Security Bulletin. 1990. *Pension Coverage among Private Wage and Salary Workers* 52(10 Oct.).

Sokoloff, Natalie. 1992. *Black and White Women in the Professions*. New York: Routledge Press.

Stanford, E. Percil. 1990. "Diverse Black Aged." In *The Black Aged: Understanding Diversity and Service Needs*, edited by Zev Harel, Edward A. McKinney, and Michael Williams. Newbury Park: Sage Publications.

Stevenson, Richard W. 1991. "States Seeking Aid on Budgets from Pensions." *New York Times*, July 21.

Taylor, Paul. 1991. "Like Taking Money from a Baby." *Washington Post*, National Weekly Edition, March 4: 31.

Torres-Gil, Fernando. 1990. "Diversity in Aging: The Challenge of Pluralism." *Aging Connection*, April/May.

Turner, John A., and Daniel J. Beller. 1989. *Trends in Pension*. Washington, D.C.: U.S. Department of Labor.

U.S. Bureau of the Census. 1989. *Projections of the Population of the United States by Age, Sex, and Race: 1988-2080*. By Gregory Spencer. Current Population Reports, ser. P-25, no. 1018. Washington, D.C.: U.S. Government Printing Office.

————. 1990. *Household Wealth and Asset Ownership: 1988*. Current Population Reports, ser. P-70, no. 22. Washington, D.C.: U.S. Government Printing Office.

————. 1991a. *Poverty in the United States: 1990*. Current Population Reports, series P-60, no. 175, Washington, D.C.: U.S. Government Printing Office.

————. 1991b. *Money Income of Households, Families, and Persons in the United States: 1990*. By Carmen DeNavas and Edward Welniak. Current Population Reports, ser. P-60, no. 174. Washington, D.C.: U.S. Government Printing Office.

————. 1991c. *Poverty in the United States, 1988 and 1989*. Current Population Reports, series P-60, no. 171, Washington, D.C.: U.S. Government Printing Office.

U.S. Department of Health and Human Services. 1990. *Fast Facts and Figures and Social Security*. Washington, D.C.: U.S. Government Printing Office.

U.S. Department of Labor, Bureau of Labor Statistics. 1992. *Employment and Earnings* 39(1). January.

Willis, Clint. 1990. "Six Ways to Prevent Insurance Shocks." *Money Magazine* (December): 133–42.

Zedlewski, Sheila R., Roberta O. Barnes, Martha R. Burt, Timothy D. McBride, and Jack A. Meyer. 1990. *The Needs of the Elderly in the 21st Century.* Washington, D.C.: Urban Institute Press.

Chapter Eight

EXPANDING SOCIAL ROLES FOR OLDER WOMEN

Ruth Harriet Jacobs

The growing numbers of older women in the United States make it socially and economically necessary both to open new roles for them and view their current roles from new perspectives. Only then can older women lead productive lives for as long as possible, instead of draining national resources or being marginalized as society's discards. Our aging society has unmet needs, and older women have unrecognized and unused talents. The unpaid work performed by older women, including family caregiving and volunteer work in communities or institutions, is generally unacknowledged and undervalued. To value and expand older women's productive roles means to recognize the importance of such volunteer work and to provide more and better-paid work opportunities to help future generations of older women avoid poverty and dependence.

It will take creative thinking, planning, and programming to correct the long-standing assignment of insufficient and negative roles to older women. We must look at older women in new ways, not with old stereotypes. This chapter begins by considering the ways in which older women's roles are limited and the obstacles they face in organizing for change. It then offers a model of contemporary role types and briefly describes the mechanisms of role change. Finally, it suggests ways in which today's limited roles could be extended in the near future through public policy intervention.

LIMITATIONS ON OLDER WOMEN'S ROLES

Historically, older women's roles in the United States have been limited by patriarchy, propriety, and patterning. Patriarchy refers to "the systemic conditions of female subordination," whereas the male is privileged (Ferguson 1991). Propriety, or the societal standard of what is socially acceptable in behavior and speech, has required most older women to conform to implicit rules that they be nurturing, asexual, self-sacrificing, restrained, passive, and modest. Patterning occurs when women internalize and conform to stereotypes about the proper demeanor and potential abilities of older women. Thus, women who are no longer young are often allocated an inferior, even despised, status due to patriarchy, are constrained by powerful norms to accept narrow roles defined by propriety, and are socialized by patterning to keep their proper backstage places. This situation has improved somewhat in recent decades, but not enough to utilize the skills and wisdom older women actually possess today or to prepare for a future in which older women will constitute a much larger part of the American public.

In the broadcast and print media, in folklore, and in jokes, older women have been maligned or laughed at as witches; bitches; clinging mothers; rabid mothers-in-law; useless hags; bumbling, troublesome meddlers; garrulous, bossy workers; and childlike or hateful people. Despite sentimental lip service paid to grandmotherly figures, if older women cannot find good roles, it is they who are blamed rather than the society that deprives them of opportunities in their later years.

Because older women are denied economic security, good healthcare, and the expression of their talents, the economy suffers from the collective dependency of many older women, rather than profiting from their productivity in creative roles. Women who are unutilized, poor, and poorly served at midlife and in early old age are apt to be needy and societally expensive in very old age, often living in poverty and supported by welfare. On the other hand, women who are well integrated into the economy and other roles in midlife and early old age are more apt to be self-sufficient longer and insured for any necessary care in extreme old age. They also contribute to the country's savings, pensions, and general tax revenues.

Tangible social dividends for the nation at large could come from an increased mobilization of older women, similar to the long-term benefits from the public works and arts projects for the unemployed during the Great Depression. Younger generations will also benefit if older women feel useful and happy. Young women will not dread their own aging, and adult sons and daughters will not be burdened by dependent older mothers who lack good roles.

THE EXPENDABILITY OF OLDER WOMEN

In previous times and even today in some parts of the world, certain categories of the population have been designated as disposable. The old and weak were left behind by hunting and gathering societies, and elsewhere surplus children or those of unwanted gender have been exposed to die or have been killed. Although in the United States we do not sanction the direct destruction of citizens, some population groups are considered largely expendable. Figure 8.1 diagrams expendability as a blockage of the reciprocal relationship enjoyed by valued groups in the society.

A valued category both receives resources from society and can contribute to it (see figure 8.1). By contrast, an expendable category of low status drains the society's resources into a dead end of despair, deviance, and poverty. Whether or not a category contributes to and receives resources from the society depends upon the economic base of the society and its social values and policies. Respect or rejection depends also on the category's achieved and ascribed status and its proportionate size. Older women currently have a collective low ascribed status. Although some older women have a high status gained through extraordinary efforts, inherited wealth, or luck, most find achievement limited or blocked by age. As this volume stresses, the size of this expendable category is growing.

The Difficulty of Organizing Older Women

Figure 8.1 illustrates that in some cases an expendable category's problems can stimulate a movement to restore that group's reciprocal relationship with society. However, to organize on its own behalf, a category must be conscious of shared deprivation and have a sense of community. A social category that is maligned and joked about has to work hard to be taken seriously or even to take itself seriously. Too often, older women consider their dilemmas trivial and regard them as personal failures or strokes of fate rather than the result of bad societal arrangements. Creating a sense of shared discrimination and of suffering and turning that into social action requires charismatic, skilled leadership—which is rare in any group, but perhaps more so among older women, who have been socialized to avoid leadership

Figure 8.1 EXPENDABILITY IN THE UNITED STATES—INTERACTION OF
ECONOMY, VALUES, AND SOCIAL POLICY WITH POPULATION
CATEGORIES OF HIGH OR LOW STATUS

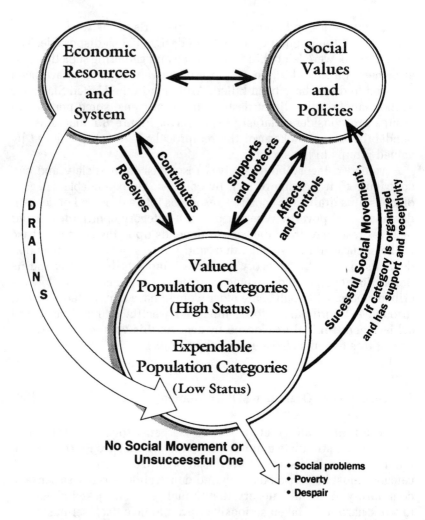

roles. Moreover, empowerment for effective action requires resources and a favorable social climate. Consciousness raising is a precondition for action, but consciousness raising alone may not guarantee empowerment or a successful outcome.

Research has shown that older people often do not identify politically with peers on the basis of age. Pratt (1976) stated that gerontophobia prevails not only among the young but also in the elderly themselves, in the form of self-hatred. Atchley (1988) and Binstock (1972) have also pointed out that the aging population is not necessarily a cohesive political group. Since there is a greater penalty for being an older woman than an older man, women tend to experience the greatest internalized ageism and do not wish to claim an unprized status. Thus, not only has the general women's movement largely ignored older women's issues (Macdonald, with Rich 1983), but older women themselves often reject organizations centered around issues arising from their aging. "Old" is not a way they want to identify themselves (Healy 1990).

To provide some examples, although the Older Women's League (OWL) has provided outstanding information, public education, and lobbying, and has attracted women with age pride, it has had trouble becoming a mass organization. Many women dislike OWL's name and fail to relate to its mission. The National Displaced Homemakers Network, another national organization, has also responded to the notion of the expendability of older women, making major contributions to their economic well-being. However, few older women want to identify themselves primarily as "displaced homemakers." The Gray Panthers, the most radical of the aging movement organizations, has also been concerned with the roles of older women. Maggie Kuhn, its founder, has been a vocal advocate and a highly visible model for older women, but, again, the result has not been a mass following. As a final example, the American Association of Retired Persons (AARP) has become the largest voluntary organization in the world, but more because it has offered such benefits as insurance, magazines, trips, and consumer discounts than because of its advocacy on aging. The AARP has had a Women's Initiative since 1985, but its focus is on disseminating educational literature and self-help information, rather than organizing or radicalizing older women; recently, however, it has become more involved in public policy issues. Overall, these organizations have considerable legislative impact nationally and in the states, and have helped numerous individual women in different ways, but they have limited power as advocates for older women's issues and have been unable to create a national movement demanding equity for older women.

It seems unlikely that in the near future our society will—without pressure—reverse the expendability of older women and enlarge their societal roles. Nevertheless, the continued aging of the U.S. population is drawing increased attention to older women's problems, and it is quite possible that some action will be undertaken in that direction.

The crucial question then will be: Will we be able to develop meaningful reforms that benefit both older women and society at large? To do this, we will have to avoid a common cycle of superficial policy reactions, as schematized in the accompanying figure 8.2. The schema presents a simplified version of the public policy response to social problems in the United States in recent decades. Unfortunately, the experience of older women in the displaced homemakers movement is a prime example.

Figure 8.2 CYCLE FOR SOCIAL EXPENDABILITY IN THE UNITED STATES

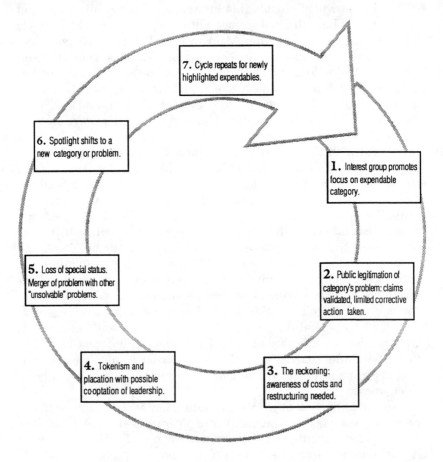

7. Cycle repeats for newly highlighted expendables.

6. Spotlight shifts to a new category or problem.

1. Interest group promotes focus on expendable category.

5. Loss of special status. Merger of problem with other "unsolvable" problems.

2. Public legitimation of category's problem: claims validated, limited corrective action taken.

4. Tokenism and placation with possible co-optation of leadership.

3. The reckoning: awareness of costs and restructuring needed.

THE CYCLE OF REFORM FOR EXPENDABLE POPULATIONS

Figure 8.2 outlines a process through which marginalized groups may achieve temporary recognition, but ultimately fail to make significant gains. In the first step, the attention of the media and of policymakers is drawn to an expendable category by interest-group organizers or a crisis. In the next step, the needs and claims of that category are legitimated after public and legislative debate. Some action ensues. (This happened, for example, in the mid-1970s when a campaign engineered by Laurie Shields and Tish Sommers of Oakland, Calif. and others identified "displaced homemakers" as older women who had been working in the home but were no longer supported by a spouse and had lost their economic security because of divorce, separation, death, or disability. After a public outcry and hard work by the displaced homemakers movement, there was a legitimation of needs and claims and some action through state and federal funding.) But then comes stage 3, the reckoning, or an awareness that the costs of solving the problem will be large and require restructuring of the resources, rewards, and values of the society. In response, stage 4 usually brings tokenism and placation, sometimes with cooptation of the movement's leadership.

In the mid-1970s, displaced homemaker lobbying groups helped pass legislation that allowed more divorced women to collect Social Security benefits by reducing the requisite former marriage length from 16 to 10 years. Some government money was allocated for training and job placement by the states and federally through the Vocational Education Act of 1976, but funding was inadequate to meet the enormous need. Some excellent training programs were initiated, and some displaced homemakers were trained for workplace roles, but all too soon the flow of funding slowed to a trickle. By 1992, only a small amount remained available through state vocational education grants.

One reason displaced homemaker programs were funded and succeeded in the late 1970s and early 1980s was that employers' needs at the time coincided with the outcry from displaced homemaker advocates. Workers were sought in the expanding high-tech and computer fields and in the rapidly growing medical and service areas. With some training, displaced homemakers and other older women became cheap labor. As new entrants to the paid work force, they occupied the bottom slots and were willing to accept low wages because of their lack of experience in the paid work force, general low self-esteem, and financial desperation. In the late 1980s, however, new waves of immigrants from Asia, South America, and the Caribbean provided additional cheap and eager labor; the older women were not the only contenders for these jobs. At the same time, the high-tech and computer fields experienced a recession in the late 1980s and early 1990s.

Unfortunately, the older women were often the first to be fired. Now even older, they are back in the unemployed pool, still experiencing sex and age discrimination. Because their training was frequently short, superficial, and job-specific, it is often obsolete now. Poorer displaced homemakers could not afford long unstipended training or higher education and so were not broadly educated. Some of their more affluent counterparts managed to get liberal arts educations and professional training that gave them greater job flexibility, but even they are suffering in the current recession.

What happened to most displaced homemaker projects is what usually happens in stage 5 of the cycle shown in figure 8.2. The special status of a formerly legitimized category of individuals is withdrawn, their problems are merged with other "unsolvable problems," public issues are redefined as private or individual problems, and "good causes" become "lost causes." Many displaced homemakers are now part of the pool of chronically unemployed.

In stage 6, the spotlight switches to another category in crisis. In this stage, the old category is forgotten, in a process accelerated by the media's thirst for a new "sob story." In the last few decades, a sequence of issues have been highlighted involving "expendables"—migrant workers, battered women, incest victims, high-school dropouts, unemployed youth, abused elders, drug addicts, abused children. All have their moment of public attention that initiates some legislation or programming, but then the entire cycle repeats itself for each category. Expendable populations continue to suffer.

However, a suffering expendable population that has good leadership and persistence—and can remain organized—can attempt to restart the cycle by again calling attention to its needs. Thus, in 1990, with prodding from the National Displaced Homemakers Network, legislation was passed by the U.S. Congress authorizing $35 million (a significant, though still insufficient amount) to train and support displaced homemakers. Yet, despite almost two years of lobbying by the network to achieve passage of the legislation, in addition to mobilization of a vigorous grassroots protest to head off a presidential veto, the act was never funded. In 1991, all new programs in the U.S. Department of Labor were left unfunded. As of spring 1992, the National Displaced Homemakers Network was still lobbying hard for funding. Thus, the renewed cycle has reached only the public legitimation phase—stage 2 in figure 8.2—and has been at least temporarily aborted at stage 3, the reckoning—awareness of costs and rationing of resources.

The remainder of this chapter attempts to provide the groundwork for expanded opportunities for older women that go beyond the circular change just described. A typology of older women's current roles is presented first, followed by a brief discussion of the ways in which the efforts of individuals can combine with changes in social policy to facilitate role changes. Finally, the chapter suggests new roles that might productively be opened to older women in different sectors of society in the near future. The list of new role options is not comprehensive, but is intended as a catalyst for further creative thinking about role expansion in our aging society.

OLDER WOMEN'S CURRENT ROLES

In the 1970s, I developed a 10-part typology of the roles possible for older women, constrained as they were by the social structure and societal values (Jacobs 1979). Almost thirteen years after the publication of this typology, the role options for older women seem to be much the same, though there has been a slight shift away from the type identified as nurturers and toward those of advocates and careerists. The types are based on an analysis of personal motivations and social structures. They are constructs for analytical purposes, attempts to understand the reality of older women's circumstances in order, perhaps, to change them, and are not intended to fully characterize any individual.

A summary of the types follows.

1. *Nurturers*, women seen by themselves and society primarily as caregivers of others—homemakers, mothers, grandmothers, volunteers, and workers in caring occupations and in other jobs where they support and help or nurture others.

2. *Unutilized nurturers*, who served in nurturing roles that no longer exist for them.

3. *Reengaged nurturers*, such as women who return to school to become teachers or social workers, or who take nurturing paid or volunteer jobs.

4. *Chum networkers and recreation-oriented women*, who may have family or work but derive their chief satisfaction from their friendships or leisure activities.

5. *Careerists*, employed and unemployed women who, though they might have families, find their primary identity in paid work. The women's movement, changes in the economy, and higher divorce rates mean that now there are more careerists among older women. However, careerist older women continue to face major obstacles. Age discrimination is stronger with each year of a woman's life. Also, many older women abandon careers to care for disabled spouses or elderly parents, thus redefining themselves as nurturers.

6. *Seekers*, women in transition looking for something to change their frequently unsatisfying lives. There are positive kinds of seeking, such as gaining a late education, finding a religion, or work. However, seeking may allow an older woman to be exploited.

7. *Faded beauties*, women who are socialized to think their only value is in their appearance, and thus dedicate themselves to mourning their lost youthful appearance or trying to preserve it.

8. *Illness-oriented women*, unhappy older women, who, in the absence of good roles, become hypochondriacs, seeking from healers the attention they cannot get elsewhere. In seeking cures for aging bodies, they seek selves more acceptable to society. They, or their insurers, pay for unneeded medical treatment because of the lack of meaningful roles.

9. *Escapists and isolates*, women who escape from loneliness, pain, or depression with drugs or alcohol. They are often abetted in drug dependency by physicians unequipped or unwilling to help with life issues.

10. *Advocates and assertive older women* who organize and work to make society better for themselves, for other older women, and for many different groups.

HOW CAN OLDER WOMEN'S ROLES BE CHANGED?

One way to move beyond our current conceptions of older women's place in society is to investigate the abilities that older women possess and what their preferences are. Another approach is to start by identifying the unmet needs of our aging society. What services and products could be provided by older women? Of course, one could simply say that, contrary to sexist and ageist stereotypes, older women are as capable as any other adults of productive activity of all kinds, with the possible exception of some extremely taxing physical labor. The intention here, though, is to draw upon observations of the roles many older women currently fulfill to suggest ways to extend, formalize, redirect, and expand these skills to better serve both older women and the entire aging society. Before suggesting new roles, though, it is useful to briefly consider the process of role-change itself.

There are two related ways in which older women's roles, or any roles, my be changed. The first is through self-change by the individual, and the second is through social policy interventions and institutional and organizational reforms.[1] Individual change may be facilitated by education, shared-strategy groups, self-help books, and/or therapists, friends, and significant others, although in some cases older women can be hurt rather than helped if the advisers are incompetent, unethical, or uninformed.[2] However, individual change, one by one or even in small groups, is no substitute for providing the societal opportunities that open up new roles to older women as a class. This can only be accomplished by public policy.

Combining Individual Effort and Societal Opportunity

Figure 8.3 models the possible interactions between individuals and society to bring about role change for older women. (Of course, real situations are more complex than this model.) In situation 1 the combination of both individual effort and societal opportunity results in a good outcome: new roles. In situation 2 the individual may be impeded by not getting support such as therapy, education (including basic literacy training, in some cases), language translation (in the case of immigrants), or even something as basic as transportation. (In some cities, public transportation can be unsafe, frightening, or even physically inaccessible for older women. Rural and suburban areas often lack public transportation altogether.) Because of poverty, older women may also lack essential items such as eyeglasses, hearing aids, or even good clothes. Without these fundamental assets, older women are unavailable for societal opportunities.

In situation 3, some assertive individuals may—with luck and better resources and contacts—win the limited good roles available to older women, but the losers will feel invalidated or unworthy. In this situation, the competition for roles will prevent older women from joining together and supporting each other. In situation 4, the individual may be able to change herself, only to find a lack of opportunities to practice her new role. The individual may then become frustrated and angry and even adopt the negative role of an escapist or

Figure 8.3 COMPONENTS OF ROLE CHANGE AND SOCIETAL OPPORTUNITY

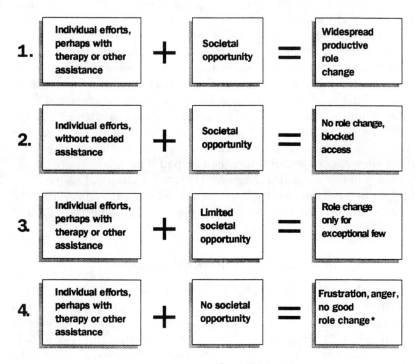

1. | Individual efforts, perhaps with therapy or other assistance | **+** | Societal opportunity | **=** | Widespread productive role change |

2. | Individual efforts, without needed assistance | **+** | Societal opportunity | **=** | No role change, blocked access |

3. | Individual efforts, perhaps with therapy or other assistance | **+** | Limited societal opportunity | **=** | Role change only for exceptional few |

4. | Individual efforts, perhaps with therapy or other assistance | **+** | No societal opportunity | **=** | Frustration, anger, no good role change* |

*Some individuals may become organizers for social change.

Components of Societal Opportunity:

☐ Job training and counseling
☐ Jobs—paid and volunteer
☐ Recognition and rewards for achievement
☐ Leadership slots in various societal structures
☐ Valued status assigned to group

illness-oriented woman. Some individuals, though, may become advocates for social change, organizing others who share their plight.

Figure 8.3 clarifies the importance of combining societal opportunities—in the form of public programs—with individual initiatives to bring about successful role change. To effectively direct resources—both public and individual—it is necessary to examine how some existing roles frequently played by older women might be improved and expanded.

Building on Current Roles

Role expansion begins with a recognition and reevaluation of the work older women currently perform, much of which has been overlooked and undervalued. Many invisible roles that older women play may seem trivial, but collectively they have a major impact and would be missed if older women suddenly stopped performing them.

The friendship roles of older women, for example, are a prime source of satisfaction to them and the society. Older women play important roles in comforting the ill and bereaved. They give measurable aid to their families and pass on history and values to grandchildren and great-grandchildren. They are the "kin keepers," as Hagestad (1986) has pointed out, sometimes creating the focal point for families. They remember birthdays. In some cases, these roles could be extended and formalized to increase their effectiveness in society and to bring older women greater rewards—in terms of economic security and social status as well as personal satisfaction.

Older women's roles in religious organizations often exemplify both the limitations and lack of recognition women encounter and their potential for effective contribution. Recently, some older women have developed vocations late in life as ministers and rabbis or in religious education. A few older women have taken national leadership roles in their denominations. However, patriarchy is very strong in many religions. Too often, older women are relegated to serving roles, providing refreshments and visiting the sick, without having power and decision-making roles. Black women have pioneered in this area, through their leadership in churches and church-based social and political movements, and could provide good models and trainers for white women.

Several years ago I conducted a multidenominational workshop for clergy and lay leaders on empowering the elderly population. Participants were asked to write on one index card what their churches, temples, and other religious groups did for older people and on a second card what the older people did for the religious groups. The cards listing what the old received were filled; however, the cards listing what the old contributed were very sparsely marked, citing mainly attendance, monetary contributions, and devotion.

This was another instance in which old people, including older women, were undervalued with many of their contributions going unrecognized and their abilities unutilized. In most religious denominations in this country, older women have raised money, sung in the chorus, cooked, worked on committees, and provided services to congregants in need. Churches and national religious organizations could and should create paid jobs as well as volunteer ones. Given that churches are a galvanizing force for many older people, such groups could make a significant contribution in this area.

Gerontologists Birren and Deutchman (1991) have listed some of the standard roles that older people currently fill, including "mentor, consultant, confidant, volunteer, historian, disseminator of the family legacy, grandparent or great-grandparent, and second- or third-career member in the work force." In the near future, how might older women build on familiar roles and develop new ways to participate in society? Considering the needs of our aging society, what enlarged roles can older women play? What kinds of training and resocialization are necessary?

RESOCIALIZATION AND EDUCATION FOR OLDER WOMEN

Although future cohorts of older women will reflect the increasing educational levels of American women today, many of today's older women and those of the near future could benefit from additional education to help them contribute productively and avoid dependency. With students of traditional age decreasing in numbers, colleges are welcoming continuing education students, but there is little financial aid available for them. After World War II, the GI Bill provided veterans an opportunity for higher education. The federal government, perhaps through the Women's Bureau of the Department of Labor, or the Department of Education, might consider administering a "W.R. Bill" (for Women Returning to Education). This would be an excellent investment in the productivity of long-lived women in an aging society.

It could be argued that public or philanthropic funding for older women's reeducation is inappropriate and unfair at a time when financial aid for young students is shrinking. Yet, it is also unfair to deny older women the education they missed while devoting themselves to bearing and rearing the young. Also, as already pointed out, it is very expensive for society to support a large and growing group of people whose abilities are not being utilized. Furthermore, people who are educated at late ages can be especially creative in approaching social problems ("Creativity in Later Life" 1991). There is an increase, not a decline, in the later years, in the ability to conceptualize and understand, though there is a decrease in rote learning ability (Atchley 1988). Without infused creativity, the United States is in danger of stagnation, as evidenced by the economic recession and the nation's declining educational, industrial, and healthcare positions relative to other countries. With higher education, some older women could use their wisdom, experience, and dedication to become problem-solvers in the near future.

Short-term motivation and education could be provided for workforce reentry and voluntary public service through a nationwide network modeled, for example, on the Elderhostel continuing education program. Elderhostels nationwide and abroad are filled with students, the majority of whom are older women, eager to learn. In the future, hostel programs could be tailored to direct older women into paid and voluntary public service. Many older women have expertise from their past work, in or outside the home, and from their avocations. "Service Hostels" might, for instance, give these women the teaching skills necessary to share their knowledge with youngsters in school settings or YWCAs. Similarly, older women could learn the skills needed to teach reading to America's illiterates or English as a second language to immigrants. Perhaps there could also be "Advocacy Hostels" where older women could learn the skills of community organizing and lobbying. "Leadership Hostels" could likewise prepare them to run for school committees or other elective offices. In this regard, a few older women have been successful candidates for state legislative, mayoral, gubernatorial, and other offices. Others have played important, though less visible, roles in political parties at the local and national levels. However, more older women need to capitalize on their political abilities by both running for office and supporting the campaigns of their peers. Legislators should also consider hiring older women as interns and legislative aides rather than only young persons just out of school.

At the grassroots level, older women often need encouragement and training to give them self-confidence and organizational skills, as well as to overcome excessive humility and internalized stereotypes of helplessness. Organizations like the League of Women Voters provide good training to women who wish to affect government at various levels. The National Association for the Advancement of Colored People (NAACP) and the Urban League have also long used the talents of older women, but even more older women need to be trained, especially for work on minority issues. Able women in nursing homes should be included in political efforts as the phone campaigners and letter writers. Indeed, the most important role for older women might be in international politics; older women's roles as peacemakers should be expanded and intensified.

Much of the remainder of this chapter speculates on specific productive work that large numbers of older women might perform in the next 15 years or so. Again, it should be stressed that the intent here is not to suggest that older women should be limited to the roles described. As previously stated, individually, older women have as many different talents, skills, and backgrounds as members of any other population group in the United States, and are able to make all kinds of productive contributions, large and small. In some cases, women have made a successful transition late in life to nontraditional jobs (for example, with training, older women who thought they had no mechanical aptitude have become manually and technically skilled).[3] However, the roles suggested here focus mainly on applying the skills many older women have acquired in performing traditional roles in the past to meet the demand for care created by growing numbers of disabled very elderly people and the children of the "baby-boom echo" generation.

In our aging society, the volunteer work of older women will be more important than ever, but paid work opportunities will also be necessary if large numbers of older women are to avoid poverty or near-poverty. Workers over the age of 65 could earn $10,200 in 1992 without affecting their Social Security benefits, and those between ages 62 and 65 somewhat smaller amounts. Those over age 70 can have unlimited earnings without losing Social Security dollars. Older women who are economically secure may get personal gratification from volunteer work, if its significance is recognized. However, stipends or part-time wages are necessary for older women who are not well off financially.

CAREGIVING AND EDUCATIONAL ROLES WITH YOUTH, FAMILIES, ELDERS, AND THE ILL

As previous chapters in this book make clear, there is a crisis in this country's system of dependent care and a need for better and more widespread educational opportunities. Older women could certainly expand their productive roles in both these areas.

Participation in Public Education

Younger age groups now constitute a smaller proportion of our population. This makes it all the more crucial that all of our children be well educated. We will need all of them in the labor force, as taxpayers, and as competent government workers and leaders. Already too many young people are unemployable because they are uneducated or functionally illiterate. Trained older women, with their sense of mission and caring for the young, could help to transform public education. They could be especially valuable in our frequently over-crowded classrooms, working with bright children or with those at risk of failure or of dropping out. Some older women have volunteered successfully in public schools, but many need to be paid for their work. Far better to have intelligent older women in such important, child-saving jobs, than unemployed or in menial, and demeaning, jobs. Minority older women would be especially valuable as teachers' aides in city schools with high proportions of minority students. But such women need training—a program and funding challenge for schools of education.

More older women could also work in higher education as teachers and administrators, as well as in supplementary roles. For example, years ago, older women were often employed as housemothers in dor-mitories. With the growth of graduate education, most such jobs have gone to graduate students who, busy with their own study and lives, are not really able to support and nurture undergraduates. Perhaps we should consider restoring the dorm adviser role to older women. Contrary to the stereotype of the naive little old lady, older women are as likely to be sophisticated as young people. With their long experi-ence, they are often quite familiar with many of the problems young people face, such as drug and liquor consumption, alienation, and anorexia. The dorm director job would also provide housing for some older women who cannot afford to maintain houses or rent suitable apartments.

Older women could also play leadership roles in higher education, a dream deferred for many because of family responsibilities. For example, in 1991 two older Quaker women in Burlington, Vt., had the courage to found an innovative college, Ovum Pacis: The Women's International Peace University. One of the founders, Alice Wiser, was in her 50s in 1990 when she received her doctorate in social psychol-ogy. Her colleague, Marcia Mason, received her master's degree in her mid-50s, writing on "How to Found, Develop, and Manage a Woman's Peace University from a Feminist Perspective." Not all older women are so ambitious in their efforts to lead education, but many do serve as local school committee members and as college trustees, and more should.

Helping Families and Individuals

Older women interested in nurturing roles can also help troubled families in numerous ways. Researchers at the Stone Center for Developmental Research and Services at Wellesley College, Wellesley, Mass., have identified mothers who are likely candidates for depression and put them in touch with peers who serve as confidants (Genero, Miller, and Angiollilo 1991). Many older women without graduate degrees in social work serve as case aides or bachelor's level social workers, and more could do so if positions were available, and funded.

Work-force support services could also be provided to families. Young working parents' time is often consumed shopping. Stores could employ older women to take telephone or written orders from young families, select the food, and arrange to have it delivered. Older women might also be paid to take children to appointments or to shop for clothes. They could also staff homelike afterschool centers; not enough such facilities exist to serve all the children who need them.

Older women—including some who live in nursing homes—are being used as volunteer telephone contacts for latchkey children. These women can become very important to children left alone. The volunteers get great satisfaction from this work, but low-income elders would also benefit if these jobs were stipended, along the lines of the Foster Grandparent program.

Older women could also lead innovative housing projects, helping young families as well as themselves. Many people cannot afford single-family homes. Other families who live in their own dwellings may be isolated from the support they need. The "cohousing" movement is just beginning in this country, although European countries have been using this shared housing model for some time. In cohousing, a group of would-be homeowners get together, find a site, and build an affordable nonprofit housing development that includes complete residences for individuals and families and also facilities shared by the community (McCamant and Durrett 1991). Such communities could allow older women who live alone (over 40 percent of those aged 65 and over now do) to live in their own homes longer and to be with other people, including children whom they may nurture. In these settings, younger people could get to know and value older women who become "extended family."

Healthcare Roles

Older women could also help fill in some of the gaps in services in the U.S. healthcare system. In this era of specialists, patients must often manage their healthcare at a time when they are least able to function. At the same time, healthcare providers often do not have the time to communicate with or listen to patients. Bright older women could be trained as liaisons between patients and healthcare professionals. They could accompany people to medical appointments, take notes for them, and intervene when people are not attended to properly. Volunteer programs that exist in some states to provide information to recipients of Medicare and other elder health insurance could be expanded. Older women who become expert in the complexities of health insurance could be paid to help younger people, including those for whom English is a second language.

HUMANIZING NURSING HOMES

The chief complaint about nursing "homes" is that they are not homelike. Would it be possible for older women, perhaps trained in the "Leadership Hostels" described earlier, to become paid or volunteer advisers to those who construct and manage nursing homes? Women who have managed homes know how to make places comfortable and attractive. Perhaps an organization concerned with better nursing home construction and management could fund a program in which older women develop ways to transform American nursing homes into friendly places, rather than places that are feared.[4] Of course, not all older women have the energy or time for leadership. Just visiting a person in a nursing home who may not have relatives can be an important role; people visited regularly generally get better staff services.

ROLES IN MENTAL HEALTHCARE

The treatment, nontreatment, and maltreatment of women's mental health is a matter of growing concern.[5] Twice as many women as men are treated for depression in the United States, and much of that results from societal injury, not from individual pathology.

Schools of social work, nursing schools, psychology departments at universities, and other training institutions might consider intensive but short-term training for older women to work in special or traditional roles in the mental health system. Perhaps this could be funded, as a trial project, by the National Institute of Mental Health, the Administration on Aging, the National Institute on Aging, and the Veterans Administration. Like physician's assistants or nurse practitioners, these women could provide some basic services and consult with doctors. This would increase access and cut costs in the crisis-ridden mental healthcare system.

It might be argued that people should have the care of top professionals when they need mental health services, but the truth is that now they often get no care at all or only perfunctory attention. Caring older women with some training could help fill the gap. Actually, in earlier times, before professionalization, older women provided a good deal of informal mental healthcare for extended families and neighbors. Older women who speak languages other than English could also be very helpful in working with recent immigrants who need care. If bilingual, they could interface with professional care providers also.

Community Service

In today's urban and suburban communities, many people do not know their neighbors and rarely call on them for help. Older women raised under an ethic of responsibility for others might well serve as models for more caring community relationships. Older women often feel frustrated that they cannot share their knowledge. In one of Boston's poor urban neighborhoods, elderly residents were surveyed to see if they would like to help their neighbors. Almost everyone said yes, yet this was in a neighborhood thought to be typically urban and uncaring (personal communication with Marjorie Glassman, former director of elder services for Family Service of Greater Boston, 1991).

A method developed by communities to increase children's safety as they walk between home and school might serve as a model for tapping older women's wisdom and understanding. In the children's safety model, certain homes are designated as "safety zones" by a large card in the house window. Perhaps willing older women in the neighborhood could also be identified as confidantes for insecure adolescents, young parents, or lonely people. However, because older women are often justifiably afraid of opening their doors to strangers, the women might be available anonymously through the phone lines, or they could have hours in a safe place such as local YWCA, community center, or senior center. Adolescents who will not confide in parents will sometimes talk with grandparents, but many do not have grandparents nearby. Older women could help fill this gap.

By the same token, perhaps a foundation could be enlisted to provide stipends to an "Older Woman Neighborhood Service Corps," in which women would use their nurturing, organizing, and other skills to assist their neighbors with information, services, and advice. With training, for example, information could be provided on AIDS and sexuality to people of all ages, including peers.

Older women's roles as caregivers to the elderly have been discussed and documented throughout this volume, and especially in chapter

3, by Foster and Brizius. Both eldercare and child-care workers in this society are paid badly and most of these workers are women. To work in these fields, unless one is independently wealthy, guarantees poverty in old age. Paid caregivers, including nurse's aides and assistants in nursing homes and paid home-health aides and homemakers for the aged, should be given more dignity and security in their roles, and wages for these jobs should be raised. Minority women and recent immigrants are often utilized in these jobs without receiving any real skill training or education. Better training is essential for the well-being of both workers and care recipients, and should be financed by employers or government agencies.

Many older women are earning a living by offering day care to the children of working parents. Often these older women's homes and backgrounds do not meet the standards for licensure or insurance. Yet, such care is all that is available to many working mothers who cannot afford child care in licensed, inspected, insured facilities. Ways could be investigated to provide such caregivers with free training and interest-free loans or outright subsidies to upgrade their establishments.

New Roles in Business

Contrary to current stereotypes, older women are not only nurturers. Indeed, many continue to fulfill caregiving roles in their personal lives and would rather assume a different type of role in the extra time they have available. They can and do perform well in administrative and technical positions. Certainly the corporate sector should be hiring older women for existing jobs. Women in their 60s, 70s, and beyond, as well as midlife women, can be successfully employed in many different jobs. By the year 2000, workers aged 55 to 64 will be the fastest-growing segment of the labor force. Older workers have been shown to be loyal and reliable and to have low absenteeism. They also continue to contribute to the Social Security fund.

In some communities, employment agencies exist that specialize in older workers. Older women could found more such agencies, thus creating jobs for themselves and promoting employment for their peers.[6]

In our society, workers previously considered inappropriate for certain jobs can suddenly be deemed appropriate if a need for them becomes apparent. For example, the fast-food industry was operated for a long time mainly with very young people, especially teenagers working after school. When changing demographics recently made fewer adolescent workers available, this industry "discovered" senior citizens. Older women may become desirable employees when specific labor shortages emerge, but they also need job developers and advocates who can identify what jobs they might do, as well as point out that age discrimination is illegal.

THE GROWING ELDER MARKET

One way that jobs might be developed for older women is to consider how innovative businesses might serve the growing market of older consumers. Several women have started businesses that offer group vacations for the fast-growing population of older women who live alone.[7] Older women who are not themselves entrepreneurial could become consultants to businesses interested in cashing in on the elder market. For instance, businesses could pay panels of older women to advise them on new ways to market developing technologies to the elderly. In addition, the fashion and beauty industry could train and employ more older women as product development consultants and sales representatives.

Businesses could also employ older women to fill in temporarily or part-time in busy departments or departments where there are absentees. Many older women now perform this kind of work through temporary-employment agencies, but corporations should consider hiring back their own retired workers who have knowledge of their operations (Travelers Insurance Company of Hartford, Conn., already has such a program). The advantage for older women is that they would have a familiar, central workplace, which temporary agencies usually cannot provide. Some companies could also benefit by recruiting a group of older women to train in child care and simple illness procedures so that these women could be sent to care for an employee's sick child or elderly parent, thus allowing the employee to come to work.

Manufacturers might support sheltered workshops where frail older women who could not be employed under regular conditions could count, inspect, or assemble products, or do other tasks for which they would be paid minimum wage or less. Such sheltered workshops would give people who cannot work in regular employment pride, companionship, structure, and needed money. Older women could manage these workshops. Such programs would combine philanthropy and self-interest, creating goodwill for sponsors.

Older women's frequent focus on health issues could be turned into a benefit for them and society by employing them, after training, as environmental aides. Chavkin (1984) and others have warned about environmental hazards in the workplace (Massachusetts Coalition 1983). Corporations could train and employ older women to discover these hazards before illness costs the companies in absenteeism, loss of good employees, and lawsuits. Perhaps the U.S. Environmental Protection Agency (EPA) might consider training older women to supplement its forces of inspectors.

Another area in which older women could be productively employed relates to home safety. Elderly people often fall in their own homes, sometimes incurring injuries that lead to institutionalization. This costs Medicare, Medicaid, and private insurers a growing amount as the population of the frail elderly continues to expand. Perhaps the American Home Economics Association, in cooperation with other agencies and educational associations, might train "home-hazard checkers." Contracts and grants could come from the EPA, the Women's Bureau of the U.S. Department of Labor, the National Institutes of Health, medical foundations, and the philanthropic sector. Manufacturers of products that can be hazardous if misused might help fund the training and employment of women to help consumers use such products safely. Older environmental spokespersons could speak to women's organizations and at senior centers, and provide consultation to individual householders.

Advisory Roles

With training, older women could also play health education roles in business, by giving lunch-hour talks on, for instance, diet, exercise, common prescription drugs, over-the-counter drugs, preventive healthcare, and long-term care services. Women who have been successful family caregivers could give talks on parenting problems and advice on elder care. Continuing education programs, county extension services, and national organizations such as the National Association of Social Workers or the American Public Health Association might sponsor training with funding from various sources.

Many older women have started small businesses, and more could do so successfully with some support services. The failure rate for small businesses is high, so older women need good counsel. The Service Corps of Retired Executives (SCORE), sponsored by the U.S. Small Business Administration, has branches in many areas and can offer advice. Retired women with executive experience are being recruited to serve in SCORE. In some areas there are helpful associations of women who are small business owners, such as NEWBO—

New England Women Business Owners, which runs conferences. For experienced older women, such mentoring provides satisfaction.

ROLES IN THE MEDIA

The media might also employ more older women. How long will it take for television to acknowledge that old women are wise, their faces showing the lines of experience? America will have come of age when we see 60- and 70-year-old anchorwomen, just as we now have venerable male broadcasters. Cable television, which is required to have local public service stations, has been utilizing older women as volunteer hosts, camerapersons, and technicians. Perhaps in the future the paying television industry will recognize their talents. Older actresses such as Katherine Hepburn, Olympia Dukakis, and Jessica Tandy have shown that older women can be portrayed in films without condescension or ridicule. As a final example, radio stations in many parts of the country have call-in shows where hosts or advisers listen and talk with callers from the broadcast audience. Older women often call in to these shows, but they are rarely the hosts or advisers. Articulate older women could host some of these programs, giving callers the benefit of their experience. Because television, films, radio, and print media influence public perceptions, they should be pioneers in utilizing the talents of older women and portraying them accurately and favorably. In the process, the overall image of older women would be enhanced.

SOME CONCLUSIONS ABOUT OLDER WOMEN'S EXPANDING ROLES

Population aging provides both significant opportunities and a great necessity to add older women's productive power to the mainstream of American society. The question is whether or not prejudice against older women will continue to blind employers, social planners, and policymakers to this potential human resource. Will the knowledge, skills, commitment, and concern of older women be utilized to fill pressing social needs, or will older women continue to suffer bad press and bad times? Will society realize that it is not only inhumane but financially disastrous to make older women obsolete and unutilized as their numbers continue to expand and their longevity increases? Programs such as RSVP (Retired Senior Volunteer Program) and Seniors in Community Service have already demonstrated that older people's skills can be utilized. Pioneering employers have found older women to be a good work force. But these are first steps in a situation calling for innovative thinking, bold strategizing, and model programs. Our best policymakers, social planners, and program developers should consider the expansion of older women's roles a priority. This chapter has only scratched the surface of older women's current and future potential.

To help older women become independent is to vitalize rather than drain society. Empowering older women may also have unforeseen benefits. Just as aging women have shown surprising ingenuity in weaving lives for themselves despite adversity, they may be able to strengthen our unraveling social fabric. To realize such a possibility, many planners will need to think creatively, policymakers will need to act on their growing understanding of the aging society's changing needs, and older women themselves will need to surpass the limits of obsolete and narrow roles. Given that the social integration of long-lived women is a worldwide problem, we should also study models from other countries.[8]

THE CONTEXT FOR FUTURE POLICY CHANGE

Prediction is always dangerous, but it seems quite realistic to be pessimistic regarding the near future for older women. The reluctance of federal and state leaders—and of taxpayers—to fund public programs, combined with increasing numbers of older women and the persistence of negative stereotypes, are powerful deterrents to social policies that would enhance older women's roles.

True, in the future, many more older women will have had higher education and careers other than homemaking, and thus may be more self-sufficient economically. However, research has demonstrated that more education for women does not equate with pay equity with men. The "glass ceiling" that blocks opportunity and mobility for younger women is even lower for older women, meaning continued lower wages and diminished job opportunity in later years. Further, women are often resented for their achievements, especially in these times of shrinking economic opportunities. In recessions, jobs that older women might hold are taken by young and older men who might have eschewed these jobs in better times.

Productive life for older women is contingent on good healthcare. Under our nation's present system, healthcare is in short supply for women who are not rich. Women have more chronic late-life illnesses than do men, and their well-being and productivity could be drastically and disproportionately affected by the current trend toward medical rationing. Moreover, the growing social approbation for suicide, assisted or self-performed, may be a subtle part of a rationing response to the aging trend. Many old women of low self-esteem, responsive to public sentiment that they are burdens, have told me that they believe they ought to die so that their children can have their money or homes or not be burdened with their care. Meanwhile, for older women who care for frail parents or spouses, relief and support services are being cut, making impoverishment and exhaustion that much more likely to continue.

Women with more education may indeed be better advocates for themselves and peers, but if the pie of opportunity gets smaller and negative images of older women persist, advocacy can be interpreted by critics as scolding and nagging, reinforcing existing canards.

Housing is a growing problem. As the homeless population increases, the number of old women in it increases, and there are no signs that the government will subsidize more low-cost housing. Luxury profit-making retirement complexes grow, but they are beyond the means of most older women alone, while those who do live in them are often resented by young people and middle-aged families struggling in hard economic times.

A more optimistic view might predict that socially aware elders will form a coalition with the disenfranchised young, as the Gray Panthers have hoped to do, to turn society around. That would require a major shift in social values, but such shifts do sometimes occur. One hopeful view is being fostered by psychiatrist Jean Baker Miller and her colleagues at the Stone Center for Developmental Research and Services at Wellesley College. These researchers postulate that women's predilection for defining the self in interrelationship and through human connection may provide a better social model than the typically individualistic and competitive model of male socialization (Jordan et al. 1991; Miller 1976). Dr. Miller developed her theory as an older woman. Perhaps her work presages that of other older women whose thinking in the future may revolutionize our view of reciprocal human interaction in an interdependent, caring—and aging—society.

Notes

I would like to thank Jessie Allen for her excellent suggestions and guidance in writing this chapter. It evolved as a collaborative process with her.

1. *Be an Outrageous Older Woman* (Jacobs 1991), presented the following schema for self-change, using an individualistic approach. "Diggers-out," "successful self-copers," or "assisted copers" generally experience eight phases in the process of change: (1) involuntary loss, such as widowhood, or voluntary rejection of the old identity, such as initiated divorce; (2) mourning of the old identity; (3) seeking models or mentors for the new identity; (4) developing and implementing strategies for identity change; (5) seeking confirmation of the new identity by others and self; (6) resisting return to the old identity; (7) gaining increasing comfort and even joy in the new identity; (8) sometimes repeating the process all over as new life contingencies require still more identity change. "Diggers in" or "noncopers" may not change, because there are no perceived or available resources to help bring such change about, or because there is investment or safety (even painful safety) in the old role.

2. A group curriculum is provided in the manual, *Older Women Surviving and Thriving* (Jacobs 1987). Facing Our Future groups are described in the manual by Deren (1985). Useful self-help books for older women include *Ourselves Growing Older*, by Doress, Siegal, and the Midlife and Older Women Book Project (1987); *Growing Older, Getting Better*, by Porcino (1983); and *Be an Outrageous Older Woman*, by Jacobs (1991).

3. In 1988, the American Association of Retired Persons (AARP), in cooperation with the National Displaced Homemakers Network (NDHN), prepared *Partners in Change*, a video portraying late-life women in nontraditional jobs and traditional work. Also available from the AARP is the bimonthly publication *Working Age*, covering the latest employment facts and demographic trends affecting employees aged 50 and over (AARP Worker Equity Department, 601 E Street, NW, Washington, DC 20049). The NDHN, at 1411 K Street, NW, Suite 930, Washington, DC 20005, can connect employers with local programs in their communities.

4. In Arlington, Mass., a pioneering program, Living is for the Elderly (LIFE), provides advocacy training for nursing home residents and also conducts workshops that help them deal with their situations.

5. In June 1989, as one of five members of the AARP national task force on aging and mental health, I attended a congressional forum on mental health and aging, sponsored by the AARP, the American Psychological Association, and the American Psychiatric Association. Participants pointed to the great need for better mental health services for older Americans in general and older women in particular.

6. A national network of employment agencies specifically for older people includes Operation ABLE in Boston, Detroit, Chicago, Little Rock, Ark., and Lincoln, Neb.; the Vermont Association for Training in St. Albans; and Career Encore in Los Angeles. In California, Jane Pond, of Irvine, started Adult Careers, an agency that has placed more than 3,000 older adults in 1,400 local companies (American Association of Retired Persons 1991).

7. Judy Rowe, herself an older woman, recently started North Country Journeys for Women Over 40, in Shelburne, Vt.

8. *Empowering Older Women: Cross-Cultural Views* (Chaney 1990), published by the Women's Initiative of the AARP in cooperation with the International Federation of Aging, includes selections from workshops at the "Conference on Coping with Social Change Programs that Work," held in Acapulco in June 1989, and from the "Conference of the Association of Women in Development," held in Washington, D.C., in 1989.

References

American Association of Retired Persons. 1991. *Bulletin,* (Summer). Washington, D.C.: Author.

Atchley, Robert. 1988. *Social Forces and Aging.* Belmont, Calif.: Wadsworth.

Binstock, Robert H. 1972. "Interest Group Liberalism and the Politics of Aging." *Gerontologist* 12: 265–80.

Birren, James, and Donna E. Deutchman. 1991. *Guiding Autobiography Groups for Older Adults.* Baltimore, Md., and London: Johns Hopkins University Press.

Chaney, Elsa M, ed. 1990. *Empowering Older Women: Cross-Cultural Views.* Washington, D.C.: American Association of Retired Persons, in cooperation with International Federation on Aging.

Chavkin, Wendy, M.D. 1984. *Double Exposure: Women's Health Hazards on the Job and at Home.* New York: Monthly Review Press.

"Creativity in Later Life." 1991. *Generations* (Journal of American Society on Aging, San Francisco) 15 (2, Spring).

Deren, Jane M. 1985. *Facing Our Future.* Washington, D.C.: National Council on the Aging.

Doress, Paula Brown, Diana Laskin Siegal, and the Midlife and Older Women Book Project. 1987. *Ourselves Growing Older.* New York: Simon & Schuster, Touchstone Books.

Ferguson, Kathy. 1991. In *Women's Studies Encyclopedia,* vol. 1, edited by Helen Tierney (266–67). New York: Peter Bedrick Books.

Genero, N., Jean Baker Miller, and Dea N. Angiollilo. 1991. "Peer Support in High-Risk Mothers of Young Children. A Three-Year Study Funded by the Federal Maternal and Child Health Bureau and the Stone Center." Wellesley, Mass.: Wellesley College.

Hagestad, Gunhild. 1986. "The Family: Women and Grandparents as Kin Keepers." In *Our Aging Society: Paradox and Promise,* New York: W. W. Norton & Co.

Healey, Shevy. 1990. "Listen to the Old Women." Session presentation at annual meeting of the National Women's Studies Association, Dayton, Ohio,

Jacobs, Ruth Harriet. 1979. *Life after Youth: Female, Forty What Next?* Boston: Beacon Press.

———. 1987. *Older Women Surviving and Thriving: A Manual for Group Leaders.* Milwaukee, Wis.: Family Service America.

———. 1991. *Be an Outrageous Older Woman: A R.A.S.P.* [Remarkable Aging Smart Person]. Manchester, Conn.: K.I.T. Press.

Jordan, Judith, Alexandra G. Kaplan, Jean Baker Miller, Irene P. Stiver, and Janet L. Surrey. 1991. *Women's Growth in Connection: Writings from the Stone Center.* New York and London: Guilford Press.

Macdonald, Barbara, with Cynthia Rich. 1983. *Look Me in the Eye: Old Women, Aging and Ageism.* San Francisco: Spinsters.

Massachusetts Coalition for Occupational Safety and Health and the Boston Women's Health Collective. 1983. *Our Jobs, Our Health: A Woman's Guide to Occupational Health and Safety.* Boston: Author.

McCamant, Kathryn, and Charles Durrett. 1991. "Building a Cohousing Community." *Co-op America Quarterly* (Spring); also in *Utne Reader* (May/June).

Miller, Jean Baker. 1976. *Toward a New Psychology of Women,* 1st ed. Boston: Beacon Press.

Pearson, Judy Cornelia. 1985. *Gender and Communication.* Dubuque, Iowa: William C. Brown.

Porcino, Jane. 1983. *Growing Older, Getting Better.* Reading, Mass.: Addison Wesley Publishing Co.

————. 1991. *Living Longer, Living Better. Adventures in Community Housing for Those in the Second Half of Life.* New York: Continuum Publishing.

Pratt, Henry J. 1976. *The Gray Lobby.* Chicago: University of Chicago Press.

Rosenthal, Evelyn, ed. 1990. *Women, Aging, and Ageism.* Binghamton, N.Y.: Haworth Press.

Chapter Nine

CARING WORK AND GENDER EQUITY IN AN AGING SOCIETY

Jessie Allen

From time to time social theorists have suggested that population aging might influence gender relations. As far back as the 1950s, Alva Myrdal and Viola Klein (1956: 13) pointed to extended life expectancy and decreasing family size as the two main forces pushing "the equality of women an essential step nearer to becoming a reality." Alice Rossi (1986) has speculated that an aging society may bring increased gender equity because, as she sees it, gender role differences are less pronounced later in life and because women, with their greater longevity, would be a growing majority in an aging population. In a more recent article, Annemette Sorensen (1991) has argued that changes in the life-course due to greater longevity, low fertility, and the gender gap in life expectancy will provide new opportunities to develop more equitable gender relations, but that these opportunities can only be realized if child care is no longer exclusively assigned to women. This chapter explores the possibility that another aspect of our aging society—the increasing demand for eldercare—may have complex implications for gender equity.

Without changes in societal attitudes and policies, the rising numbers of disabled elderly Americans who need care threaten to set back women's recent gains in social and economic equality. However, there are some characteristics of this new caregiving demand—especially in combination with women's increased labor-force participation—that, if recognized, could spark changes in all dependent care that would actually increase gender equity.

The discussion in this chapter centers on how different aspects of the demand for eldercare—and some policy responses to it—might tend to promote or obstruct the integration of all family care with paid employment and the distribution of caring work between women and men. Changes in the overall caregiving experience in an aging society are considered, along with some of the differences between child care and eldercare, in order to uncover possible openings for developing the integration and redistribution of caring work. This chapter concludes with a brief sketch of some gender equity implications of two frequently suggested policy responses to the growing eldercare demand.

The pressure of the aging trend is just beginning to be widely felt. This time of transition provides a unique opportunity to observe the ways in which current demographic trends undermine old assumptions about the nature and place of caring work in our society. Such observations could be crucial if we hope to redress long-standing gender inequities in dependent care and its interaction with women's work-force status.

DEPENDENT CARE, PAID EMPLOYMENT, AND GENDER EQUITY

Forty years ago, most dependent care—for children and for chronically disabled adults—was provided by unpaid women at home, and most women were not in the paid labor force. Today, most caring work is still done by women at home, even though women now make up nearly half the paid labor force. Incredibly, there have been no major public policy reforms regarding dependent care and no broad-based changes in labor-force schedules or structures in response to this enormous social and economic change.

The question of how women's continued caregiving roles affect their fortunes in the labor force is highly politicized. From one perspective, it is argued that in choosing to provide family care, women also choose to forgo educational opportunities, challenging work that requires and builds skills, and continuous full-time employment, with the rational consequence that they receive lower wages. The other side argues that women's clustering in lower-paid occupations and lower pay levels within occupations is virtually unconnected to their actual caregiving responsibilities. Rather, it is claimed, women's disadvantages in the labor force are the result of discriminatory attitudes on the part of employers who (wrongly) perceive that family care prevents women from being fully "committed" to high-quality paid employment and so shunt them into less desirable jobs and even deliberately create low-quality, low-productivity (low-cost) jobs with women in mind.

This chapter does not choose sides in this ongoing debate. Instead, the basic premise here is the more mundane observation that as long as most women are doing two jobs—one paid, one unpaid—while most men do just one job, for pay, men have an advantage in the world of paid work. Conversely, so long as women's position in the labor market is less favorable than men's, strong economic pressures reinforce the traditional assignment of unpaid caregiving work to women. One can argue about whether or not the current situation is a matter of choice—and about whose choice it is—but it is illogical to claim that an unpaid caregiver's work-force opportunities equal those of someone who does not provide care. Of course, work-force equity is not equivalent to gender equity. Still, now that most women and men are in the labor force throughout their adult lives, women's fortunes in the labor market are increasingly aligned with their overall social and economic power.

CHANGES IN CARING WORK IN AN AGING SOCIETY

How could there have been so little change over the past several decades in the distribution and accommodation of caring work while women's labor-force participation has increased so dramatically? Perhaps part of the answer is that for much of the time, birthrates were either falling or were fairly stable at unprecedentedly low levels. From 1960 to 1980, the number of children under age five was actually declining, so conceivably there was a general sense of harmony between large social trends (i.e., fewer young children needing care, more mothers in the work force—no matter how much conflict individual working parents and their employers might have felt). To be sure, during this period, the elderly population was already growing fast, but, possibly because the numbers of the very old were extremely small to begin with, Americans were somewhat slow to register the significance of this countertrend.

Without informed policy changes, the growing numbers of very elderly Americans only compound women's caregiving burden. In the coming decades the added caring work could slow women's progress toward a labor market position equal to that of men and pose a serious obstacle to achieving more equitable gender relations in our society. Studies have shown that many caregivers to the elderly reduce their hours of paid work or quit their jobs altogether to provide such care (Stone, Cafferata, and Sangl 1987). Women may sacrifice job earnings, health insurance, and pension coverage when they take on the job of caring for disabled elderly relatives. In the process, they become more vulnerable to impoverishment as they age, part of the reason women constitute three-quarters of the elderly poor.

Increases in the very elderly population both add to the total number of people who need care and create a demand for more different kinds of care. The aging trend means that there will be caregivers of many different ages—including the mothers of preschool children, middle-aged women with disabled parents, and very aged spousal caregivers. The growing prevalence of eldercare also means that caregiving practices are branching out from the central model of motherhood. The aging trend extends the period in a woman's life during which she can expect to be called upon to provide dependent care, it makes the timing of demands for care less predictable, and it adds to the ranks of primary caregivers a new group of men—the husbands of disabled elderly women. All of these effects could have ramifications for policy reforms that are needed to better integrate dependent care and workforce participation and for the distribution of dependent care among women and men.

A More Diverse Dependent Population

The change in dependent care in our aging society is not primarily one of quantity. Even by 2050, the overall "dependency ratio" (the number of people under age 20 and aged 65 and over per 100 people aged 20–64) will not quite reach the high levels of the 1960s, when the baby boom swelled the ranks of young children (U.S. Bureau of the Census 1989). The big difference is that instead of being over 80 percent children, the "dependent" population will be more than half elderly people, and will include an unprecedentedly high number of the oldest old. In the period from 1990 to 2010 there will be a doubling of the very elderly population (aged 85 and older), among whom disability is far more prevalent than in any other age group: nearly a quarter now require institutionalization (Rivlin and Wiener 1988: table I-1).

The very elderly today form a group that is about one-third the size of the youngest group (under age 5). However, assuming low fertility rates persist, by 2010 that proportion will rise to 60 percent, and by the middle of the next century, there will be more Americans aged 85 and over than children under the age of five. Thus, in the future, instead of a situation in which caring work is centered on children with a small additional proportion of disabled adults, the population that requires care will be nearly equally divided between the disabled elderly and very young children.

Age and Employment Status of Caregivers

The addition of large numbers of people caring for disabled elders should broaden the age range of providers of dependent care. Most eldercare providers themselves are middle-aged and elderly. One study estimates that about three-quarters of *potential* caregivers to the elderly (the sons, daughters, and spouses of disabled elders) are between the ages of 35 and 64, and 59 percent were under age 55. The likelihood of actually being a caregiver, however, increases with age up to age 75. Still, two-thirds of active eldercare providers are under age 65 (Stone and Kemper 1990). In contrast, with today's small family size and even despite the much-reported trend toward delayed childbearing, most mothers of preschool children are in their 20s and early 30s.[1]

Many caregivers of the disabled elderly and young parents are in the labor force, though people providing eldercare might be somewhat less likely to be employed. One evaluation has shown that about a third of people actually providing eldercare were employed and that another 9 percent had quit their jobs to provide care (Stone et al. 1987). In contrast, 59 percent of married women with children under age six and 74 percent of single mothers of children under age six were in the labor force in 1990. Stone and Kemper (1990) have estimated that about half of potential caregivers to the elderly—that is, spouses and children of disabled elders—work full-time.

In the future, the rise of full Social Security eligibility to age 67 should tend to increase the proportion of elder caregivers in the usual work-force ages. Even now their presence in the workplace is significant, though estimates vary widely, depending on definitions of disability and of what constitutes care—from 2 percent to 23 percent of the work force (Stone 1991). Stone and Kemper (1990) estimate that *potential* caregivers to the elderly constitute 9 percent of the full-time work force. By comparison, mothers with children under age 6 made up about 17 percent of full-time workers in 1987.[2]

It is important to keep in mind that the age differences at any given moment between the caregivers of children and of the elderly signify another kind of similarity over time. In many cases, the caregivers of young children one year will be eldercare providers at a later date; they are the same women at different points in their lives.

Extending the Period of Potential Caregiving

Clearly, a demand for eldercare typically occurs at a later—though sometimes overlapping—stage in a woman's life than the need to care for young children. Since most women continue to have children, and since they may also have to provide care to several different elderly relatives, potential caregiving demand now appears to be spreading over a longer period in women's lives. This would appear to reverse the long-term shrinkage—because of smaller family size and increased longevity—of the portion of a woman's life during which she may be called upon to provide dependent care.

In *Women's Two Roles*, written in the 1950s, Alva Myrdal and Viola Klein (1956) argue convincingly that, because of increasing longevity and lowered birthrates, the average proportion of a woman's life spent on nurturing dependent children has decreased dramatically, leaving more time for work-force participation after children are grown. They also point out that women's increasing chance of being widowed, due to the gender gap in life expectancy, is an additional reason for women to support themselves independently through paid employment. Finally, they identify married women as the greatest labor reserve available to compensate for the rising dependency ratios of an aging society.

The prescience of this early work on the social impact of population aging is striking, and the authors' predictions of further increases in women's labor-force participation have come to pass. Equally striking, however, is the convergence of three trends they did not foresee: further decreases in fertility that have slowed the growth of overall dependency ratios; dramatic declines in mortality at old ages, leading to widespread demand for care of disabled elderly family members; and very large increases in the labor-force participation of married mothers of young children. These last two factors combine to produce the increasing number of workers who are actual or potential caregivers for growing lengths of time while also being in the paid labor force. Thus, instead of compartmentalizing paid employment and unpaid caregiving in successive stages of women's lives, the aging trend has tended to overlap and intersperse these two kinds of work.

Another aspect of the expanded potential caregiving period seems noteworthy. That is, the increasing number of people—and workers—who must regard dependent care as something they perhaps look forward to, rather than as something they can put behind them fairly early in their careers. This is a considerable change from a situation in which one's caregiving duties were usually limited to the care of young children. Even those women who delay childbearing until their mid-30s, for example, might look forward to a full 20 years of employment from age 45 to 65, relatively free of intense child-care responsibilities. Not so with eldercare.

The extended period of potential care demand does not mean that most women will necessarily be providing care for longer periods. For some individuals this will indeed be the case, depending on the number of children they have, the number of older relatives who eventually require care, and the number of other potential caregivers available. Data do not exist to allow us to accurately estimate the lifetime chances of being called upon to provide unpaid eldercare, now or in the future, or to predict the average length of time people will devote to such care. Still, if the population projections are correct, and if most women continue to have children, it seems certain that the span of time during which a woman could be reasonably sure that she would *not* be called upon for care is virtually disappearing.

The reversal of the more-than-century-long compression of the potential caregiving proportion of women's lives is a profound social change. Little has been written, though, about the possible implications of this largely unforeseen development.

Caregiving by Choice and by Chance

The growing demand for eldercare creates changes in the duration and timing of caregiving. In addition, the assumption of eldercare duties differs from the decision to provide child care in ways that, if recognized, may help reshape traditional attitudes about the allocation and meaning of all caring work.

The view that childbearing—and by extension, childrearing—is primarily a matter of individual choice may have been gaining strength recently. For example, this attitude seems to underlie the recent decisions by two states to deny increased subsidies to mothers who give birth to additional children while on welfare. At the other end of the economic spectrum is the frequent portrayal of successful professional women with children as greedy individuals who "want it all." What these attitudes disregard is the clear need for a society to reproduce its population in order to sustain itself. Nevertheless, there is undoubtedly a sense in which parenthood is a personal choice.

In contrast, the need to care for a disabled relative arises from factors entirely outside the control of the person called upon to provide that care. One does not choose, for instance, to have a mother who gets Alzheimer's disease. If, in fact, a much greater portion of dependent care demand in the future is perceived to be the result of chance rather than choice, this may influence societal attitudes about

the responsibility of the community—and especially of employers—
to support caregivers. It may also tend to undermine the perception
that women's disadvantages in the labor force, including their lower
earnings, are primarily the result of their choice to provide family
care.

Diverging from the Motherhood Model

Traditionally, eldercare has been viewed as an offshoot of the central
caring role of a mother. This attitude persists today in the assumption
that women will "naturally" respond to the needs of disabled elderly
relatives. However, as eldercare moves from the margins to the center
of caring work, this view may be challenged.

If we recognize that a variety of eldercare relationships and situations are becoming increasingly "normal," it becomes harder to view
motherhood as the transcendent paradigm of all dependent care. This
could help alter a perspective that has worked from two directions at
once to limit the integration of family care and paid employment and
to block the redistribution of caring work between men and women.
The reluctance to view caring work as something that can be performed by both sexes equally well, given pragmatic adjustments in
workplace practices, is buttressed by deep-seated societal attitudes
equating caregiving with motherhood and identifying motherhood as
the natural vocation of women. As Nadine Taub (1985: 389–90) put
it, the "stereotypic qualities associated with childbearing and childrearing have been invoked to limit women's opportunities in the
workplace. At the same time, that view has prevented structuring the
workplace in a way that takes account of the actual difficulties experienced by women as a result of their assigned role."

It should furthermore be noted that in many ways, eldercare falls
outside the developmental, nurturing model of mothering. For example, some writers have stressed the critical difference that whereas a
young child grows toward independence, an elderly disabled person
typically becomes ever more dependent and eventually dies (Brody
1985).

Finally, the wide range of activities and relationships that eldercare
encompasses make it harder to conceive as variations on any single,
essential model. The situations in which "normal" eldercare occurs
vary greatly. For instance, the care recipient might live with the caregiver, independently, or in an institution. The intensity and duration
of care are also much more variable than is the basic, necessary care
for young children. Most importantly, perhaps, the relationships be-

tween caregiver and care recipient are more varied. Among unpaid, family caregivers, biological connection does not necessarily take precedence. Daughters-in-law, for instance, may provide care even when adult sons are present (Brody 1981).

Men as Caregivers

The vast majority of eldercare is provided by women, who make up 90 percent of paid caregivers and about three out of four unpaid family caregivers. However, this distribution obscures the interesting finding that when a disabled person has several close relatives who might provide care, it is not always a woman who provides the main source of care. Specifically, when a disabled person has a spouse—man or woman—that person is most likely to become the primary caregiver (Stone and Kemper 1990).

The fact that men usually die sooner than their typically younger and longer-lived wives means that a relatively small number of husbands actually become eldercare providers. Still, according to a study of the 1984 National Long-term Care Survey (Stone and Kemper 1990), husbands comprise 21 percent of primary caregivers. It seems likely that this regular assumption of primary caregiving work by men is a situation unique in history. That is, for the first time ever on a regular basis, a group of men are providing hands-on dependent care, not as surrogates for women but based on their own family relationship with the person who needs care. It would be interesting to find out more about the men who are fulfilling this new role—new, at least in the sense of something that is becoming a kind of social norm if not an altogether common situation. There may be significant patterns regarding their age, employment status, and the duration and type of care they provide. For instance, since more women get Alzheimer's disease, husband caregivers may be more likely to be caring for a person who suffers from this degenerative disorder (Kaye and Applegate 1991).

Recorded gender differences among eldercare providers may be deceptive. It has been reported, for instance, that women are more likely than men to provide the most personal kinds of care, such as bathing, dressing, and helping elders go to the toilet, while men generally do more instrumental tasks. However, we cannot conclude that this is true of husband caregivers in particular.

Interestingly, one examination of the 1982 National Long-term Care Survey found that a larger proportion of husbands (89 percent) reported doing household tasks because of a spouse's disability than did wives (74 percent). However, as the authors point out, this result may actually indicate that husbands are more likely to perceive any household work as out of the ordinary and related to care, whereas many wives may simply see such tasks as part of their normal gender-assigned role—regular housework rather than a part of caregiving per se (Stone et al. 1987). Such distinctions not only point to the importance of how survey questions are framed, but they suggest just how significant gender roles are for the meaning of caring work in a person's life. It should be of great interest for anyone concerned with gender equity and family structure to learn more about the growing group of husband caregivers—pioneers, if not volunteers, in the world of "women's work." Their experiences might also be a crucial link for broader coalitions to press for policy change to support caregiving.

There seems to be growing cultural endorsement—in theory—for the notion that family life, including dependent care, should be a shared project between men and women. Still, study after study reports that—in practice—even among married couples who are both in the labor force, women continue to do most of the housework and child care (Gerson 1985; Hochschild 1989). Not only that, despite increased theoretical support for shared child care, because of high divorce rates and increasing births out of wedlock, higher and higher proportions of children live in households where no man is even present, let alone performing hands-on care (Hagestad 1986). By the year 2000, over half of all children will have lived for a time with a single parent—almost always a mother (Waldrop 1990). In this context, it seems especially important to look closely at the experiences of a group of elderly men who may be actually practicing the values espoused by a younger generation.

Implications for Policy

The fact that the need for eldercare occurs later and less predictably than child care seems particularly relevant for so-called "work–family" policy. Especially in an aging and increasingly feminized work force, there is likely to be a growing proportion of workers who face the possibility of being called on for dependent care at unpredictable times relatively late in their careers. This would seem to strengthen arguments for policy changes that foster the integration of paid employment with a wide variety of unpaid caregiving work across a long period in the average worker's life.

The new extension of the proportion of life open to caregiving demands would seem to preclude a dependent care approach that treats paid work and family care as separate worlds that women could move in and out of at successive stages of their lives. In the year 2000, as was true in 1900, there will be no substantial life stages for average adult women that are reliably empty of potential caregiving demand. A hundred years ago, this fact supported the exclusion of most women from the labor force at most ages. In the present situation, in which the national standard of living depends on women's paid employment, it underlines the increasing need to integrate paid work with family care and to redistribute caring work more equitably between the sexes.

I have described several factors inherent in the nature of eldercare that might unsettle traditional attitudes, such as the beliefs that family care is primarily a matter of individual choice, that all caregiving is essentially an extension of motherhood, and that women are the only "natural" caregivers. Such attitudinal changes could, in turn, affect the goals of policies that address caregiving and partially determine public support for reforming the structure of dependent care.

GENDER EQUITY ISSUES OF TWO PROPOSED REFORMS

Proposals to reform our anachronistic system of dependent care and workplace structures cover a wide range of policies and practices, all of which are certain to have some impact on gender equity. The following discussion considers some gender equity issues raised by just two frequently recommended reforms. The first is expanding the provision of paid home care for the disabled elderly. The second is creating government mandates for job leaves for family care, including care for disabled elderly relatives. The discussion here focuses on a stated goal of both these policies: to allow Americans to continue productive paid employment while providing family care. It should be noted, though, that both of these policies have an additional aim— often stated as the primary reason for expanding home healthcare but usually unstated for employee leave mandates—of decreasing the rate of institutionalization among the very elderly, a key policy objective in an aging society.

The future costs of institutional care could be astronomical, assuming that current disability and demand levels persist while the aging trend increases the numbers of the very elderly in our population. Also, institutional care is generally perceived to be a last resort for both the people who need care and their families. Decreasing insti-

tutionalization is a policy goal with complicated gender equity implications of its own. On the one hand, it would add to the already heavy
burden of family caregivers, most of whom are women. On the other
hand, elderly women are currently twice as likely to be institutionalized as elderly men (Rivlin and Wiener 1988: table I-1). The gender
equity implications of institutional versus home care for the disabled
elderly should be studied closely. This chapter, however, focuses only
on how increasing paid home care and mandating employee leaves
might directly affect the family care burden and labor-force status of
women.

Increasing Paid Home Care

Policy analyses of the aging trend are full of assertions of the "tremendous need for home-care services and paid caregivers to replace
some of the care now being provided by family members" (Zedlewski
et al. 1990: 120). To be sure, most of these family members are women,
and many of them are unfairly overburdened by the demands of combining paid work and unsupported unpaid caregiving. Still others
must actually quit their jobs to provide care. To address this situation,
increasing paid home care is a strategy that might foster better conditions for women in the labor force and, ultimately, gender equity.
However, whether or not expanding home healthcare would actually
increase gender equity also depends on the conditions under which
this occupation would be expanded.

One might assume that with increased demand, job compensation
in this occupation would rise. Unfortunately, this has not been true
for home healthcare workers in the past. For instance, a considerable
demand increase in large cities (notably Boston and New York) in the
1980s did little to improve wages and benefits because much of this
care is subsidized by a single payer—Medicaid—which is able to set
low wage ceilings. In the late 1980s, a large-scale campaign by healthcare unions did manage to call attention to these workers' problems,
and raised compensation somewhat for unionized home healthcare
workers. However, it will be hard to organize many of these isolated
workers at a time when union rolls and resources are shrinking and
there is strong political opposition to organized labor.

One innovative home-care agency in New York City seems to have
demonstrated that raising wages, providing good benefits, and up-
grading work conditions can raise care quality and patient satisfaction
and greatly reduce worker turnover (to 15 percent from an industry-
wide average of 45–50 percent). This worker owned cooperative has

also developed a training program for home-care workers that allows them to obtain nursing credentials and thus advance professionally. Similar programs exist in Oakland, Calif., and Waterbury, Conn. (Cooperative Home Care Associates 1990, and personal communication with Rick Surpin 1992). However, public support to integrate most home healthcare workers into the mainstream of the professional healthcare sector would require a major shift in the way these jobs are usually viewed.

The current low investment approach to home healthcare has been justified (economically, if not ethically) by its status as a marginal occupation. To expand this job sector greatly in the future, without raising compensation, providing better benefits, and improving training and promotion opportunities and working conditions, would apparently marginalize one group of women in low-quality, low-productivity jobs in order to provide better work-force opportunities for another group of women.

Current home healthcare workers are almost all (90 percent) women and disproportionately women of color and recent immigrants (Older Women's League and American Federation of State, County, and Municipal Employees 1988). The U.S. Department of Labor (1992) conservatively projects that the number of jobs in the "homemaker-home health aides" category will nearly double in the period from 1990 to 2005, and announces that in this occupation, "job opportunities are excellent." As things now stand, these are "opportunities" to perform exactly the kind of low-pay, no-benefits, low-training, high-turnover jobs that exemplify the worst characteristics of the service occupations in which so many women workers remain segregated. If paid home health care must be expanded in the future—and given the rising eldercare demand, the desire to prevent or delay institutionalization, and women's growing labor force participation, it probably must—the quality of these jobs will have to be raised, if the potential positive gender equity effects are not to be neutralized, or actually reversed.

Work-Force Leaves

Employee leave for family care is a strategy that has been proposed and selectively implemented to minimize the friction between paid employment and unpaid caring work. Foster and Brizius (chapter 3 of this volume) have catalogued the different types of parental, family, medical, and maternity leaves that have been mandated by different states. These are all unpaid leaves. In addition, five states have mandated temporary disability insurance (TDI), which provides partially paid leave without job protection for a disabling condition that temporarily disrupts employment, including childbirth.

All of these leave policies have immediate practical benefits for many women workers. However, such policies will only benefit women in the long run in terms of overall gender equity if they support women's continuous work-force attachment and their increased movement into better-paying occupations. Leave policies could conceivably wind up disadvantaging women if, instead, they tend to move women out of the work force for longer periods of time, reinforce the separation of male and female workers into different occupations or "tracks" within occupations, or otherwise weaken women's labor market position.

As discussed earlier here, the rising demand for eldercare is broadening the age range during which a person may be called on to provide intense family care and expanding the pool of potential caregivers (and, thus, leave-takers). The greater diversity of caregiving needs in an aging society could become a force for gender equity, provided that diversity is reflected in policy. Broadening eligible leave relationships to include not only care for children but for disabled parents and spouses as well reduces the chance that any one group of workers can be singled out as likely leave-takers and marked as undesirable by employers. Structuring work-force leaves to include eldercare may thus benefit not only actual eldercare providers but all women—and especially those of childbearing age—because it would mean that employers would be less likely to try to exclude them from their work forces or to marginalize them in low-quality jobs.

Recent research seems to indirectly support this notion (Trzcinski 1990). Long-term positive effects for women were found as a result of state-mandated TDI leave, which can be described as an "equal-treatment" policy—one that is equally available to men and women. The same study also found negative effects of leave structured as a "special treatment" benefit for women, namely, state-mandated maternity leave. The findings suggest that the narrowly defined separate treatment approach encouraged employers to adjust to mandated leaves in ways that undermined women's labor market position, whereas broadly structured disability leaves apparently actually improved women's average job tenure and job compensation (Trzcinski 1990).

We might expect to see the positive effects of equal treatment magnified as the basis for leave eligibility expands. Proposed federally mandated family and medical leave is very broadly structured, including leave not only to care for a disabled parent or spouse, a newborn, or a newly adopted or sick child but also for an employee's own disabling condition. This should substantially increase the number of men who would take advantage of the policy.[3] However, even such a broadly defined "equal treatment" benefit might still have a decidedly unequal effect on women and men regarding their assumption of family care. Whenever possible, most working couples would certainly make the rational economic decision for the lower-paid partner to exercise the unpaid leave option, in order to preserve the maximum family income. So long as the gender gap in employment income persists, that lower-paid person is likely to be a woman. Still, a significant number of women who have no job-protected leave must now risk losing their jobs if they leave them, even briefly, to provide family care. Thus, whereas on the one hand, unpaid leaves might reinforce the prevailing pattern that it is women, and not men, who withdraw from paid work to provide unpaid care, they also, on the other hand, make it much easier for those women to return to work.

The net effect of broadly structured, equal-treatment leaves would seem to be to increase women's attachment to the work force. Such leave policies might also tend to promote women's movement into male-dominated occupations, because they would make it easier to combine these jobs with family care. At the same time, they could also encourage employers in female-dominated occupations to improve job quality and restructure jobs to improve productivity, because they would reduce worker turnover and improve women's job tenure. However, leaves that are more narrowly defined—for example, maternity leaves, or leaves only for child care and not eldercare and worker disability—might have the opposite effect, because they would encourage employers in male-dominated occupations to avoid hiring people (that is, women) who would be most likely to use leave (Trzcinski 1990).

Finally, supporters of federally mandated family and medical leave point out that such a policy would, in effect, set a new "labor standard which assumes that the average worker gets pregnant, cares for young children and elderly parents, and experiences illness" (Spalter-Roth and Hartmann 1991: 43). In other words, for the first time, a public policy would recognize as normal the typical work experience of women in an aging society.

Pay Equity and Dependent Care

Another type of employment policy could help alleviate potential gender equity problems associated with both expanding paid home care and providing unpaid family care leaves. Comparable-worth, or pay-equity, policies set salary levels according to scales that rate jobs by their relative degree of difficulty and skill requirements. Such policies have been adopted in a few state and local government work forces and are being explored by others. Comparable-worth policies are not much in the news these days, and are not likely to be instituted on a national scale any time soon. Still, it is worth noting that besides direct effects on job compensation, a comparable-worth approach might lead to a fairer distribution of both paid and unpaid caregiving work. Most comparable-worth scales would probably raise the notoriously low wages of paid caregivers, directly benefiting large numbers of women workers and perhaps even drawing some men into these traditionally female occupations. Then, expanding home healthcare would not also expand the proportion of working women in poorly paid jobs. At the same time, comparable-worth schemes would tend to reduce the economic disincentive for many men in couples to take advantage of unpaid work-force leaves for family care.

The interaction of comparable-worth and work-force leave policies should be studied. For instance, it would be interesting to look at the effect of comparable-worth policies on the use of family leaves among the state work forces where both of these policies are mandated. What are the numbers of men and women taking unpaid leaves? How do they compare with leave use by men and women in states that have mandatory unpaid leave but whose public jobs are not indexed by comparable worth? Is there a difference in terms of who is using leaves for child care versus eldercare?

Regarding the primary goal of comparable-worth policies—job income equity for men and women—one thing seems clear: caregiving is a part of this issue that will not dissolve. No practice of uniform pay scales, and likewise no amount of higher education and wider job opportunities for women, will result in real income equity until family care—and in an aging society this increasingly means eldercare—is equitably distributed. In light of this, policymakers concerned with gender equity must consider the potential impact of all proposed work-family policies on the distribution of caregiving between men and women.

THE OUTLOOK FOR EQUITY

This chapter has suggested some ways to look at caring work in an aging society, ways that may reveal new opportunities for promoting gender equity. If we fail to recognize and respond to such opportunities, the growing numbers of disabled elderly Americans will amplify the dissonance between an obsolete system of dependent care that relies on the unpaid work of women and a labor force that relies on women's increasing participation.

If population projections are correct, if disability rates do not miraculously decline, and if we do not significantly alter the way we are now providing care, the situation for women will surely worsen. However, if the pressure of the rising demand for eldercare can be applied to reforms shaped by a recognition of the changing nature of caregiving, we may be able to shift long-standing inequitable attitudes and policies. There will then be a chance for gender relations to become more equitable than they have been at any time in the nation's history.

Notes

The ideas expressed in this chapter were developed in part through discussions with Alan Pifer. Thanks are due Lucy Winner and Felicity Skidmore for helpful comments on an early draft. Douglas Schulkind's rigorous arguments and thoughtful editing made all the difference.

1. A look at natality statistics shows that in 1989, 71 percent of births were to women aged 29 and under and 58 percent of births were to women between the ages of 20 and 29 (National Center for Health Statistics 1990). Given that the median age of childbirth is thus probably somewhere around 27, one might estimate that the average age of mothers caring for young children is around 30.

2. Author's calculations from data in tables B1-24 and B3-10 in Taeuber 1991.

3. Another interesting aspect of the current version of the proposed federal family and medical leave legislation is that it provides leave to care for a disabled spouse or parent—but not for a parent-in-law. Thus, it might increase the likelihood that an adult son would take time off to care for his disabled parent, since his wife would not be eligible for leave to care for her in-laws.

References

Brody, Elaine M. 1981. " 'Women in the Middle' and Family Help to Older People." Gerontologist 21(5): 471–80.
————. 1985. "Parent Care as a Normative Family Stress." Donald P. Kent Memorial Lecture. Gerontologist 25: 12–29.

Cooperative Home Care Associates. 1990. "Cooperative Home Care Associates: A Status Report." Bronx, N.Y.: Author.

Gerson, Kathleen. 1985. *Hard Choices: How Women Decide about Work, Career, and Motherhood.* Berkeley, Calif.: University of California Press.

Hagestad, Gunhild O. 1986. "The Family: Women and Grandparents as Kin-Keepers." In *Our Aging Society: Paradox and Promise,* edited by Alan Pifer and Lydia Bronte. New York: W.W. Norton & Co.

Hochschild, Arlie. 1989. *The Second Shift: Working Parents and the Revolution at Home.* New York: Viking Press.

Kaye, Leonard W., and Jeffrey S. Applegate. 1991. "Components of a Gender-Sensitive Curriculum Model for Elder Caregiving: Lessons for Research." *Gerontology & Geriatrics Education* 11(3): 39–56.

Myrdal, Alva, and Viola Klein. 1970. *Women's Two Roles: Home and Work.* London: Routledge & Kegan Paul.

National Center for Health Statistics. 1990. *Advance Report of Final Natality Statistics, 1989. Monthly Vital Statistics Report,* vol. 20, no. 10. Washington, D.C.: U.S. Department of Health and Human Services.

Older Women's League and American Federation of State, County, and Municipal Employees. 1988. *Chronic Care Workers: Crisis among Paid Caregivers of the Elderly.* Washington, D.C.: Older Women's League.

Rivlin, Alice M., and Joshua M. Wiener. 1988. *Caring for the Disabled Elderly: Who Will Pay?* Washington, D.C.: Brookings Institution.

Rossi, Alice S. 1986. "Sex and Gender in the Aging Society." In *Our Aging Society: Paradox and Promise,* edited by Alan Pifer and Lydia Bronte. New York: W.W. Norton & Co.

Sorensen, Annemette. 1991. "The Restructuring of Gender Relations in an Aging Society." *Acta Sociologica* 34: 45–55.

Spalter-Roth, Roberta M., and Heidi I. Hartmann. 1990. *Unnecessary Losses: Costs to Americans of the Lack of Family and Medical Leave.* Washington, D.C.: Institute for Women's Policy Research.

Stone, Robyn. 1991. "Defining Family Caregivers of the Elderly: Implications for Research and Public Policy" (Editorial). *Gerontologist* 31(6): 724–25.

Stone, Robyn I., and Peter Kemper. 1989. "Spouses and Children of Disabled Elders: How Large a Constituency for Long-term Care Reform?" *Milbank Quarterly* 67(3–4): 485–506.

Stone, Robyn, Gail Lee Cafferata, and Judith Sangl. 1987. "Caregivers of the Frail Elderly: A National Profile. *Gerontologist* 27 (October).

Taeuber, Cynthia. 1991 *Statistical Handbook on Women in America.* Phoenix: Oryx Press.

Taub, Nadine. 1985. "From Parental Leaves to Nurturing Leaves." *New York University Review of Law & Social Change* 13(2): 381–405.

Trzcinski, Eileen. 1990. "Separate versus Equal Treatment Approaches to Parental Leave: Theoretical Issues and Empirical Evidence." In

Second Annual Women's Policy Research Conference Proceedings. Washington, D.C.: Institute for Women's Policy Research.

U.S. Bureau of the Census. 1989. "Projections of the Population of the United States, by Age, Sex, and Race: 1988 to 2080," by Gregory Spencer. Current Population Reports, ser. P-25, no. 1018. Washington, D.C.: U.S. Government Printing Office.

U.S. Department of Labor, Bureau of Labor Statistics. 1992. "20th Edition of Occupational Outlook Handbook Published." News Release. Washington, D.C.: Author, May 29.

Waldrop, Judith. 1990. "You'll Know It's the 21st Century When . . ." American Demographics (December) 23–27.

Zedlewski, Sheila R., Roberta O. Barnes, Martha R. Burt, Timothy D. McBride, and Jack A. Meyer. 1990. The Needs of the Elderly in the 21st Century. Washington, D.C.: Urban Institute Press.

Chapter Ten

MEETING THE CHALLENGE: IMPLICATIONS FOR POLICY AND PRACTICE

Alan Pifer

Most Americans would agree on the elements of a good society. They would include such things as a strong economy capable of providing an adequate standard of living for all; an effective educational system for young people and a safe environment in which to raise them; good health care for everyone; decent housing for all; equal opportunity irrespective of race, gender, or age; a foolproof safety net for the unfortunate; economic protection for the elderly; and freedom from crime.

There would, however, be no agreement on how to bring such a good society into being. Some would leave it largely to the workings of a market economy, some would depend on our traditional mixed economy, and some would favor much heavier state intervention than we have seen in recent years. Nearly all of us, however, want the good society without having to pay for it in increased taxes. Because of this basic disagreement over ways and means, most of the attempts at social reform, in the public sphere, tend to be narrow and confined to a single sector, based on a perception of impending crisis in that sector, addressed to symptoms rather than underlying causes, and underfinanced. Almost inevitably, they lead to disappointment and, usually, failure.

Nonetheless, there have been times in our history, such as in the mid-1930s when the Social Security Act and other New Deal legislation was passed, and in the 1960s with its civil rights and Great Society measures, when accumulated public anger and impatience with the usual obstacles to reform have created an overriding force great enough for the institution of broad new policies that amounted to a veritable social revolution. Today we face social and economic problems that are so extensive and of such magnitude and that have stimulated such public anger that we may well be entering a major new reformist period—despite budget constraints and a lack of the visionary national leadership we enjoyed in the 1930s and 1960s. The growing political empowerment of women is a critical element in this nascent revolution.

This book approaches the question of social reform through analysis of a particular, though widely pervasive, underlying force in society—the impact of the inexorable aging of our population specifically on women. Stated more precisely, it examines the ways population aging intensifies both women's traditional concerns, especially caregiving for the elderly, and new concerns that arise from the many, often competing, roles women now play in our national life. The preceding chapters offer some specific recommendations for policy change. However, the book is primarily descriptive of the present situation and speculative of the future and is only broadly prescriptive.

This final chapter does not, therefore, attempt to provide a comprehensive, detailed set of policies designed to be responsive to the many ways population aging affects women. That sort of effort would be both presumptuous and hazardous, given the enormous difficulties inherent in prescribing public policy "solutions" to large new social problems. On the one hand, one simply cannot foresee the longer-range consequences of new measures—however promising they may be in the short run. On the other hand, one faces the dilemma that because recommendations for policy reform in one area inevitably reach into other areas, they are almost certain to seem simplistic, unless those other areas are themselves analyzed in depth, which is clearly beyond the scope of a volume such as this.

Finally, there is the challenge posed by all programmatic innovations that require spending—namely, how to *pay* for what is recommended. Increase the deficit? Cut the defense budget? Tax the rich? Reduce funding for welfare, student aid, mass transit, farm subsidies? Possible answers to the question are infinite, but in the end, from a longer-range perspective, the question is not only meaningless but dangerous, because it paralyzes objective, politically uninfected, and, most important, creative thought about the future.

There must, therefore, be forums for consideration of social reform that are essentially exploratory, that can propose possible changes in policy and practice without pretending to have complete and final answers, that are broad in scope, and that are free of any obligation to confront immediately the stultifying question of *who pays*. This book, in its overall character, is intended to be just such a forum for exploring the consequences of population aging for women.

There are, of course, other perspectives one can use to shed light on the concerns of women today and to indicate how these can be alleviated. Women's basic right to fair treatment would certainly be one perspective, and their continued assumption of special responsibilities for the welfare of children would be another. This volume makes no claim that analysis of the impact of population aging on women is necessarily a superior approach or one that should be used exclusively. It seeks to demonstrate, however, that such an analysis offers unique insights into current human resource issues, and that these insights are of great importance, not only for women but for all Americans, regardless of age or gender.

For example, population aging, as it becomes more pronounced, is constantly shifting the nature of the interface between the nation's paid work force—nearly half of which is now composed of women—and the American family, where women are the traditional homemakers and caregivers. Understanding this dynamic is important in the framing of new policies affecting both employment and families. Another example is the need in designing a national health insurance program to understand the priority population aging places on an effective provision for long-term care.

The recommendations for policy changes in the preceding chapters cover a number of topics, resting on a series of premises that are the book's foundation. There are ten main premises:

First, the powerful consequences of population aging affect women more heavily than men. This is not only because women live longer than men but also because so many of them are now in the paid labor force while continuing to be the society's principal caregivers for growing numbers of disabled elderly family members.

Second, the consequences of population aging do not affect all women equally because of the great diversity among women in regard to such characteristics as age, marital status, number of siblings, number and age of children, race, employment status, and income.

Third, the greatest recent change in the lives of women, along with a long-term decline in the fertility rate, has been their entry in large numbers into the paid labor force. This will not change, for three reasons—because women are essential to the maintenance of a productive economy, because the nation's standard of living has become dependent on the presence of two earners in most families, and because in a growing number of families a woman is the sole source of support.

Fourth, although the fertility rate of women is likely to remain relatively low, indicating stability in their child-care responsibilities, the burden of eldercare will continue to increase because of steady growth in the numbers of the very old, among whom the incidence of disability is high. Further advances in treatment of diseases that principally affect the elderly, allowing them to live much longer with chronic ailments, could increase this burden dramatically over the coming decades, especially after about the year 2030 when baby-boom cohorts enter the oldest age groups.

Fifth, the life-expectancy advantage of women over men, currently about seven years, will perpetuate the imbalance between men and women among older Americans. Although men's longevity is expected to improve in the next century, women will continue to predominate numerically in the oldest age groups. Both the total number of elderly women and the proportion they represent of the entire population will continue to rise. Unless significant changes are made, many of these women will live out their final years in poverty or near poverty.

Sixth, in part because women live longer than men, they have chronic health problems over longer periods, consume greater amounts of healthcare, and incur greater healthcare costs. They are also, numerically, by far the greatest providers of healthcare. For example, approximately three-quarters of the people employed in the healthcare industry are women, to which must be added the vast amount of unpaid healthcare provided by women to family members at home.

Seventh, because of long-standing inattention to the healthcare needs of women, both in treatment and research, women suffer chronic illness in their older years that could in many cases have been avoided or ameliorated.

Eighth, preventive healthcare programs designed specifically for older women can be cost-effective. For this reason, they merit much wider attention.

Ninth, continued low fertility in the future, following on the low fertility of the past quarter of a century, will, even with increased immigration, result in a relatively small proportion of young workers in the labor force well into the next century. By rights, this should create needs and opportunities for older workers, including older women.

Tenth, because of the great increase in longevity in the past three or four decades, a new stage has, in effect, been added to the average life span, in which large numbers of older people who would once have been decrepit or deceased are now still vigorous in mind and body. These older people represent an enormous resource to the nation because of the education and training many of them have received and because of their collective experience. Well over half of these "young-old" citizens are women.

This list of premises and the analysis in the preceding chapters make clear that when we speak of the consequences of population aging, we are referring to the impact of an ever-older population on women of all ages, and, through them, on society at large, as well as the consequences that relate immediately to the lives of the growing numbers of older women themselves.

The effects for women are bound to be diverse. For example, responsibility for the care of an elderly parent at home over a long period of time would almost certainly restrict a woman's opportunity for full-time employment outside the home, resulting very probably in reduced earnings, no health insurance, and a lack of pension eligibility. These conditions, in turn, would make it more likely that the woman would later become one of the expanding population of single older women, living alone, often in poverty, suffering chronic health problems and consuming costly healthcare at public expense over many years.

In another case, the shortage of young workers characteristic of an aging population might create such a need for the skills of more experienced, better-educated older women that their employers, rather than easing them out of the work force as they aged, would be motivated to offer them retraining, promotion, and improved pay. Those same women some years later might then show up as part of a new body of independent "young-old" people in the society, financially secure because of full Social Security eligibility, a private pension, and savings, and in good health partly as a result of adequate health insurance coverage in previous years.

The overriding question, as noted by Jessie Allen in chapter 1 of this book, is how to articulate the varied consequences of the aging trend for women in America in such a way as to command an effective national response in the form of new attitudes and practices. This task is, of course, complicated by the reality that other social and economic factors interact with the aging trend's impact on women's lives—forces such as gender and age discrimination, responsibilities for homemaking and children, lack of pay equity, inadequate opportunities for training or retraining in employment, the availability only of part-time employment offering no health or retirement benefits, and divorce or premature widowhood.

In spite of these complexities, there is no question that the impact of population aging is a powerful new driving force in our society that must be reckoned with in any attempt at overall social and economic improvement. If the prescriptions for dealing with the negative consequences of this phenomenon alleviate other ills, so much the better. For example, equal pay for jobs of comparable worth might be instituted specifically to help prevent poverty among older women and the heavy public costs this entails. However, comparable-worth policies would also help address the long-standing problem of pay inequity in general and thereby enable women to earn the income needed to do more for their children.

Indeed, as previously mentioned, recognition of the impact of population aging on women and an effective national response to it could become a powerful lever for creating a better society for all Americans. This view may seem rather fanciful and even naive in the present climate of political indifference to the real and pressing needs of large numbers of women, especially low-income minority women. Nevertheless, the aging trend is a relatively new phenomenon, and its full consequences are not yet understood by most Americans. Over the next decade or two, as population aging becomes steadily more pronounced, and especially by 2020 or 2030, when the trend becomes extremely heavy, its impact will be undeniable, and a broad societal response will become inevitable. The issue now is how to prevent needless suffering by women and general harm to society in the intervening years by speeding up an effective response to the problem.

A hint of growing awareness of the need for such a response is evident in the results of a survey of nontraditional benefits for the work force of the year 2000 conducted by the International Foundation of Employee Benefit Plans (1990). Of the 463 employers who responded to the survey—roughly one-third in manufacturing and two-thirds in service industries—well over half anticipated a shortage of workers by the end of the 1990s. Of that group, 77 percent believed that women would take over the jobs left vacant, and 55 percent believed that the elderly would fill the vacancies. A majority of the respondents also said that by the year 2000 they would be offering benefits advantageous to women and families, such as child-care resource/referral, subsidies for child-care expenses, elder services resource/referral, flextime, family leave, job sharing, and a compressed workweek. The respondents also felt that part-time employment would be offered almost universally, but this, of course, is not necessarily advantageous to women because of its traditional lack of benefits such as health insurance and pension rights.

Regarding training and education, the survey showed that by the year 2000 virtually all the responding employers would be offering tuition reimbursement and technical, management, and professional training, and that a majority would provide basic skills training, retraining, gender/minority sensitivity workshops, family counseling, and mentor career counseling—all of which would be beneficial to women. The widespread adoption of private-sector measures such as these, which are obviously a response to anticipated labor shortages and productivity problems, should be encouraged, even if it necessitates public assistance, in the form, possibly, of tax advantages or subsidies, to enable smaller companies to play their part.

Despite promising signs such as the results of the survey just described, the present situation of many women, especially lower-income women and, disproportionately, women of minority background, remains bleak, and the impact of population aging is clearly a contributing factor. The problems these women have always faced have been exacerbated by growing numbers of frail, dependent, and often impoverished elderly family members who must be cared for at home. This added burden has limited the opportunities of women for full-time paid employment, on-the-job training, career advancement, improved earnings, and pension eligibility—thereby substantially increasing the possibility that they will end up in poverty in their own old age.

Limited earnings have also generally meant a lack of health insurance and, therefore, inadequate medical care, leading to chronic disabilities in later life and a burden on Medicaid and Medicare funds that might have been avoided. Finally, poor earnings by women have in many cases so reduced family income that the life chances of children have been destroyed. Few families these days can provide a decent home, adequate healthcare, and, in time, higher education for their children without two incomes, and in the increasing number of cases where a woman is the principal or sole breadwinner, her reduced earnings are, of course, devastating to her family's welfare. Indeed, it makes only limited sense to try to improve the lot of children without first improving the lives of their mothers.

One can easily see in this chain of misfortune many points where new policy interventions could significantly alter the outcome. Employers, for example, could grant both women and men time off to care for elderly family members; they could provide more liberal benefits for part-time workers (many of whom are women), including benefits such as health insurance, retraining programs, opportunities for advancement, and pension eligibility; and they could more rigorously adhere to equal opportunity in employment regulations. Most important, they could go much farther in instituting pay equity for women. Few employers, of course, will institute such measures for purely altruistic reasons. Practical necessity will be the motivating force. A key point here is the relationship between women's lower earnings and their roles as caregivers. Specifically, as argued by Allen in chapter 9, in an aging society real income equity between men and women will not be possible until the burden of eldercare is more equally distributed.

More widely available, publicly provided home care for the elderly, and especially an insurance program to cover the costs of long-term care, would provide desperately needed relief to many women. The establishment of some form of national health insurance would, of course, make a huge difference to the many women, and their families, who are currently uninsured or underinsured. In designing such a system, attention must be paid to women's more often intermittent work-force attachment, largely due to family care demands at home. This is particularly the case if the plan is to be based on employer-provided insurance.

Furthermore, far more attention must be given to preventive health-care programs, especially for older women. Prevention programs generally must include not only service delivery but also research, public education, and outreach efforts, and should be targeted to particularly vulnerable groups. It is especially important for physicians and other healthcare workers to receive more extensive training in the health needs of older people and in preventive healthcare in general.

In the area of individual behavior, men could help women by sharing to a much greater extent than they do now responsibility for home care of the elderly. Government might encourage this through tax concessions, which, of course, would also be made available to women. Men must begin to recognize that in the future they may not always be able to count on a spouse or sister to care for their parents or, indeed, themselves.

The other major manifestation of population aging has been the development of an ever-growing number of older single women, the result of greatly increased longevity and women's longer life expectancy. A significant proportion of single women live alone and in poverty or close to it. Single women in the United States aged 65 and over now number about 11 million, but are expected to increase to well over 16 million in the next 30 years. In general, society tends to ignore the roles these women play in our national life. To the extent that they are given an opportunity to be productive, their roles are generally confined to housework, child care, and the care of other old people, usually on an unpaid basis. Many of these women lead lonely, fearful lives, almost totally cut off from the life of the surrounding community.

This dismal situation could be greatly alleviated by changes in prevailing policies and practices, some of which would also do much to help younger women cope with the burdens imposed on them by an aging population. There may not be much that can be done for the very oldest, frailest, and poorest of this group of women except, in cases where they do not qualify for Social Security benefits, to raise their incomes by increasing their Supplemental Security Income (SSI) payments, ensure that they qualify for and receive Medicaid, and, where they wish it, arrange for them to move to congregate living quarters or, if necessary, into good nursing homes.

There are, however, many women in a less-advanced age bracket, roughly 60 to 75 years of age or even younger, who have been largely sidelined by society but remain healthy and vigorous and who, if given the chance and encouragement, have the energy and skills to still contribute significantly to the nation's productivity and to its quality of life, either in paid employment or voluntary work. Although some of these women may wish to be caregivers, paid or unpaid, either for children or the very old, they must not automatically be assigned this role, as they tend to be now. It is, of course, easier to say that a choice should be available to them than to realize it in practice, since so much caregiving for the very old is for a spouse, parent, or other close relative and is largely inescapable. Only a comprehensive system of home care and the availability of affordable high-quality institutional care, where needed, can provide this opportunity for choice.

Despite women's increased labor-force participation, the economic outlook for tomorrow's elderly women is not much improved, because most women continue to work in traditionally female jobs for relatively low wages, and because Social Security and pension policies continue to favor typically male patterns of continuous employment. There is little to indicate that large numbers of today's younger women—members, for example, of the baby boom, now aged about 28 to 46—will not later be in the same predicament as so many of today's elderly women. That is, they will eventually find themselves living alone and struggling to get by with inadequate and dwindling resources. Certainly, no significant policy changes have yet been made to help prevent this.

There are, nevertheless, two important ways in which the lives of younger women today differ from those of their mothers and grandmothers, and that offer at least the possibility of a better future for them. The first is that younger women are, on the whole, a much better-educated group. Nearly 25 percent of the third of our population composed of the baby-boom generation are college graduates, and, of these, just under half are women. Women, however, have outnumbered men in higher education since 1979 and by an ever-growing margin, and, according to projections by the National Center for Educational Statistics, they will outnumber men by close to 2 million by the year 2001. At that time, there will be a projected 8.9 million women actually in college (as opposed to 7 million men). In terms of advanced degrees, women today are earning substantially more master's degrees than are men, and by the year 2001 it is projected that they will be earning almost as many doctorates (National Center for Educational Statistics 1991).

If these trends continue, the cumulative effects of women's educational differential will mean that in the decades ahead women will constitute a large stock—in time well over half—of the nation's best-educated people. Furthermore, the buildup will be occurring during a period when higher education will become an even more important qualification for a good, well-paid job. Theoretically, therefore, well-educated women will be in a strong competitive position in the labor force and will be able to command the salaries and pension rights that will prevent them from falling into poverty in their older years.

Such a prognosis, however, is subject to two important qualifications. The first is that until now, because of job discrimination and pay inequity, higher education has not paid off adequately for women. Female college graduates are still, on average, paid considerably less than men. Second, too few women are getting a strong background in mathematics and science at the precollege level, and too few, therefore, are training as scientists, engineers, and technologists in college, which limits their opportunities for better-paying jobs later. These are serious human resource issues that should be commanding top-level attention, not simply in the interest of fairness to women but, more broadly, in the national interest, because they are fundamental to our future competitiveness as a nation and our future standard of living.

Despite the importance of higher education, however, there will be many women, especially minority women, who, principally for economic reasons, are not afforded an opportunity for a college education and therefore will be likely to end up in poverty or near-poverty in their later years. Some policy changes that could prevent this happening have already been discussed here. Another change, clearly, would be an increase in financial aid from public and private sources sufficient to enable every interested and qualified woman (and man) to attend a higher educational institution.

The other important factor that may make the economic future of today's younger women more comfortable than that of their mothers is their better competitive position in the labor market as a result of a diminished supply of young male workers. From 1980 to 1990 there was a 20 percent decline in the number of 14- to 17-year-olds in the population and a 12 percent decline in the number aged 18 to 24, about half of whom would have been male and half female (National Center for Educational Statistics, 1991). However, the improved competitive position for women may prove illusory if the law of supply and demand does not function because of continued discrimination against women in hiring, pay, training, and advancement, and if their employment continues to be clustered in certain "female occupations" such as office work and caregiving.

Much has been written about an inevitable conflict in our national life between the economic welfare of older Americans and the interests of the young. Spending on the former, it is said, automatically reduces the life chances of the latter. A companion claim is that spending on the elderly, which, apart from defense and interest payments on the national debt, constitutes about half of the federal budget, comes at the expense of investment in the nation's future— investment in such things as research, education, training, infrastructure, and productive capacity.

These claims have only a superficial validity and, if subjected to the deeper analysis made possible by the perspective of population aging's impact on women, have no validity whatsoever. Women, in fact, are the critical link between the interests of the young and those of the old. If they have better jobs, higher earnings, and improved benefits, they can—along with their husbands, if present—provide their children with safer homes, better nutrition, needed health care, and, eventually, the postsecondary education required for access to good jobs. This, in itself, is an investment in the nation's future.

At the same time, better jobs, higher incomes, and improved benefits for women will enable them not only to lessen the likelihood of poverty for their parents but also to safeguard their own old age through savings and retirement benefits. Both results would help greatly to create a sound and fair basis for a reduction of public spending on the elderly, if in time that proves necessary.

Finally, better employment prospects for women would, indirectly but importantly, contribute to national investment by providing increased tax revenues to enable government at all levels to spend more on infrastructure, research, education, and training.

The aging of the American population, which will increase further in the decades ahead, is a neutral phenomenon, not intrinsically bad or good. Its effects today and in the future depend entirely on the nation's response to it. The aging trend's negative consequences for women can be counteracted by recognition of the changing realities of their lives and implementation of new policies and practices. Similarly, the trend's possible benefits for them can be realized by other new policies and practices. That these policies and practices have yet to be realized is evidence of society's continuing indifference not only to fairness but to serious human resource issues as well—issues that are as important to men as to women. Accommodation to the impact of population aging, possibly the greatest social and economic force of our time, has, thus far, been almost entirely at the expense of women. That this should continue makes a travesty of our vaunted claim to be the leading nation in the world. Only through much greater attention to the needs and potential of our women can we make real progress toward the good society to which all of us, as Americans, aspire.

References

International Foundation of Employee Benefit Plans. 1990. *Nontraditional Benefits for the Workforce of 2000.* Brookfield, Wisc.: Author.
National Center for Education Statistics. 1991. *Projections of Education Statistics to 2002.* NCES 91-490. Washington, D.C.: U.S. Department of Education.

ABOUT THE EDITORS

Jessie Allen directs the Southport Institute's Project on Women and Population Aging. She began studying the societal effects of population aging while serving as project associate on the Aging Society Project of Carnegie Corporation of New York. A graduate of New York University's School of the Arts, Ms. Allen is a writer, director, and performer of experimental theatre works, which often focus on women in history.

Alan Pifer is chairman of the Southport Institute for Policy Analysis, an organization he founded in 1987. From 1967 to 1982, he was president of Carnegie Corporation of New York. Mr. Pifer is co-editor of *Our Aging Society: Paradox and Promise* (Norton 1986) and co-author of *Government for the People: the Federal Social Role* (Norton 1987). He has spoken extensively on population aging to academic, voluntary, and business groups and chaired and served on numerous national panels and advisory councils in the areas of education, health, and philanthropy. He is a past director of the Federal Reserve Bank of New York, McGraw-Hill Inc., and numerous non-profit organizations.

ABOUT THE CONTRIBUTORS

Kimberly Allshouse holds a master's degree in social work from Boston University. Her primary research interests are issues related to women's employment. Prior to pursuing graduate studies, Ms. Allshouse worked for several years in human services management. She has also conducted research on the quality of hospital care in the United States.

Robert J. Blendon is chairman of the Department of Health Policy and Management at Harvard University's School of Public Health in Boston. He is also deputy director of the Division of Health Policy Research and Education at Harvard. He is the author of numerous articles on health care access, quality, costs, and funding approaches. Formerly senior vice president and director of the program of The Robert Wood Johnson Foundation, Dr. Blendon has also served in the U.S. Department of Health, Education, and Welfare as a special assistant for policy development. He is on the editorial board of the *Journal of the American Medical Association*.

Jack A. Brizius is a public affairs consultant, self-employed in the firm of Brizius and Foster. He specializes in public finance, government reorganization, and planning for the public sector. He was previously director of the National Governors' Association Center for Policy Research and the Office of State Planning and Development of the Pennsylvania Governor's Office. He holds a Ph.D. from Woodrow Wilson School of Public and International Affairs, Princeton University.

Marriane C. Fahs is director of the Division of Health Economics and an associate professor in the Department of Community Medicine at Mount Sinai School of Medicine in New York City. She holds joint appointments in the International Leadership Center on Longevity and Society (U.S.), Ritter Department of Geriatrics and Adult Development, Mount Sinai School of Medicine and the Doctoral Program in Economics, Graduate Center, City University of New York. She received her MPH and PhD from the University of Michigan. The author of numerous papers on cost-effectiveness analysis and prevention services, she served on the National Advisory Panel on Payment for Preventive Services for the Elderly under Medicare for the Office of Technology Assessment and also served on the U.S. Preventive Services Task Force Subcommittee on Cost Effectiveness Analysis.

Susan E. Foster is half of the independent consulting team of Brizius and Foster. Her consulting assignments to state government have recently included work for the governors' offices of Alabama, Arizona, Indiana, Maryland, Mississippi, Rhode Island, and West Virginia. Prior to establishing her private consultancy, Ms. Foster was Deputy Under Secretary for Intergovernmental Affairs in the U.S. Department of Health, Education, and Welfare. She holds an MSW in Social Policy and Administration from Rutgers Graduate School of Social Work.

Ruth Harriet Jacobs is a sociologist and gerontologist affiliated with the Wellesley College Center for Research on Women in Wellesley, Massachusetts. She was previously chair of sociology at Clark University in Worcester, Massachusetts, and a professor at Boston University. Her books include *Life After Youth: Female, Forty, What Next?* published by Beacon Press in 1979; *Older Women Surviving and Thriving*, Family Service America Publications, 1987; and *Be An Outrageous Older Woman: A R.A.S.P*, published in 1991 by Knowledge, Ideas & Trends Inc. of Manchester, Connecticut. She currently teaches sociology, gerontology, and counseling at Regis College, Weston, Massachusetts; Massachusetts School of Professional Psychology in Dedham; Springfield College School of Human Services in Manchester, New Hamphsire; and the Boston University School of Social Work continuing education program.

Jo-Ann Lamphere-Thorpe is on the faculty of the Department of Health Policy and Administration at the University of North Carolina at Chapel Hill. Collaboration for the chapter began while she was a research associate in the Department of Health Policy and Management at Harvard University's School of Public Health. Ms. Lamphere-Thorpe's experience with the health care sector spans academic medical center management, policy analysis and program development for the New York State Department of Health, and private consulting to various health care providers. She is a doctoral candidate at Columbia University's School of Public Health.

Dr. Julianne Malveaux is an economist, writer, and syndicated columnist whose weekly column appears nationally in some 20 newspapers through the King Features Syndicate. She is a regular contributor to *Ms.* and *USA Today*, and a weekly contributor to the *San Francisco Sun Reporter*. Her academic and popular writing also appears in other magazines, newspapers, and journals. She provides regular radio and television commentary on sociopolitical issues, especially on CNN's *Crier and Company*, and on the PBS show *To The Contrary*. As a scholar, Dr. Malveaux has most recently been a visiting faculty member at the University of California, Berkeley, in the African American Studies Department. Her research focuses on the labor market and on public policy and its impact on women and minorities. She co-edited the book, *Slipping Through The Cracks: The Status of Black Women* (Transactions Publications 1986), and has completed a manuscript on the status of black women in the labor market.

Paula Rayman, Ph.D., is an associate professor of sociology at Wellesley College and director of the Pathways for Women in the Sciences project at Wellesley's Center for Research on Women. Her research on women's attachment and retention in science has been supported by the Alfred P. Sloan Foundation and the National Science Foundation and continues her longstanding interest in the meaning of work in modern society. She is the author of *The Kibbutz Community and Nation Building*, and co-editor of the *Labor and Social Change* series of Temple University Press. She has written extensively on unemployment, workplace education, and older workers. Professor Rayman has held fellowships from the National Institute of Mental Health and the Bunting Institute. She chairs the Older Worker Task Force of the Massachusetts Jobs Council.

Cynthia M. Taeuber is chief of the Age and Sex Statistics Branch of the Population Division at the U.S. Bureau of the Census. She has written extensively on women, the current older population, and the aging of the baby-boom generation. Her major publications include *America in Transition: An Aging Society*, "Demographic Dimensions of an Aging Society" (in *Our Aging Society*), *America's Oldest Old*, *America's Centenarians*, *An Aging World*, *Women in the American Economy*, *Statistical Handbook on Women in America*, and *Sixty-five*

Plus in America. Ms. Taeuber holds an MA in sociology/demography from Georgetown University. She received the Department of Commerce (DOC) Bronze Medal Award for her development of statistics on women and the elder population and the DOC Silver Medal Award for the development of the 1990 Census program for statistics on the homeless population.

ABOUT THE INSTITUTIONS

THE SOUTHPORT INSTITUTE FOR POLICY ANALYSIS was founded in 1987. With offices in Southport, Connecticut and Washington, D.C., it provides objective, nonpartisan analysis of public and private policy issues of national importance. It is the successor organization to the Project on the Federal Social Role and the Aging Society Project which operated from 1982 to 1987. The Southport Institute's primary interest is in policies to advance human resource development and, in particular, those issues that affect the quality of the American work force.

Human resource questions have long been of only marginal importance to public and private policymakers, despite their central importance to building a productive economy and insuring the welfare of all Americans. The program of the Southport Institute is devoted to helping public and private agencies find solutions to human resource issues that will best advance the national interest.

◆

THE URBAN INSTITUTE is a nonprofit policy research and educational organization established in Washington, D.C. in 1968. Its staff investigates the social and economic problems confronting the nation and public and private means to alleviate them. The Urban Institute has three goals for its research and dissemination activities: to sharpen thinking about societal problems and efforts to solve them, to improve government decisions and performance, and to increase citizen awareness of important public choices.

Through work that ranges from broad conceptual studies to administrative and technical assistance, Institute researchers contribute to the stock of knowledge and the analytic tools available to guide decision making in the public interest.

The Institute disseminates its research and the research of others through the publications program of its Press.

BLS, see U.S. Bureau of Labor
  Statistics
Boston Women's Health Collective,
  219
Boyd, Robert, 26, 45
Branch, L.G., 129
Branson, M.H., 129
Breslow, L., 106, 127
Brizius, Jack A., 6, 9, 81, 211, 233
Brody, Elaine M., 51, 71, 127, 228,
  229, 237
Buchmann, Anna Marie, 155, 163
Burnett, W., 129
Burns, Roberta O., 104
Burt, Martha R., 45, 73, 104, 131,
  166, 190, 238
Butler, Robert N., 97, 100, 106, 128

C

Cafferata, Gail Lee, 51, 103, 223,
  238
Cain, Glen G., 135, 163
Callaghan, Polly, 154, 155, 163
Callahan, Daniel, 97, 100
Campbell, Nancy Duff, 157, 158,
  163
Career Encore, 217n.6
careerists, 200
caregiving, 47–71; and aging
  population, 48, 49–50; and
  changing family structure, 48–
  49; and changing workforce, 48,
  49; and choices, 61–70; and
  fairness, 69–71; and financing,
  68–69; and prevention, 60–61;
  and responsibilities of men, 59–
  60; and the workplace, 62–67;
  comprehensive caregiving
  policy, 55–60; for the elderly, 51–
  55; in the family, 88–89;
  national caregiving policy, 59–
  71; paid caregivers, 52–54, 57–
  59; role of caregivers, 54–55;
  services available, 67–68
caregiving accounts, 68–69
caring work, 221–37; age of
  caregivers, 225; by choice and by
  chance, 227–28; changes in
  caring work, 223–31; dependent

care, 222–23; diverse dependent
  population, 224; eldercare, 228–
  29; employment of caregivers,
  225; implications for policy,
  230–31; men as caregivers, 229–
  30; potential period of
  caregiving, 225–27
Cartwright, W.S., 124, 129
CASS, see Coronary Artery
  Surgery Study
CEA, see cost-effectiveness
  analysis
Center for Policy Alternatives, 65,
  72
Chaney, Elsa M., 217n.8, 218
Chavkin, Wendy, 213, 218
Chou, Marylin, 72
chum networkers, 199
civil rights, 241
Collins, A.M., 128
Collins, Barbara Rose, 177
Commonwealth Fund Commission
  on Elderly People Living Alone,
  5, 10
compression of morbidity, 78
Cooperative Home Care
  Associates, 233, 238
Coronary Artery Surgery Study
  (CASS), 122
cost-effectiveness analysis (CEA),
  110, 113–14
Cowan, Cathy A., 101
Cowell, Carol S., 100
Cowell, Daniel D., 100
Cummings, S.R., 123, 128

D

Daily, Theresa, 103
Davis, K., 106, 128
de Lissovoy, Gregory, 100
Deluty, Philip, 72
dementia, 124–25
DeNavas, Carmen, 22, 38, 42
dependency, 31–36; and disability,
  34–36; parent support ratio, 32;
  social support ratio, 32–34
dependent care, 62–63
Deren, Jane M., 217n.2, 218
Deutchman, Donna E., 204, 218

DiCarlo, Steven, 84, 100
differences among elderly, 3–5, 9,
    11–31; economic status, 4, 19–
    26; educational attainment, 31;
    health status, 5; living
    arrangements, 28–30; marital
    status, 4, 22–23, 26–28; race
    and ethnic differences, 4, 17–18;
    19–20; 21–22
disability, 117
Dolinsky, Arthur, 12, 44
Donelan, Karen, 99, 100
Dooley, Martin D., 135, 163
Doress, Paula Brown, 217n.2, 218
Dukakis, Olympia, 214
Durrett, Charles, 208, 219
Dynamic Simulation of Income
    Model (DYNASIM), 22–23, 157
DYNASIM, see Dynamic
    Simulation of Income Model

E

Early Retirement Incentive Plans
    (ERIPS), 136
economic policies, 9
economy and the low-income
    elderly, 184–86
education, 31, 37–38, 206–07,
    249–50
Ehrenburg, Ronald G., 156, 163
eldercare, 5–6, 9, 221–37, 244, 248.
    See also caregiving *and* caring
    work.
elderly in the workplace, 19–20,
    249
Employee Retirement Income
    Security Act of 1974, 181
Epstein, A.M., 123, 131
ERIPS, *see* Early Retirement
    Incentive Plans
Ernst, Maurice, 72
escapists, 200
ethic of caring, 6–7
Executive Life, 181

F

faded beauties, 200
Fahs, Marianne C., 5, 9, 108, 109,
    110, 124, 128, 129, 130

Families USA, 160, 163
Feldman, Jacob J., 78, 94, 95, 102
Ferguson, Kathy, 192, 218
Fernandez, John P., 62, 72
Fierst, Edith U., 157, 158, 163
Figart, Deborah M., 138, 140, 164
Financial Accounting Standards
    Board, 84
Fingerhut, L.A., 18, 42
Finney, C.P., 130
Fisher, L.D., 129
flextime, 66–67
Foege, W.H., 121, 128
Folman, S.J., 128
Forrest, C., 136, 165
Foster D.A., 123
Foster, Susan E., 6, 9, 81, 211, 233
Fox, N., 130
Fox, P.J., 130
Frankel, David, 185, 188
Fried, L.P., 106, 128
Friedman, Dana E., 63, 72
Friedman, Emily, 86, 100
Fries, James F., 77, 95, 101, 106, 128
Fuchs, Victor R., 96, 101
Fullerton, Howard N., Jr., 19, 39,
    43, 49, 72, 133, 134, 164
functional limitations, 34–35

G

Gabel, John, 100
Gagen, Mary G., 135, 164
gender equity, 231–37, 248; paid
    home care, 232–33; pay equity,
    235–36; work-force leaves, 233–
    35
Genero, N., 208, 218
German, P.S., 106, 128
Gerson, Kathleen, 230, 238
Gibeau, Janice L., 52, 72
Gillette, M.K., 128
Gitter, Robert J., 135, 164
Glasse, Lou, 159, 164
Glassman, Marjorie, 210
Gleason, H.P., 106, 128
GNP, *see* gross national product
Goldbloom, R.B., 115, 128
Gordon, Jeanne, 71
Gray Panthers, 195